HITLER'S LAST DAY

— MINUTE BY MINUTE —

Praise for *D-Day: Minute by Minute*:

'Studded with extraordinary detail, it's the most joltingly vivid account ever written of the day the Allies gambled everything... Heartbreaking and thrilling by turns.' – **Daily Mail**

'This blow-by-blow account of Allied troops' storming of the Normandy beaches highlights the poignant moments, personal stories and individual scenes that make key moments in history... The chaos, the horror and the bravery of the battlefield are all here.' – **Daily Express**

'An accessible history that conveys the havoc and vast international spread of D-Day.' – **Kirkus Review, US**

'This book creates a remarkably vivid picture of one of the most important days in modern history.' – **The Good Book Guide**

Praise for *The Assassination of JFK: Minute by Minute*:

'Reads like a pacey, page-turning, cold war political thriller.' – **Dermot O'Leary**

'You forget you are reading a factual description of a historical event, as it feels like a gripping crime thriller.' – **Edinburgh Evening News**

'A blow by blow account of a moment that changed history... The pictures come thick and fast as the tragedy unfolds and some of the images painted are painfully powerful.' – **Radio Times**

'A gripping account of those blood-soaked few days in November 1963.' – **Daily Express**

HITLER'S LAST DAY

— MINUTE BY MINUTE —

JONATHAN MAYO
& EMMA CRAIGIE

First published in 2015 by Short Books
Unit 316, Screenworks
22 Highbury Grove
London N5 2ER

10 9 8 7 6 5 4 3 2 1

A CIP catalogue record for this book is available from the British Library.

ISBN 978-1-78072-233-7

Printed and bound in Great Britain by CPI Group (UK) Ltd, Croydon, CR0 4YY

Photo credits:

Cover Photo
Mold covered Nazi SS officers cap on floor
inside Adolf Hitler's command bunker
Getty Images, © William Vandivert

Back Cover Photo
London celebrating the announcement
of Hitler's death 1945
Getty Images, © Keystone-France

Endpapers
April 1945: American soldiers standing along
the barrel of a captured German gun
Getty Images © MPI

Pages 6-7, Battle of Berlin map by Two Associates

Page 29, bunker layout by Two Associates

Page 14 (Introduction)
Getty Images, © Popperfoto

Page 30 (Sunday 29th April 1945)
© Bundesarchiv, Bild 183-V04744

Page 184 (Monday 30th April 1945)
Getty Images, © Fred Ramage

Page 286, (After April 1945...)
© Imperial War Museums (BU 8955)

The 'Minute by Minute' format is applied to this publication with the permission of TBI Media

TBI ✳
The Big Idea

For David, Maud, Wilf, Myfanwy and Samuel
EC

For Hannah and Charlie
In memory of Derek Mayo and Michael Scott-Joynt
JM

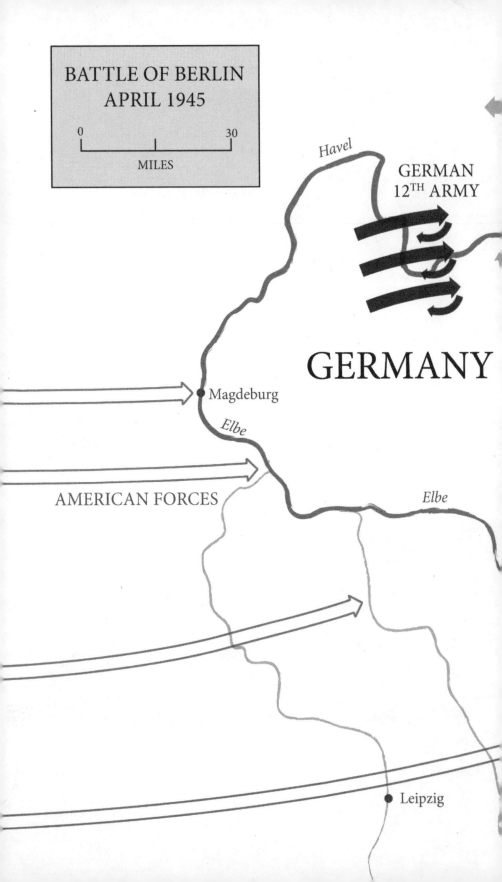

SOVIET FORCES

BERLIN

otsdam

Frankfurt

GERMAN
9TH ARMY

Spree

Triebel

Torgau

Contents

Cast of Characters

American

Major-General Walter *Bedell Smith* — General Eisenhower's Chief of Staff
General Simon Bolivar *Buckner* — Commander of the US forces on Okinawa
Alistair *Cooke* — Journalist for the *Manchester Guardian*
Joseph E. *Davies* — Former ambassador to Moscow
General Dwight D. *Eisenhower* — Supreme Commander of the Allied Forces
John *Eisenhower* — Officer in the 3323rd SIAM company; son of Dwight D. Eisenhower.

Flight Lieutenant Alexander *Jefferson* — P-51 pilot and POW
John F. *Kennedy* — Journalist for the *Chicago Herald-American*
Lieutenant Wolfgang F. *Robinow* — German-born US army soldier
Franklin D. *Roosevelt* — President of the United States March 1933 to April 1945

Lieutenant Marcus J. *Smith* — US army medical officer working in Dachau
Lieutenant Colonel Felix L. *Sparks* — US 45th Infantry Division
Harry *Truman* — Succeeded Roosevelt as President on 12th April 1945

Lieutenant Bill *Walsh* — US 45th Infantry Division, serving under Lieutenant Colonel Felix Sparks

Australian

Wing Commander Lionel 'Bill' *Hudson* — POW in Rangoon jail

Belgian

Albert *Guerisse* — Doctor for the SOE under pseudonym Pat O'Leary; POW in Dachau

British

John *Amery* — Journalist and son of Cabinet Minister Leo Amery
Winston *Churchill* — British Prime Minister since May 1940
Lieutenant Commander Patrick *Dalzel-Job* — Member of Ian Fleming's 30 Assault Unit
Richard *Dimbleby* — BBC correspondent in Germany
Major-General Sir Francis *de Guingand* — Montgomery's Chief of Staff
Michael *Hargrave* — Medical student heading to Bergen-Belsen
Clara *Milburn* — Diarist and mother of POW Alan Milburn
General Sir Bernard *Montgomery* — Senior ground force commander for the invasion of Europe

Alan *Moorehead* — *Daily Express* journalist in Germany
George *Orwell* — Journalist and author
Captain Sigismund *Payne-Best* — British agent for the Secret Intelligence Service
Robert *Reid* — BBC correspondent in Germany
Corporal Bert *Ruffle* — POW in Stalag IV-C
Jack *Swaab* — Gunnery officer in the 51st Highland Division
Wynford *Vaughan-Thomas* — BBC correspondent in Germany
Major Elliott *Viney* — POW in Stalag VII-A at Moosburg
Second Lieutenant Alan *Whicker* — British Army Film and Photo Unit
Tony *Wigan* — BBC correspondent in San Francisco

Danish
Hans Henrick *Koch* .... Danish Ministry of Social Welfare

Dutch
Audrey *Hepburn-Rushton*
  (aka Edda van Heemstra) .... Actress
Jacqueline *van Maarsen* .... Friend of Anne Frank
John *Schwartz* .... First cousin of Audrey Hepburn

German
Ruth *Andreas-Friedrich* .... Berlin resident; member of anti-Nazi resistance group
Artur *Axmann* .... Head of Hitler Youth
Nicolaus *von Below* .... Luftwaffe officer and adjutant to Hitler; last person to leave bunker before Hitler's death
Gerhard *Boldt* .... Military intelligence officer working for General Krebs; leaves bunker on mission to contact General Wenck
Colonel Bogislav *von Bonin* .... One of the *Prominente* group of prisoners
Martin *Bormann* .... Hitler's private secretary
Eva Hitler née *Braun* .... Hitler's wife
Gretl *Braun* .... Hitler's sister-in-law, Eva's sister
Wernher *von Braun* .... Inventor of the V2
General Wilhelm *Burgdorf* .... German army general; witness to Hitler's last will and testament
Gerda *Christian* .... Hitler's secretary
Captain Willi *Dietrich* .... U-boat captain in the *Faust* wolfpack off Norwegian coast
Admiral Karl *Dönitz* .... Head of German navy, named Hitler's successor in the Führer's last testament
General Alexander *von Falkenhausen* .... Former German army Commander-in-Chief in Belgium; one of the *Prominente* group of prisoners
Hermann *Fegelein* .... Himmler's SS representative in the bunker, married to Eva Braun's sister, Gretl
Sister Erna *Flegel* .... Nurse in Reich Chancellery emergency hospital
Karl Hermann *Frank* .... Secretary of State and Chief of Police in Prague
Lieselotte *G.* .... Berlin resident and anonymous diarist
Joseph *Goebbels* .... Hitler's Propaganda Minister
Magda *Goebbels* .... Wife of Joseph Goebbels
Helga, Hilde, Helmut, Holde, Hedda, Heide *Goebbels* .... Children of Joseph and Magda
Hermann *Göring* .... Recently deposed head of the Luftwaffe
Robert Ritter *von Greim* .... Hitler's last Luftwaffe chief
Clara *Greenbaum* .... Prisoner at Bergen-Belsen
Hermann *Gretz* .... Technician in the bunker
Otto *Günsche* .... SS officer and adjutant to Hitler
Dr Werner *Haase* .... Surgeon in Reich Chancellery emergency hospital
Fey *von Hassell* .... One of the *Prominente* group of prisoners
Marta *Hillers* .... German journalist; anonymous author of memoir, *A Woman in Berlin*
Heinrich *Himmler* .... Recently deposed SS chief attempting to negotiate with the Allies

11

Hitler's Last Day: Minute by Minute

General Rudolf *Holste* — General supposed to be attacking Russian forces from the north-west of Berlin

Willi *Johannmeier* — SS officer, one of the couriers of Hitler's last testaments

Margaret *Joyce* — Wife of William Joyce; German citizen from 1940

William *Joyce* — Broadcaster for the Reich Broadcasting Company; German citizen from 1940

General Alfred *Jodl* — Chief of Operations Staff of the Armed Forces High Command; signed German unconditional surrender on behalf of Admiral Dönitz

Traudl *Junge* — Hitler's secretary

Erich *Kempka* — Hitler's driver

General Wilhelm *Keitel* — Supreme High Command of the German Armed Forces

Karl *Koller* — Luftwaffe liaison officer in the bunker

General Hans *Krebs* — Chief of Army General Staff

Armin *Lehmann* — Hitler Youth runner

Dr Hans Graf *von Lehndorff* — Doctor in Königsberg

Ewald *Lindloff* — SS officer who buries Hitler's remains

Heinz *Linge* — Hitler's personal valet

Heinz *Lorenz* — Hitler's press officer, one of the couriers of Hitler's last testaments

Bernd Freytag *von Loringhoven* — Adjutant to General Krebs; leaves bunker with Boldt on mission to contact General Wenck

Constanze *Manziarly* — Hitler's cook

Emil *Maurice* — Hitler's former chauffer

Ernst *Michel* — Former Auschwitz prisoner

Rochus *Misch* — Bunker switchboard operator

General Wilhelm *Mohnke* — Battle Commander of Berlin's central government district, including the bunkers

Heinrich *Müller* — Head of the Gestapo

Liesl *Ostertag* — Eva Braun's maid

Harald *Quandt* — Magda Goebbels' son from her first marriage

Hanna *Reitsch* — Aviatrix who flies Robert Ritter von Greim in and out of the bunker

Walter *Schellenberg* — SS intelligence officer working for Heinrich Himmler, organising negotiations with Count Bernadotte

Dr. Ernst *Schenck* — Doctor in the Berlin Reich Chancellery emergency hospital

Anni Antonie *Schmöger* — Munich resident

Captain Adelbert *Schnee* — U-boat commander

Field Marshal Ferdinand *Schörner* aka Blutiger (Bloody) Ferdinand — Named Commander-in-Chief of the German army in Hitler's last testament

Claus *Sellier* — Lieutenant in the 79th Mountain Artillery Regiment

Arthur *Seyss-Inquart* — Reich Commissioner in the Netherlands

Albert *Speer* — Architect and Minister for Munitions

Richard *Strauss* — Composer

Dr Ludwig *Stumpfegger* — SS doctor in the Berlin Reich Chancellery emergency hospital

Fritz *Tornow* — Hitler's dog handler

Walther **Wagner** .... Civil magistrate who marries Adolf Hitler and Eva Braun

General Helmuth **Weidling** .... Commandant of Berlin, leading the defence of the city against the Russians

Rudolf **Weiss** .... Assistant to General Burgdorf who leaves the bunker with Boldt and von Loringhoven on a mission to contact General Wenck

General Walther **Wenck** .... Commanding forces south of Berlin, Wenck was Hitler's last hope for relief of the capital. He was actually trying to give Berliners safe passage out of the city

Henry **Wermuth** .... Prisoner in Mauthausen concentration camp

Sisi **Wilczek** .... Nurse escaping Vienna for her family home Moosham Castle

August **Wollenhaupt** .... Hitler's barber

Walther **Wulff** .... Astrologer who advises Heinrich Himmler

Wilhelm **Zander** .... One of the couriers of Hitler's last testaments; assistant to Martin Bormann

Japanese

General Isamu **Cho** .... General Mitsuru Ushijima's Chief of Staff on Okinawa

Yasuo **Ichijima** .... Kamikaze pilot

Haruo **Ito** .... Commander of Rangoon jail

General Mitsuru **Ushijima** .... Commander of Japanese forces on Okinawa

Colonel Hiromichi **Yahara** .... Responsible for the strategy for the defence of Okinawa

New Zealander

Major Geoffrey **Cox** .... Intelligence officer with the 2nd New Zealand Division

Russian

Vasily **Grossman** .... Journalist accompanying the Russian forces attacking Berlin

Nina **Markovna** .... Taken to Germany as a forced labourer, together with mother and brother

Vyacheslav **Molotov** .... Russian Foreign Minister

Yelena **Rzhevskaya** .... German language interpreter working for SMERSH, the Russian intelligence unit

Captain Stepan **Neustroev** .... Commander of the 1st Battalion in the 756th Regiment of the 150th Rifle Division whose unit stormed the Reichstag

General Vasily **Shatilov** .... Commander of the 150th Rifle Division of the Soviet army

Joseph **Stalin** .... Leader of the Soviet Union; real name Iosif Vissarionovich Dzhugashvili

Swedish

Count Folke **Bernadotte** .... Swedish diplomat negotiating the release of Scandinavian Jews from German camps

Felix **Kersten** .... Swedish masseur treating Heinrich Himmler and encouraging peace talks with Count Bernadotte

13

Adolf Hitler greets members of the Hitler Youth behind the Re
Chancellery building on his 56th birthday, 20th April 19

Introduction

In April 1941, Al Bowlly, one of Britain's best-loved singers, recorded a new Irving Berlin song at Abbey Road Studios in London. 'When That Man Is Dead and Gone' was to become one of the most popular songs of the war. In it he looked forward to the day when the 'news'll flash / Satan with the moustache' is buried 'beneath the lawn'. The song, although written by an American, summed up the mood of the British people in 1941, who regarded Hitler as a ridiculous yet dangerous figure, whose death they would happily celebrate. But it had not always been the case.

Even as late as the 'Phoney War' or what some called the 'Bore War' of the winter of 1939–40, there was considerable support for reaching an agreement with the German dictator. Within a year that changed. Attitudes hardened because of the humiliation of the Dunkirk evacuation in May 1940, and the Battle of Britain of the summer and autumn that followed, but most especially because of the Blitz, which brought terror to cities such as Bristol, Coventry, Glasgow, Liverpool and London.

The singer Al Bowlly himself was a casualty. A week after

recording 'When That Man Is Dead and Gone', a bomb exploded outside his flat near Piccadilly. Lying on his bed reading a cowboy book, Bowlly was killed outright.

The British public first heard about Adolf Hitler in November 1923 when he attempted to seize control of the Bavarian government as a first step towards overturning the Weimar Republic. But his political awakening began in the First World War.

> *The idea of struggle is as old as life itself, for life is only preserved because other living things perish.*
>
> *Adolf Hitler, 1928*

On 1st August 1914 Hitler was photographed in a crowd which had gathered to celebrate the outbreak of the First World War in the Odeonsplatz, Munich. He later wrote in *Mein Kampf* that he 'thanked heaven from the fullness of [his] heart for the favour of having been permitted to live at such a time.' The war was 'a deliverance from the distress that had weighed upon me during the days of my youth'.

That distress began in early childhood. Adolf Hitler was born in 1889 in the town of Braunau am Inn in Austria. His father Alois was a bad-tempered, authoritarian and unpredictable man, frequently drunk. According to Adolf's younger sister Paula, her brother received daily thrashings. Their mother Klara was much younger than their father, and closely related to him. She addressed him as "Uncle". Hitler later told people that she would sit outside the room, waiting for the beatings to finish so that she could comfort her son. She was, in Paula's words, 'a very soft and tender person' and Adolf adored her. His father died when Adolf was 14 and his mother when he was 18. Her doctor, who had attended many deaths, later recalled, 'I have never seen anyone so prostrate with grief as Adolf Hitler.'

Hitler had already faced disappointment when he failed to get a place to study architecture at the Vienna Academy of Fine Arts shortly before his mother's death. After her funeral in 1907 he returned to the Austrian capital. He lived in cheap lodgings and then, after a period of sleeping on park benches, moved into a men's hostel. He fraudulently claimed financial support – pretending to be a student – and supplemented this by selling small paintings and sketches, but lived an indolent life. He rose at noon and stayed up late at night working on grandiose architectural projects, designing castles, theatres and concert halls. He wrote operas and plays. Each project began with manic euphoria, but none were finished. His ambitious dreams alternated with periods of depression.

> *Was there any shady undertaking, any form of foulness, especially in cultural life, in which at least one Jew did not participate? On putting the probing knife to that kind of abscess one immediately discovered, like the maggot in a putrescent body, a little Jew who was often blinded by the sudden light.*
>
> *Adolf Hitler,* Mein Kampf

Hitler frequently got into furious arguments at the night kitchens where he went for bread and soup. According to one of his early flatmates in Vienna, Jewish-Czech August Kubizek, the 19-year-old Hitler quarrelled with everyone and had frenzies of hatred. The anti-Semitism of Vienna, crudely expressed in endless cheap pamphlets, gave Hitler the relief of a focus for his feelings of fury and resentment. Writing *Mein Kampf* 15 years later, he claimed that this was the period when his view of life took shape: 'since then I have extended that foundation very little, and I have changed nothing in it.'

This festering aggression found a new outlet in the First World War. Hitler was accepted into the German army as a regimental staff runner and suddenly his aimless life had a structure and purpose. In the next four years he was twice wounded and twice decorated but he never rose above corporal. According to one of his fellow soldiers he sat in a corner 'with his helmet on his head, lost in thought, and none of us could coax him out of his apathy'. He was seen as a loner, a dreamer. His only friend was a dog, a white terrier he called Foxl which had wandered over from the English trenches. According to his military chief, Fritz Wiedemann, Hitler was brave but odd, and couldn't be promoted further because it was clear that he couldn't command respect.

> **In these nights hatred grew in me – hatred for the originators of this dastardly crime.**
>
> **Adolf Hitler,** Mein Kampf

On 10th November 1918, the day before Armistice Day, Hitler was in hospital in north-east Germany convalescing after his second injury. As he recalled in *Mein Kampf,* a pastor came in to address the patients. With regret he told them that Germany had become a republic; the monarchy had fallen; the war was lost. To Hitler the news was unbearable:

'I could stand it no longer. It became impossible for me to sit still one minute more. Again everything went black before my eyes; I tottered and groped my way back to the dormitory, threw myself on my bunk and dug my burning head into my blanket and pillow.

'Since the day when I had stood at my mother's grave, I had not wept... But now I could not help it...

'And so it had all been in vain... Did all this happen only that a gang of wretched criminals could lay hands on the Fatherland?... I, for my part, decided to go into politics.'

> *A man – I've heard a man, he's unknown, I've forgotten his name. But if anyone can free us from Versailles then it's this man. This unknown man will restore our honour!*
>
> *Rudolf Hess, May 1920*

After leaving hospital Hitler went to live in Munich and started attending political meetings. He made his first public speech on 16th October 1919 in a beer cellar in a Munich suburb to an audience of 111 people. He spoke till he was sweating and exhausted, unblocking a dam of hatred towards the political establishment, frustration at the humiliation of the defeat of the 1914–18 war and determination to overturn the traitors who, in June, had signed the Versailles Treaty. Hitler was thrilled to discover 'what I had always felt deep down in my heart... proved to be true. I could make a good speech'. The audience was electrified by his raw intensity. He was voicing the pain of people who felt powerless and offering hope of a glorious future to people who felt battered by defeat. Within weeks he was attracting audiences of 400; the following February he addressed 2,000 people crammed into a huge beer hall in the centre of the city. People stood on the tables and roared as he shrieked abuse at the Jews. There was tumultuous applause as he declared, 'Our motto is only struggle! We go forward unshakably to our goal!'

By July 1921, Hitler had assumed leadership of the

Nationalsozialistische Deutsche Arbeiterpartei, NSDAP, later known as the Nazis. By the autumn of 1923 he had gathered more than 55,000 followers, a thousandfold increase from when he joined as the 55th member. Intoxicated by this success, and inspired by Mussolini's successful 'March on Rome' the previous October, Hitler decided to attempt a coup – later known as the Beer Hall Putsch – and assert his position as the leader of all the anti-Republican protest groups in Munich. The putsch was planned one day and executed the next.

> *A little man… unshaven with disorderly hair and so hoarse that he could hardly speak.*
>
> **Description of Hitler in a Times *report***
> ***of the Munich Beer Hall Putsch***

On the evening of 8th November, Hitler burst into a Munich beer cellar where 3,000 people were listening to speeches by Bavarian politicians. He was accompanied by one of his most glamorous supporters – the war hero and ace fighter pilot Hermann Göring – and a team of helmeted storm troopers pushing a heavy machine gun. Hitler leapt onto a chair, waving a dog whip and brandishing a pistol. In order to make himself heard he fired a shot at the ceiling and then shouted across the vast room, 'The national revolution has broken out in Munich! The whole city is at this moment occupied by our troops! The hall is surrounded by 600 men. Nobody is allowed to leave!'

The city was not occupied by Nazi troops and the putsch fizzled out after a 30-second exchange of gunfire in which four policemen and 14 Nazis were killed. One of the activists was a young chicken farmer with a soft pudgy face and glasses. He held his head high and carried a standard bearing a swastika. His name was Heinrich Himmler.

Hermann Göring was shot in the leg. Adolf Hitler tripped and dislocated his shoulder. Both men fled the scene. Göring managed to escape to Austria where he was treated for his injuries and given morphine for the pain. It was the beginning of a lifelong addiction. Hitler only managed to get as far as a friend's house outside Munich and was arrested two days later. Together with several other organisers of the march he was tried for treason. Hitler was given the minimum sentence of five years and in April 1924 was sent to Landsberg Prison.

In Landsberg, Hitler had a large room with windows looking out over beautiful countryside. Many of the prison guards were Nazi Party members and secretly showed their respect with greetings of *Heil Hitler*. He was allowed to receive flowers and gifts and had so many visitors that once numbers topped 500 he decided to restrict them. He spent most of his time writing, or rather dictating, *Mein Kampf*, setting out a political ideology which he never revised. He argued that the future success of the German nation required triumph over the evil conspiracies of the Jews and communists and territorial expansion in the east.

After the shambles of the 1923 putsch, Hitler spent ten years building up the Nazi Party and, with the support of the former chicken farmer Heinrich Himmler, developed the SS as an effective military elite. The focus of his ambition turned from Bavarian politics to national leadership.

That is the miracle of our age, that you have found me, that you have found me among so many millions! And that I have found you, that is Germany's good fortune!

Adolf Hitler, 13th September 1936

Hitler's appointment as Chancellor of Germany on 30th January 1933 was greeted by huge, orchestrated torchlight processions. The reality was that the Nazi Party had come to power with minority support following an election that failed to deliver a majority government. Germany was suffering catastrophic inflation and high unemployment, which Hitler tackled with a massive programme of road building, construction and military rearmament. The expansion was funded by huge borrowing, the seizure of assets and printing money.

At the same time Hitler introduced policies designed to destroy opposition. Trade unions and all other political parties were banned. Opponents were murdered or sent to newly created concentration camps. In pursuit of a notion of racial perfection, laws of 'Racial Hygiene' were brought in. Sex was forbidden between so-called Aryans and Jews or 'gypsies, negroes or their bastard offspring'. A eugenics programme for the medical murder of people with disabilities was secretly established.

The changes were enforced by violence, delivered by the SS and the newly formed Gestapo, and by extravagant propaganda. A young journalist with a PhD in Romantic Literature, Joseph Goebbels, was put in charge of controlling the media. A young architect, Albert Speer, was brought in to design the visual impact of mass rallies and marches.

> *My dear wife.*
> *This is hell. The Russians don't want to leave Moscow. It's so cold my very soul is freezing. I beg of you – stop writing about the silks and boots I'm supposed to bring you from Moscow. Can't you understand I'm dying?*
>
> *Adolf Fortheimer, German Soldier, December 1941*

In 1939 Hitler reflected on the achievements of the first six years of his leadership in a speech to the German parliament, the Reichstag:

'I have restored to the Reich the provinces grabbed from us in 1919; I have led millions of deeply unhappy Germans, who have been snatched away from us, back into the Fatherland; I have restored the thousand-year-old historical unity of German living space; and I have attempted to accomplish all that without shedding blood and without inflicting the sufferings of war on my people or any other. I have accomplished all this, as one who 21 years ago was still an unknown worker and soldier of my people, by my own efforts...'

By the end of 1938 the Rhineland, Austria and Sudetenland in Czechoslovakia had all been pulled into a greater Germany without any international opposition. But the invasion of Poland triggered the British and French declarations of war on Germany on 3rd September 1939. Undeterred, in April 1940, Hitler invaded Denmark and Norway, again without encountering significant opposition. Then in the spring of 1941 German troops were sent into the Balkans, Yugoslavia, Greece, North Africa and the Middle East, and later into Iraq and Crete. The beginning of the end of this massive expansion came in June 1941 when, in contravention of a non-aggression pact of 1939, Hitler launched a massive attack on Soviet Russia. Six months later he declared war on the United States. By Christmas 1944 Germany was pincered between these two advancing superpowers.

On 15th January 1945, Hitler retreated from the hideous reality of defeat. He rushed back to Berlin, and buried himself in his Führerbunker, giving orders to Albert Speer that all German infrastructure and industry be destroyed. There would be no surrender. Victory or destruction were the only options.

There were two bunkers beneath the Reich Chancellery building in Berlin. The older one, the upper bunker, had been designed by Albert Speer as an air raid shelter in the early 1930s. It was built beneath the cellars of the old Reich Chancellery and was ready for use by 1936. A lower bunker, which became known as the Führerbunker, was constructed in 1944. It was located 8.5 metres below the garden and protected by a 3-metre-deep concrete roof.

During January 1945 Hitler slept in the Führerbunker but worked in the remaining rooms of the Reich Chancellery. In the early afternoon of 3rd February 1945, the US Air Force undertook a mass bombing attack on Berlin, creating a fireball which burned for five days and inflicting the worst damage that the capital had yet suffered. From this point Hitler stayed underground.

Most of the senior Nazis had sent their families to safety and had moved out of the capital. Only Joseph Goebbels remained in Berlin, sleeping in a luxurious bunker built beneath his family home. The head of the SS, Heinrich Himmler, had been living in a sanatorium in the beautiful resort of Hohenlychen since January, receiving treatments for stress and severe stomach pain. Himmler held a very inflated view of himself as a figure of international stature and had become convinced that he was the best person to negotiate the peace and lead Germany into the future. At the suggestion of his Swedish masseur, Felix Kersten, who took advantage of his relationship with the SS chief to try and get concentration camp prisoners released, Himmler had two secret meetings: one with Count Folke Bernadotte, a Swedish diplomat, and one with Norbert Masur, the Swedish representative of the World Jewish Congress. Ostensibly the purpose of both meetings was to discuss the release of prisoners, but Himmler's motive was to open up a channel of communication with the

Western Allies. He hoped that Masur would put the issue of the Final Solution behind him.

You know what I wish? I wish they had killed Hitler and then there would be a chance to end the war!

Albine Paul, Nazi Party supporter, spring 1945

On 11th March 1945 there was a service of remembrance for the war dead in the village of Markt Schellenberg, close to Hitler's mountain retreat in Obersalzberg. At the end of his speech the local army commander called for a *Sieg Heil* to the Führer. There was a deadly silence. None of the civilians, Home Guard or soldiers responded. On this cold morning everyone kept their mouths shut and their right arms tightly by their sides. At hundreds of rallies held during the previous 12 years these people, and millions of others, had leapt, mesmerised, to their feet to "*Sieg Heil*" the close of Adolf Hitler's rousing speeches. But the spell had been broken.

Hitler went outside for the last time on his 56th birthday, 20th April 1945. He dragged himself up the concrete steps from the Führerbunker to the Reich Chancellery garden to inspect a group of young boys, members of the Hitler Youth. The boys had been instructed to look straight ahead, so 16-year-old Armin Lehmann was shocked at the Führer's decrepit appearance when it finally came to his turn and his leader was standing right in front of him. His hands were shaking as he grabbed Lehmann's arm and clutched at his sleeve before enclosing the boy's right hand in both of his. 'I could not believe,' Lehmann later wrote, 'that this withered old man in front of me was the visionary who had led our nation to greatness.'

> **If the German people cannot wrest victory from the enemy, then they shall be destroyed... they deserve to perish, for the best of Germany's manhood will have fallen in battle. Germany's end will be horrible, and the German people will have deserved it.**
>
> *Adolf Hitler, summer 1944*

In the following days the Russian army encircled Berlin and entered the suburbs. An attempt by Göring to clarify his position as Hitler's successor triggered one of the Führer's ferocious outbursts and Göring's dismissal as head of the air force. Hitler felt betrayed on all sides. He blamed the disaster of the war on the incompetence of his generals, and ultimately a failure of the German people. When he learned about Himmler's attempts to negotiate with the West he turned purple with rage and ordered his arrest and execution.

That evening, 28th April 1945, Hitler started to get his personal affairs in order. He instructed Joseph Goebbels to find an official with the authority to conduct a civil wedding and to source some wedding rings. After a lifetime insisting, 'for me marriage would have been a disaster... it's better to have a mistress', Hitler had decided to marry Eva Braun, the woman who had been his secret mistress for 14 years. He then asked his secretary Traudl Junge to take down his final testament and will. Adolf Hitler, who for the past 12 years had kept Germany under his spell, who had masterminded some of the most extraordinary battles in modern history, was preparing to end his life.

This book tells the story of Monday 30th April, the day Hitler commits suicide, and also the day before, when so many extraordinary things happen both inside the bunker and across the world that help place that last day in context.

On D-Day, 6th June 1944, hundreds of Allied soldiers wrote about the life and death events happening around them. Sometimes, as soon as they'd scrambled to the top of the beach, having dodged bullets and mortars, out would come a diary and pencil. These diaries provided perfect source material for the book *D-Day: Minute by Minute*. In contrast, we were expecting first-hand accounts of the end of April 1945 to be hard to come by – few people had any idea these two days would be so historic. And yet we found scores of diaries and memoirs. It's as if, amongst the chaos, one way of coming to terms with the experience was to keep a diary – some updated theirs four or five times a day.

However, that chaos also meant that those involved had little sense of time. Armin Lehmann, describing his first visit to Hitler's bunker, wrote, 'I was in a daze, not knowing whether it was night or day. Time had come to be a meaningless concept.' Sometimes we've had to estimate when events occurred or rely on statements such as 'just before sunset'. When we've come across interesting events with little indication of when exactly they took place, we have indicated an approximation by adding the word 'about' before the time listed in the text. But very often we have been able to give precise timings to events because military personnel like to keep a record of such things – even in a prisoner-of-war camp.

For the events that occurred in Hitler's bunker we have been able to draw on a large number of memoirs and interviews given by survivors. Some of these eyewitnesses are more reliable than others but by reading their different points of view and cross-checking for discrepancies we have pieced together the sequence of events. Unless indicated otherwise, times given are German local times.

Al Bowlly sang how hellish the world of 1941 was but what 'a heaven it will be / When that man is dead and gone.' That one man could be the cause of such suffering almost defies belief. As Hitler ended his life, hundreds of thousands of people across the world were trying to save theirs. The world, for all involved, was indeed hell. This is their story..

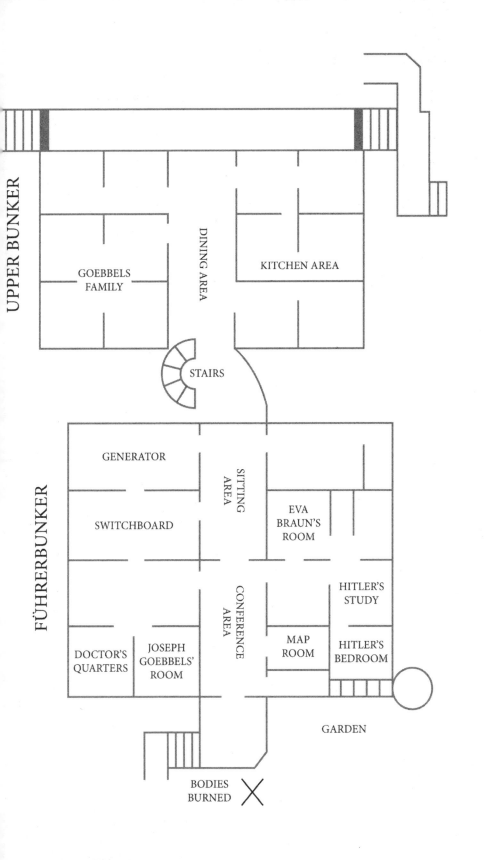

UPPER BUNKER

GOEBBELS FAMILY

DINING AREA

KITCHEN AREA

STAIRS

FÜHRERBUNKER

GENERATOR

SWITCHBOARD

SITTING AREA

EVA BRAUN'S ROOM

CONFERENCE AREA

HITLER'S STUDY

DOCTOR'S QUARTERS

JOSEPH GOEBBELS' ROOM

MAP ROOM

HITLER'S BEDROOM

GARDEN

BODIES BURNED ✕

Entrance to the Führerbunker from the Reich Chancellery garden, July 19

Sunday 29th April 1945

Everyone now has a chance to choose the part which he will play in the film a hundred years hence.

Joseph Goebbels, 17th April 1945

Midnight local time/8.00am Tokyo Time

Eva Braun is in her bedroom having her hair done by her maid, Liesl Ostertag. Braun keeps it lightly peroxided, cut in short waves, with her long fringe pinned up on the right side. Her face is carefully made up to look natural, as Adolf Hitler likes it. She has chosen her outfit: a long black silk taffeta dress which she is going to wear with her favourite diamond watch, a gold bracelet with pink tourmaline gems and a topaz necklace. She has decided on some black suede Ferragamo shoes, one of the scores of pairs she has bought from the exclusive Italian designer since her first visit to Italy in 1936. She wants to look her best. Tonight she is marrying the man she has loved since she was 17. They have been conducting a secret affair for the last 14 years.

Braun's room is the most comfortable in the bunker complex. She has furnished it entirely with pieces designed for her by the architect of the bunker, Albert Speer. As well as the dressing table and chair, there's a straight-backed sofa, upholstered in a floral fabric, a wardrobe and a single bed. Everything is marked with her four-leaf clover monogram, also designed by Speer, the two sides of the clover created out of a curved E facing a curved B. Her monogram is stamped on the furniture, embroidered on her clothes and engraved on her silver combs and brushes, on her jewellery and on the broach clip which Liesl is pinning into her hair.

Hitler's favourite architect, Albert Speer, designed the massive new Reich Chancellery, which has been used from 1939, beside the old Reich Chancellery, a rococo palace on Berlin's Williamstrasse which had served as an official Chancellery building since 1875, as well as the bunker complex beneath both buildings. Both Chancellery buildings have suffered bomb damage and are largely abandoned, but in the cellars there is an emergency hospital and a field kitchen plus garages and a network of rooms for secretaries, officers, officials. The cellars are connected to the Führerbunker by a long passageway which has been shelled in the past few days, but is still passable.

Twenty-eight feet above Eva Braun's head, the body of her brother-in-law, Hermann Fegelein, is being placed in a shallow grave in the Reich Chancellery garden. The gravediggers are working by the light of the firestorms illuminating the Berlin night sky. There is heavy Russian artillery bombardment as Soviet forces have just succeeded in establishing a crossing over the River Spree and the guns are giving cover to the stream of tanks entering the centre of Berlin. Braun's brother-in-law has been executed during the evening on the orders of the man she is about to marry. She pleaded for his life for the sake of her younger sister Gretl who is expecting Fegelein's child any day, but Hitler had dismissed her furiously, forcing her to concede, 'You are the Führer.'

Hermann Fegelein, an obsequious cavalry officer, has been working in the bunker as Himmler's liaison officer. He had attempted to cement his position in Hitler's inner circle by marrying Gretl Braun the previous summer. However, he had no wish to die at the Führer's side and had disappeared from the bunker during the previous week. He had been caught with a woman, not his wife, in his Berlin apartment. Apparently preparing to flee the capital, he was found stuffing German marks and jewellery into a suitcase. He had been held by the Gestapo ever since and when news of Himmler's attempts to negotiate with the Allies reached the bunker Hitler had no hesitation in ordering the execution of the SS chief's representative.

At the Kanoya Naval Air Base in the south of Japan, 23-year-old Yasuo Ichijima is in his room updating his daily diary. He's due to fly in a few hours, and he knows he is not coming back. For the past year, most of the flights from Kanoya have been kamikaze missions. A few days ago Ichijima was told that his suicide mission was imminent, and has spent his time swimming, going for walks and saying goodbye to friends. Last Tuesday night he was kept awake by rowdy and drunk kamikaze pilots next door. Ichijima wrote in his diary, 'They probably have the right idea. Personally I prefer to wait for death quietly. I am anxious to behave well up to the last moment... I am very honoured and proud to have the opportunity of offering to my country, which I love more than I can say, a pure life.'

Ichijima's mission is to fly a plane loaded with explosives and fuel towards the US fleet which is part of the invasion force slowly overrunning the Japanese island of Okinawa, 500 miles to the south. The Americans have advanced steadily through the Pacific and if they take Okinawa, the invasion of Japan will soon follow. He must fly at low altitude and, avoiding anti-aircraft guns, crash into a warship – preferably close to, or into, one of its funnels. Ichijima knows that he must not close his eyes at the last moment, however much he wants to, as it will make him less accurate. He's a devout Christian, and is writing what will be the final entry in his diary – words from the Gospel of Matthew: 'Then Jesus said to his disciples, "Whoever wants to be my disciple must deny themselves and take up their cross and follow me."'

So far in April there have been over 1,000 kamikaze missions against the US and Royal navies, with about 20 ships sunk with the loss of hundreds of Allied lives. The kamikaze pilots only have minimal training as they make only one flight. They are escorted by experienced pilots who return to base to pick up the next wave of young volunteers.

Joseph McNamara, a sailor with the USS Anthony *off the coast of Okinawa, kept a diary about what it was like to be under continued kamikaze attack. On 27th May 1945 he wrote:*

'A day of horror – unbelievable... one Jap hit the water so close to us his body was thrown up on the forward torpedo tubes. The men found him, covered with rag dolls, charms etc. He was immediately pitched into the water – sharks in schools tore him to pieces. They hang around us.'

Yasuo Ichijima is part of a small Christian community in Japan. Catholic missionaries first arrived in the middle of the 16th century and were initially persecuted for their faith. In 1873 a ban on Christianity was lifted, but it is still only practised by a minority – Yasuo Ichijima is seen by his fellow pilots as unusual to hold such beliefs.

In the Führerbunker switchboard office the telephonist Rochus Misch is watching Hans Hofbeck of the Reich Security Service describing Hermann Fegelein's killing. Hofbeck witnessed the shooting in the Reich Chancellery cellar corridor about half an hour ago. He acts out what he witnessed: he raises his arms, holding an imaginary machine gun, and aims at shoulder height, shouting the sound effects 'Ratatatata!'

'If it succeeds, very well; if it fails, we'll hang ourselves!'

00.10am

Adolf Hitler is standing in the conference room of the Führerbunker leaning both his hands on the broad side of the empty map table. Traudl Junge, one of the two secretaries remaining in the bunker, sits on the other side of the table taking down his words in shorthand. The Führer has nearly finished dictating his 'Political Testament'. Junge had been very excited when she started. She thought that she was going to be the first person to learn why the war had become so catastrophic. As she later told the makers of the documentary *The World at War*, 'I was heart thumping (sic) when I wrote down what Hitler said.' But as Hitler drones on in a flat monotone she feels increasingly disappointed. There are no revelations, neither expressions of guilt nor justifications, just the recycled accusations she has heard many times before: 'It is untrue that I, or anybody else in Germany, wanted war in 1939. It was wanted and provoked exclusively by those international politicians who either came of Jewish stock, or worked for Jewish interests...'

He boasts how he has forced the Jews to pay for all the

suffering they have caused: 'I ... left no one in doubt that, this time, millions of children of Europe's Aryan peoples would not die of hunger; millions of grown men would not suffer death; and hundreds and thousands of women and children not be burned and bombed to death in the towns, without the real culprit having to atone for his guilt, even if by my more humane means.'

Hitler goes on to explain his planned suicide: 'I will not fall into the hands of an enemy who wants to create a new spectacle, organised by the Jews, to entertain the hysterical masses. I have therefore decided to remain in Berlin, and there to choose death voluntarily at the moment when I believe that the residence of the Führer and the Chancellor can no longer be held...'

Traudl Junge wrote down her memories of the bunker in 1947–8, but in the following years she was ashamed of the manuscript and her failure to distance herself critically from the events. For many years she tried not to think of this period of her life. She told herself that she was too young – 25 in 1945 – to be held responsible for her involvement in the murderous regime. However, one day, when she was in her forties, she walked past a plaque in memory of Sophie Scholl in Munich. Sophie Scholl had been a member of the White Rose group which distributed anti-Nazi leaflets. Junge noticed that Scholl had been born in 1920, as she had herself, but in 1942, the year when Junge started working for Hitler, Scholl had been executed for her anti-Nazi activities. She later said, 'At that moment I really realised that it was no excuse that I had been so young.' She went on to rewrite and publish her memoirs in 2002.

Hitler barely looks up as he dictates. He nominates a successor government with Grand Admiral Dönitz, the head of the navy, as its leader. Hermann Göring, head of the Luftwaffe, and Heinrich Himmler, head of the SS, are formally expelled from the party and from their posts for negotiating with the enemy 'without my knowledge and against my wishes'. The list of new appointments is long. As she jots down the names in shorthand, Junge can't understand the point of all these appointments if, as he insists, all is lost.

The Führer pauses briefly and then launches into the dictation of his personal will.

He sets out a number of legacies and then explains that he has decided to 'take as my wife the young woman who after long years of friendship voluntarily came to this practically besieged city in order to share her destiny with mine'. The news shocks Junge. Hitler has always insisted he will never marry because women have a destructive influence on great men. Hitler regarded it as a crucial part of his public persona that he was a single man, devoted to his country and without a wife standing in the way of the fantasies of the women of Germany.

He continues, 'I and my wife choose death in order to escape the shame of deposal and surrender. It is our will that our bodies be burned immediately in the place where I performed the greatest part of my daily work in my 12-year-long service to my people.'

Suicide has always been an option in Hitler's mind. Just before the Beer Hall Putsch of 1923, he told his supporters, 'If it succeeds, very well; if it fails, we'll hang ourselves!' He has always seen the choice being between absolute success and absolute defeat. There is no middle ground.

Hitler pauses for a moment, then moves away from the table. 'Type that out for me in triplicate and then bring it in to me.' He has never before ordered triplicate copies without first checking a proof copy.

Earlier in the evening, while Hitler was ordering the execution of Fegelein, Traudl Junge had dozed off on a camp bed in the Führerbunker conference room. Since the bombing of the passageway which links the bunker with the cellars of the Reich Chancellery, Hitler insisted that the two remaining secretaries, Traudl Junge and Gerda Christian, come and sleep in the Führerbunker. They have been snatching odd hours of rest, sleeping in their clothes.

Traudl Junge thinks the Führer must have asked for her and left her undisturbed because when she went to his room at about 11.30pm to drink tea, as the secretaries do every evening, he asked her, 'Have you had a nice little rest, child?' He then asked her if she would take some dictation. Hitler often calls her 'child', and she thinks of him as 'a kindly paternal figure', who gives her 'a feeling of security, solicitude for me, safety'. She grew up without a father and his protective attitude is something she has always longed for.

Traudl Junge takes off the typewriter cover. It seems such an undignified end, 'the same phrases, in the same quiet tone, and then... those terrible words about the Jews. After all the despair, all the suffering, not one word of sorrow, of compassion'. She thinks, 'He has left us with nothing. A nothing.'

'You are all going up to a hotel in the mountains tomorrow which, after you have all been shot, will be set on fire.'

In the kitchen of the Hotel Bachmann in the centre of Villabassa, a small town in the Italian Alps, two SS guards are getting drunk with a British secret agent. One of the guards has already passed out. The other, called Fritz, pulls out a piece of paper from his pocket and shows it to the Englishman.

'Here is the order for your execution; you won't be alive after tomorrow.'

The extravagantly named Captain Sigismund Payne-Best of the SIS (Secret Intelligence Service, also known as MI6) takes the news calmly. 'What nonsense... Surely no one is going to be such a fool as to shoot any of us at this stage of the war. Why, the whole lot of you will be prisoners yourselves in a day or two.'

Payne-Best knows the SS well. For five and a half years, the 59-year-old agent has been held in chains by the SS, mostly in solitary confinement in Sachsenhausen concentration camp. In November 1939 he was captured at the Dutch–German border while in the middle of what he'd thought were peace negotiations between the German government and the British government of Neville Chamberlain. Britain and Germany had been at war for two months, and Chamberlain was still eager to find a peaceful solution. Churchill, then First Sea Lord, was sceptical about the talks and was vindicated when the Germans broke off the negotiations and arrested Payne-Best and his colleague Major Richard Stevens, in order to find out about British secret intelligence networks in Europe. It was a highly successful kidnapping from the German point of view. Stevens was carrying an uncoded list of British agents in Europe.

Payne-Best is a remarkable man, and in the words of a fellow prisoner, 'the caricature of the Englishman. Very tall, very gaunt, and even stooping a little through emaciation, with hollow leathery cheeks, prominent teeth, monocle, flannel trousers, a check jacket and a cigarette.' His teeth are in fact dentures, his original teeth having been replaced by a Sachsenhausen dentist, due to decay caused by the appalling camp diet. Payne-Best didn't mind the process, despite the lack of anaesthetic, because it got him out of his cell. He speaks fluent German, having been an intelligence

39

officer in the First World War, and he used every opportunity in Sachsenhausen to get to know his SS guards. He speaks with such confidence and authority that his drinking partners assume that he has connections inside the SS and so they seek his friendship.

As Payne-Best tries to read the piece of paper Fritz is waving around, Fritz assures him that all the SS will fight to the last and will never be taken prisoner. What Payne-Best can just make out is a long list of names and an order that they should be executed if there is a risk of them falling into Allied hands. The other guard mutters drunkenly, half fumbling for his pistol, 'Shoot them all – bump them all off is best.'

The names on the list are the most famous of Payne-Best's fellow prisoners – 120 of them – currently asleep upstairs in the Bachmann and other hotels and houses around Villabassa. They are all considered by the Germans to be *Prominente* – prisoners who are politically or socially well connected and could be used as bargaining tools in negotiations with the Allies. The 120 range in age from three to 73. For the past few weeks they have been moved by the Germans away from the advancing Russians. Last Wednesday, they left Dachau concentration camp where they'd been for eight days.

The prisoners on Fritz's list include Léon Blum, former Prime Minister of France and his wife; Pastor Martin Niemoller, an outspoken critic of Hitler and a founder of the Confessing Church – a Protestant movement founded to oppose Nazism, and a fellow prisoner with Payne-Best in Dachau a few weeks ago – and Kurt von Schuschnigg, the former Chancellor of Austria, his wife and three-year-old daughter. Part of von Schuschnigg's punishment for trying to assert Austria's independence before Hitler annexed the country was to clean the toilets of his SS guards with his own toothbrush and towel. They would then force him to clean his teeth.

'Now Fritz,' Payne-Best says, 'surely you don't intend to take part in my killing?'

'*Ja,* Herr Best – but what can I do? You are all going up to a hotel in the mountains tomorrow which, after you have all been shot, will be set on fire.'

Then Fritz has an idea.

'I will tell you what I will do. I will give you a sign before they start shooting and you can come and stand near me so I can give you a shot in the back of the head... You won't know anything about it.'

He pulls out his pistol.

'Turn around and I will show you.'

'Don't be silly! How can I see what you're doing behind my back – why, you might have an accident and shoot me now!'

Fritz turns to his drunk colleague.

'You turn your head so I can show Herr Best how to give the *Nackenschuss*.'

But the SS man just mutters about 'bumping them all off', knocks everything from the table and collapses onto it.

Fritz then starts to tell Payne-Best how his wife and children back home have no idea of all the atrocities he's committed, that he's killed 'hundreds, no thousands of people', and that the war is a terrible thing but that it's the fault of the Jews and plutocrats in England and America. Hitler is a good man and only wants peace.

Payne-Best has heard enough. He makes his excuses and heads to his room.

On 22nd April 1945, Hitler, realising the hopelessness of Germany's situation, screamed at his generals that the Prominente *should all be shot. They no longer had any value as negotiating pawns and he wanted to hurt the Allies in whatever way was left to him. The value of hostage exchanges diminished in Hitler's eyes after Stalin's son*

Yakov Dzhugashvili was captured. Hitler offered to exchange him for German Field Marshal Friedrich Paulus who'd been captured at Stalingrad. Stalin declined the offer: 'I will not trade a marshal for a lieutenant,' he replied. Yakov Dzhugashvili died in a concentration camp.

Stalin's real name is Iosif Vissarionovich Dzhugashvili. Stalin is a pseudonym. It comes from the Russian word for 'steel'.

The Prominente *also included British prisoners, some of whom were held in Colditz Castle, like Churchill's nephew Giles Romilly, John Elphinstone, a nephew of the Queen, and Michael Alexander who, when he was captured in North Africa, pretended he was related to British Field Marshal Sir Harold Alexander.*

In the Führerbunker the conference room is being set up for the wedding ceremony. Five chairs are positioned at the large map table. Traudl Junge has had to take her typewriter and work into the common room outside Joseph Goebbels' room.

The civil magistrate and Home Guard volunteer Walther Wagner arrives in the bunker clutching a two-page typed document. He came to the bunker earlier in the evening, having been summoned by Joseph Goebbels. When he discovered that he was required to conduct a civil wedding service he insisted on returning to his office to prepare the proper paperwork. Wagner is dressed in his Nazi uniform with his Home Guard armband. Hitler's valet, Heinz Linge, reckons that Wagner is as excited as the bride.

About 00.15am

The new Commander of the Luftwaffe, Robert Ritter von Greim, is struggling on his crutches as he climbs the concrete steps out of the bunker. Von Greim has just spent two days with the Führer, having been summoned so that Hitler could personally appoint him to replace the disgraced Luftwaffe chief, Hermann Göring.

Göring's downfall was triggered by a telegram which he sent to Hitler on 23rd April. At the military briefing on the previous afternoon, Hitler had learned that the Russians had broken the inner defence cordon and were in the suburbs of north Berlin. There was no news of a German counter-attack. Hitler started to yell. He ranted, without pausing, for half an hour. He screamed about failure, lies, corruption and betrayal until he finally collapsed, sobbing, into an armchair. He declared that the war was lost. It was the first time he had actually said it. Everyone was free to go, he murmured, but he would stay in Berlin until the end. His only remaining duty was to die.

'There's not much more to fight for,' he concluded, 'and if it's a matter of negotiations, the Reich Marshal can do better than I.'

The Reich Marshal was Hermann Göring, who had been named as Hitler's successor in 1941. The comment was meant to be dismissive, but Göring's representative in the bunker, Karl Koller, took it seriously and immediately set off to Bavaria to inform his boss.

When Göring heard the news he was astonished and excited. He attempted to compose a telegram to the Führer in order to clarify and confirm the situation. He was, however, too verbose to draft anything brief enough for a telegram, so his message was rewritten by Koller:

'FÜHRER! – In view of your decision to remain at your post in the fortress of Berlin, do you agree that I take over, at once, the total leadership of the Reich, with full freedom of action at home and abroad, as your deputy, in accordance with your decree of 29th June 1941? If no reply is received by ten o'clock tonight, I shall take it for granted that you have lost your freedom of action, and shall consider the conditions of your decree as fulfilled, and shall

*act in the best interests of our country and our people. You know
what I feel for you in this gravest hour of my life. Words fail me to
express myself. May God protect you, and speed you quickly here
in spite of all. Your loyal – HERMANN GÖRING.'*

*When the telegram reached the bunker on the evening of 23rd
April, it triggered another Führer rage about corruption and betrayal.
Hitler's private secretary, Martin Bormann, a personal enemy of
Göring, drafted the response, which stripped him of his position as
successor, and demanded immediate resignation on health grounds
in order to avoid further measures. Göring resigned within half an
hour. Hitler then ordered Bormann to summon Robert Ritter von
Greim, one of Germany's most decorated pilots.*

*Robert Ritter von Greim made an almost impossible flight into
Berlin, arriving on 26th April. By now the Russians had control of
the sky above the German capital and the bottom of von Greim's
plane was torn apart by anti-aircraft guns. He suffered a serious leg
injury and his companion, the tiny aviatrix Hanna Reitsch, had to
lean over his shoulders to land the plane safely on the temporary
runway by the Brandenburg Gate, a 400-metre stretch of uncra-
tered road running through Berlin's central park, the Tiergarten.*

As Reitsch now tries to help von Greim up the bunker steps
she is protesting miserably – she wants to stay in the bunker
and 'die at our Führer's side'. Von Greim, however, looks posi-
tively jolly – whether cheered by his appointment, or by the
fact that he is getting out of the bunker. Telephonist Misch
feels sick as he watches them leave. He had hoped that von
Greim would be asked to fly the Führer out of Berlin, and then
they would all have been able to make their escape.

*Misch is one of a number of gentle giants in Hitler's entourage. He
is six foot tall but by his own account has been chosen to work for
the Führer as 'someone who gave no trouble'. Having been badly*

injured during the invasion of Poland in 1939, he had been deter-
mined to do nothing that would jeopardise his work for the Führer.
'Heavy field boots sinking into mud and filth instead of extra-light
dazzling made-to-measure boots on thick carpet – no thank you.'
Here in the bunker, though, he feels claustrophobic. He thinks
constantly of his wife Gerda and their baby daughter. It has been
six days since he managed to contact Gerda by telephone. He sips
cognac constantly and keeps his pistol to hand.

Hitler is sending von Greim, as head of the Luftwaffe, on two missions. Firstly, he is to mobilise the Luftwaffe to break through the Russian encirclement: 'Every available plane must be called up by daylight!' Secondly, he is to arrest and arrange the execution of Fegelein's boss, SS chief Heinrich Himmler.

When he learned the news of Himmler's overtures to the Allies the previous day, Hitler had shouted at von Greim, 'A traitor must never succeed me as Führer! You must get out to ensure that he will not.'

'Is it not better to live a fine, honourable, brave but short life than drag out a long life of humiliation?'

As she leaves the bunker the aviatrix Hanna Reitsch is carrying a number of personal and official letters. Eva Braun has given her a final letter to her sister Gretl who is staying with their parents in Hitler's mountain home in Obersalzberg. The letter makes no mention of Fegelein's death. The Propaganda Minister Joseph Goebbels and his wife, Magda, have given Reitsch letters for Magda's oldest son Harald, who is being held as a British prisoner of war in Britain.

Magda Goebbels is dressing in her bedroom in the upper bunker. This older bunker is starker than the Führerbunker and her small room is typical with its concrete walls and minimal furnishings: a single bed, a chest of drawers and only a bare bulb for light. Magda proudly pins the golden party badge that Hitler gave her two days ago onto the front of her dress. It is his personal badge, marked with the number 1; the badge of the premier figure in the Nazi Party. She feels it is the greatest honour of her life. Hitler has worn the badge on his uniform for 12 years. During his chancellorship Magda has often stood in as an unofficial first lady, accompanying the Führer on formal occasions, sitting in pride of place at official dinners while Eva Braun is hidden away, confined to her room. The badge confirms her status in the hierarchy.

Magda Goebbels was born in Berlin to an unmarried chamber-maid. Her mother went on to have a long-term relationship with a Jewish hotel manager, Richard Friedlander. They lived as a family in the Jewish quarter of Berlin; Magda went to a Jewish school and celebrated Jewish festivals. As a teenager she chose to take her stepfather's surname. Her first love was a young man called Victor Arlosoroff who was a charismatic leader of the Berlin Zionist movement. Magda became a keen supporter, attending Zionist meetings. When she was 19 and he was 20, Magda and Victor became engaged, but the relationship ended suddenly on Victor's 21st birthday and within months Magda was engaged to a man she had met on a train the day after their break-up.

The man on the train was Günther Quandt, a hugely wealthy industrialist. He was 38, twice Magda's age, when they married in 1921. As a condition of their marriage Magda reverted to her original surname, Richter, as Günther didn't want to appear to be marrying a Jew. Magda's mother separated from Richard Friedlander at the same time. He was not invited to the wedding. That year

Günther and Magda had a son, Harald, who would be 18 in 1939 and immediately join the Luftwaffe. They divorced amicably after seven years and Magda was given a generous settlement.

Shortly after her divorce Magda was taken by a friend to a Nazi rally where she heard Joseph Goebbels speak. She was electrified by his high-octane oratory and approached him afterwards, offering to work for him as a volunteer. They started a relationship, and in 1931 the girl who grew up in the Jewish quarter of Berlin married the man who spearheaded the exclusion of all Jews from the city and instituted the regulation yellow star whereby all Jews were identified. Adolf Hitler was their best man.

Magda never saw her stepfather Richard Friedlander again. His name is on the list of those who died in Buchenwald.

The six Goebbels children, Helga, Hilde, Helmut, Holde, Hedda and Heide, who are aged between four and 12, are sleeping in three bunk beds in the room next door to their mother. Joseph Goebbels' bedroom is separate from theirs, down the main staircase and at the far end of the Führerbunker, next door to Adolf Hitler and Eva Braun's suite. When the children arrived a week ago they were told that Germany was on the verge of winning the war and that they had come to the bunker to be ready to join in the victory celebrations with the Führer. In fact Joseph and Magda decided to join their leader when they realised that defeat was imminent. They want to face death at his side. They have come to end their lives, and the lives of the children.

Magda has spent much of the week lying in bed. She suffers from angina. She can bear to see the children only for brief periods. Most of the work of looking after the children has fallen to the secretaries and kitchen orderlies. Magda has confided to the other women in the bunker that she is terrified that when the time comes she will be too weak to bring herself to kill them.

This evening Magda has written to her oldest son, Harald. When his plane was shot down over Italy in 1944, he was missing for several months. The Goebbels were delighted when they finally learned that he had been captured by the British, which they consider the safest possible outcome, though they don't know where he is being held. He is in fact in the prisoner-of-war camp in Latimer House, Buckinghamshire, where he is very popular with the young RAF officers who interrogate him. Latimer House is a camp for high-ranking Germans and Harald, who is there because of his family connections rather than his rank, is much younger and more affable than most of his fellow prisoners.

Magda Goebbels tries to explain to Harald why she has brought his younger brother and sisters into the bunker:

'The world which will succeed National Socialism is not worth living in and for this reason I have brought the children here too. They are too good for the life that will come after us and a gracious God will understand me if I myself give them release from it...

'Be proud of us ... Everyone must die one day and is it not better to live a fine, honourable, brave but short life than drag out a long life of humiliation?

'My Beloved Son

'Live for Germany!

'Your Mother'

Joseph Goebbels has also written to his stepson. He tells him that he should be proud of his mother. He also warns him:

'Do not let yourself be disconcerted by the worldwide clamour which will now begin. One day the lies will crumble away of themselves and the truth will triumph once more. That will be the moment when we shall tower over all, clean and spotless, as we have always striven to be and believed ourselves to be...

'May you always be proud of having belonged to a family

which, even in misfortune, remained loyal to the very end to the Führer and his pure sacred cause.'

He signs off with the words, 'All good things and my heart-felt greetings, Your Papa.'

Magda and Joseph entrust these letters to Hanna Reitsch, and Magda also gives her a diamond ring. Hitler's parting gift to Reitsch is a cyanide capsule.

'I couldn't have a better master.'

In his study, Hitler is talking to Heinz Linge, his valet.

'I would like to let you return to your family.'

'*Mein Führer*, I have been with you in good times, and I want to stay with you in the bad,' Linge replies.

Thirty-two-year-old Linge was a bricklayer in Bremen when the glamour of the Waffen SS inspired him to join up. Having been sent to guard Hitler's mountain residence, the Berghof, he was selected to be Hitler's chief valet shortly after war broke out in 1939. Linge is a subdued, steadfast man with a large, round face and pale-blue eyes. He is devoted to the Führer, and tells people, 'I couldn't have a better master.'

Hitler looks at him calmly. 'I did not expect anything else from you.'

He pauses and leans against his writing desk. 'I have another personal job for you. What I must do now is what I have ordered every commander to do: hold out to the death. This order also applies to me, since I feel that I am here as the Commandant of Berlin...'

Linge's head is swimming.

'You should put two blankets in my bedroom and get hold of enough petrol for two cremations. I am going to shoot myself here together with Eva Braun. You will wrap our bodies in woollen blankets, carry them up to the garden, and there burn them.'

Linge is trembling. He stutters his reply: *'Jawohl, Mein Führer!'* and leaves the room.

During these last weeks in the Führerbunker Hitler has spent most of his time in his study. It is a small room with an oppressively low ceiling. There's a desk and a stiff upright sofa, more like a wooden bench, upholstered in blue and white linen. There is a small rectangular table where he eats his meals with the secretaries, and a side table with a radio. He has a portrait of Frederick the Great on the wall. The wall of the corridor outside is also hung with valuable paintings which have been brought down from the Reich Chancellery for safety. The concrete floor of the corridor is lined with a red carpet and there are comfortable armchairs in which Hitler's generals often drink and sleep. The bunker's diesel generator is across the corridor and fills the Führerbunker with the drone of its engine and the stench of its fuel.

In London, thousands of people are sleeping on the platforms of the Underground. Over the last five years a real community spirit has flourished – there are bunk beds, toilets and even libraries. The menace of V1 (*Vergeltungswaffe-1*, Retaliation Weapon 1) flying bombs and V2 rockets is over. Churchill himself said so in the House of Commons on 26th April.

The last fatality as a result of Hitler's vengeance weapons was on 27th March. Thirty-four-year-old Ivy Millichamp of 88 Kynaston Road, Orpington (the town had suffered disproportionately as the Germans had been fooled into setting the wrong coordinates in order to hit central London) had gone into the kitchen to boil a kettle when a V2 landed on the street. Seventy people were injured. Ivy Millichamp's husband, asleep in the front room, survived. Ivy was killed outright.

Despite Churchill's announcement that the threat is over, thousands are choosing to stay underground at night. Mass Observation – an organisation set up to gauge public opinion explained the appeal: 'Some come from solitary bed-sitting rooms with a gas-ring, and find they can spend evenings in light and gaiety, surrounded by company.'

00.35am

In Berlin Robert Ritter von Greim and Hanna Reitsch climb out of the armoured vehicle which has brought them to the Brandenburg Gate, where a light aircraft is waiting. They squash into the small two-seater plane. Reitsch is at the controls with von Greim behind her, his crutches jammed down by his feet. They set off down the makeshift Tiergarten runway. The plane picks up speed and soars into the night sky. It's immediately illuminated by Russian searchlights and comes under fire – but they make it into the clouds. Reitsch looks down at the cloud bank, shining in the silver moonlight, 'still, serene, idyllic', and thinks that it looks like a giant quilt wrapped over the flaming city. She heads for Rechlin airfield, where von Greim will issue his first instructions for the Luftwaffe.

Hanna Reitsch is the only woman to be awarded the German Iron Cross (First Class). She won it for her bravery as a test pilot. Before and after the war she set more than 40 gliding and altitude records. In February 1944 she suggested to Hitler that the Luftwaffe develop a plan she called Operation Suicide, in which pilots sacrificed their lives for the Fatherland in the style of Japanese kamikaze pilots.

> Hitler agreed to the plan but, to Reitsch's disappointment, felt that
> it wasn't the right 'psychological' moment to put it into operation.

00.45am

Following Hitler's instructions, Heinz Linge puts through a
call to Hitler's driver, Erich Kempka, in the underground car
park, to ask him to source some petrol.

'Petrol?'

'Yes, petrol. We need about 200 litres.'

'A mere 200 litres?' Kempka quips sarcastically. Petrol is
desperately scarce. 'Is this a joke? What are you going to do
with 200 litres of petrol?'

'Believe me, Erich, I cannot tell you on the phone, but this is
not a joke. We need 200 litres of petrol delivered to the exit of
the Führerbunker as soon as possible. Do whatever you need
to do to get hold of it.'

Linge puts down the phone and pours himself a couple of
glasses of schnapps to help him get over the shock of the implication of this order.

Kempka orders an assistant to syphon off whatever remnants
of petrol he can find in the cars in the underground garages.
The concrete roof has fallen in and most of the cars are covered
in masonry.

'When the Chief has won the war, I can play my own part in the film of our life story.'

1.00am

Eva Braun and Adolf Hitler emerge from their rooms, her arm
through his. She is in her black dress. It is a simple, elegant

dress, decorated around the neck with sequins. Black is the traditional colour of German wedding dresses, though white is now more fashionable. As a girl, dreaming of marriage, Eva was photographed dressing up in her grandmother's black lace wedding dress. Hitler has not changed his clothes and is wearing his usual black trousers and grey military jacket. Walther Wagner, the civil magistrate, greets them nervously. The couple take their seats on one side of the empty map table, flanked by their witnesses; Wagner sits opposite.

Braun and Hitler met in October 1929 at the Hoffman photographic studio in Munich shortly after she had started working there as an assistant. Hitler was one of Hoffman's main customers, commissioning endless propaganda portraits. She was 17 and he was 40. One day he came into the studio, wearing his beige belted Burberry raincoat just as she was climbing a ladder to reach some files from a top shelf. Braun was embarrassed because she had shortened her skirt that morning and she could tell that the man with the 'funny moustache' was looking at her legs. She was worried that he would notice that her hem was uneven.

1929 was the year when Hitler became a household name in Germany and the Nazi Party's popularity began to soar as German unemployment rose in the wake of the Wall Street Crash. Eva Braun was soon in love with this increasingly powerful man and did all she could to insinuate herself into his circle. From about 1931 Hitler started to invite Braun to cafés, to the opera, and eventually to stay.

The first four years of their relationship were very difficult for Eva Braun. Hitler showed her very little interest or concern. She stayed in Munich, working at the photographic studio, living with her strict Catholic parents, while he worked in Berlin, surrounding himself with adoring fans. He rarely called. He frequently let her down. Twice she attempted suicide, and it was after the second attempt in May 1935, when her sister Ilse found her in a coma, after she had taken an overdose of the sedative Vanodorm, that he decided to accept her as his official mistress.

Hitler's relationship with Eva Braun was always hidden from the public, but it was now made known to his staff and immediate circle. He bought her a house in Wasserstrasse in Munich and in the following months had a suite of rooms refurbished for her in the Berghof, his mountain home in Obersalzberg. She still had to hide away when there were official visitors, but privately she became mistress of the Berghof. Their relationship became steady, comfortable. She knew that her job was to keep him relaxed, and she was good at it. He loved her quality of 'Gemütlichkeit', cosiness. He used to say, 'Eva gives me a rest. She keeps my mind off things I don't want to think about.' Always a passionate photographer and film maker who loved to star in her own home movies, Eva Braun dreamed of Hollywood. She would tell people, 'When the Chief has won the war, I can play my own part in the film of our life story.'

Braun's nickname for Hitler is Chief (German 'Chef'); he calls her 'Tschapperl' which translates as 'wench, bumpkin or idiot'.

The two-page marriage certificate is laid out on the map table in the Führerbunker conference room. Wagner reads out the preliminary questions about the couple and fills in the information with a thick blue-ink pen. Hitler omits the names of his parents and gives his address as the Reich Chancellery. Braun, apparently flustered, gives two different street numbers – 8 and 12 – as her address on Wasserstrasse (12 is correct). Joseph Goebbels and Martin Bormann give their details as witnesses. The bride and groom are then asked to confirm that they are of 'pure Aryan descent and free of any hereditary diseases that would exclude them from marriage'.

Hitler's descent, and in particular the absence of any hereditary diseases, was in fact very much in doubt. His paternal grandmother was unmarried at the time of his father's birth and the identity of his paternal grandfather was never confirmed, but it was widely believed to be his foster father, Johann Nepomuk Hiedler, whose surname he took. The change of spelling to Hitler was thanks to a phonetic transcription by the pastor of Döllersheim who kept the register of births and deaths. Johann Nepomuk Hiedler was also the grandfather of Hitler's mother, Klara, so that Hitler's parents seem to have been uncle and niece. The family was certainly beset with health issues. Adolf was one of only two of their six children to survive childhood. The other, his sister Paula, had a learning disability. Hitler himself is believed to have had two forms of genital abnormality: an undescended testicle and a rare condition called penile hypospadias in which the urethra opens on the underside of the penis or, in some cases, on the perineum. The popular British army marching song, sung to the tune of Colonel Bogey, that began, 'Hitler has only got one ball/The other is in the Albert Hall', may have been more accurate than the troops ever imagined.

Having received satisfactory responses, Walther Wagner then reads out the marriage vows: '*Mein Führer*, Adolf Hitler, are you willing to take Fräulein Eva Braun as your wife? If you are, answer, "I do".'

Adolf Hitler repeats, 'I do.'

'Fräulein Eva Braun, are you willing to take our Führer, Adolf Hitler, as your husband? If you are, answer, "I do".'

Eva Braun repeats, 'I do.'

Hitler places a gold ring on Eva's finger, and she places one on his. The rings have been taken from the bodies of murdered Gestapo prisoners. The couple discover the rings (hastily obtained from the Gestapo treasury) are too big.

Wagner then declares 'this marriage is legal before the law'. When he drew up the document Wagner expected the ceremony would be completed before midnight and he dated it '28 April 1945'. He now handwrites '29' on top of the '28'. Then he passes the pen to Hitler as the first named and the first to sign.

The two words 'Adolf' and 'Hitler', side by side and far apart, both slope steeply downward. 'Adolf' is diminished to three zigzag lines with a cross, representing the horizontal of the 'f', on the lowest line. 'Hitler' is more ornate, beginning with a complex loop, but the following letters are tightly compacted.

Eva Braun's signature is in tidy schoolgirl italics. She automatically begins her surname with the letter B, then crosses it out and signs, 'Eva Hitler, *geb* (née) Braun'. Goebbels and Bormann then sign as official witnesses. Goebbels uses the title Dr, and like Eva writes neatly in the correct place. Martin Bormann's signature is a big confident illegible scrawl. The final signature, 'W Wagner', is easy to read.

'How I love him! What a fellow! Then he speaks. How small am I! He gives me his photograph. With a greeting to the Rhineland. *Heil Hitler*! I want Hitler to be my friend. His photograph is on my desk.'

The witnesses to the marriage are the only two senior Nazis who have stayed with Hitler in the bunker. They have been locked in a battle for primacy of position since 1933. Both are ruthlessly ambitious. Witnessing Hitler's marriage and facing death at his side is their final reward.

Goebbels is not a medical doctor but uses the title he earned by completing a doctoral thesis about 19th-century Romantic literature at the University of Heidelberg in 1921. A very short, thin, dark-haired man with a deformed foot, Goebbels was mockingly known as 'our little doctor' by those in Hitler's circle who conformed to the strapping blonde Aryan ideal which his propaganda promoted.

As Minister of Propaganda, Joseph Goebbels has been instrumental in creating the myth of the Führer, the great leader who will save the nation, whom he has frequently presented in biblical terms, calling Hitler 'holy and untouchable' and even anticipating his death in Christ-like imagery: 'An hour may come when the mob rages around you and roars, "Crucify him!" Then we shall stand firm as iron and shout and sing "Hosanna!"'

Goebbels' personal relationship with Hitler is intense. In 1926 Goebbels demanded that 'the petty bourgeois Adolf Hitler' be expelled from the National Socialist Party. But three weeks later Hitler embraced him publicly and Goebbels swept away his previous objections to Hitler's views on communism, foreign policy and private property. His private diary takes on a homoerotic charge, and an adolescent tone: 'How I love him! What a fellow! Then he speaks. How small am I! He gives me his photograph. With a greeting to the Rhineland. Heil Hitler! I want Hitler to be my friend. His photograph is on my desk.' Hitler initially rewards this enthusiastic little man with promotion, but later cools. Hitler never allows any of his inner circle to feel secure in their position.

Martin Bormann is the Führer's private secretary. His name is largely unknown to the public but as the person who controls communication between Hitler and the rest of the world he is arguably the most powerful person in the country, in some ways more powerful than the Führer. In the isolation of the bunker he decides what information Hitler gets, and who is allowed to communicate with the leader. He controls Hitler's finances. Among Hitler's entourage he is nicknamed the 'Brown Eminence' and is widely loathed. Eva certainly detests him. She has always felt herself in competition with him for Hitler's attention and has resented the fact that he is the person who gives her an allowance and to whom she has to go if she incurs extra expenses. He is a short, overweight, graceless man who understands the power of secrecy. He has never courted publicity and has always worked as a functionary. The only time he has ever come to the public's attention was in 1923 when, together with Rudolf Höss, who went on to become Commandant of Auschwitz, he was arrested for the murder of his elementary school teacher Walther Kadow. Kadow moved in the same far-right circles and was suspected of having betrayed a colleague. Höss and Bormann lured him into a forest where they beat him with maple saplings until he collapsed. They then slit his throat and finally shot him in the head. Höss was sentenced to ten years' hard labour, Bormann to one year in prison. On the grounds that it was impossible to decide whether Kadow had died from the beating, the throat-slitting or the shooting, both were found guilty of manslaughter rather than murder.

For the last four years Bormann has stayed constantly at Hitler's side, keeping the same unconventional hours, present but silent. His ability to listen matches Hitler's ability to speak. He is ruthlessly efficient and always carries a notebook which he whips out whenever the Führer expresses an opinion or even hints at an instruction.

1.25am

Landing safely at Rechlin airfield, 150km north of Berlin, an emotional Hanna Reitsch is exhilarated by the successful flight. Robert Ritter von Greim, pale with pain, immediately addresses the handful of staff who remain at the airfield and gives the order for all aircraft to support the relief of Berlin. His words are pointless. The airport has been devastated by Allied bombing. The few planes that are left will make no difference.

1.30am

After the marriage ceremony in the Führerbunker, the couple

go back to their private rooms for champagne, tea and sandwiches with their senior staff. Hitler goes briefly to check on Traudl Junge's progress with typing the testaments, then joins the party. He turns down the champagne but, most unusually, as he is normally teetotal, he accepts a small glass of Hungarian wine, sweetened with sugar. Walther Wagner stays for 20 minutes. He has a glass of champagne and a liverwurst sausage, and then sets off back to his Home Guard post in a wine cellar on Unter den Linden. He will be shot in the head two days later, caught in the crossfire of a street battle.

Hitler's valet, Heinz Linge, is struck by Eva's composure. He congratulates her as 'Frau Hitler' and her eyes light up. For a moment she lays her hand on his forearm and smiles.

Hitler's mind is still on his political testament; he sends both Martin Bormann and Joseph Goebbels away from the party, at different moments, to add more names to the list of appointments which Traudl Junge is still typing. Junge is tired and very frustrated by the constant changes.

> **It really makes no odds to us if we kill someone.**
>
> **Heinrich Himmler**

Three hundred kilometres away, in his headquarters in the police station in Lübeck near the Baltic coast, Heinrich Himmler is poring over astrological charts with the astrologer Walther Wulff and Walter Schellenberg, the SS head of foreign intelligence.

As soon as Himmler heard that news of his attempts to start peace negotiations with the Allies had become public, he summoned Schellenberg, who had been involved in setting up the meetings with the Swedish Count Folke Bernadotte.

As Schellenberg wrote later, 'I realised that my position with Himmler would now be so difficult that I should have to face the fact that I might be liquidated.'

In order to protect himself, Schellenberg decided to take Walther Wulff with him to meet Himmler. He knew that the deposed SS chief could never resist having his horoscope read and he hoped that Wulff would be able to keep Himmler calm.

Himmler is chewing on a fat cigar. He smells strongly of brandy and is sweating and shaking and close to tears. He is terrified that he could be arrested or simply shot on Hitler's orders at any moment. Schellenberg and Wulff are equally tense. Wulff has spent time imprisoned by the Gestapo. He has agreed to help Schellenberg but he is anxious not to aggravate the SS chief with his predictions. As agreed with Schellenberg in advance, Wulff tells Himmler that the stars suggest the best course of action is to send Schellenberg back to Count Bernadotte in Sweden. Schellenberg is committed to trying to rescue the talks about talks. Studying the charts, Himmler finally agrees that Schellenberg can discuss the ending of the German occupation of Scandinavia with Bernadotte.

Himmler's biggest concern is what the charts have to say about his personal future and that of his mistress, Hedwig Potthas, and his children. He has no idea what to do and keeps asking Wulff whether he should kill himself, or whether he could have a future. He asks Wulff to explain how safe various countries are, in astrological terms. Should he flee, for example, to Czechoslovakia? Wulff advises that the charts aren't looking good for Czechoslovakia. It is the position of the stars, rather than the position of the Russian army approaching the Czech capital that concerns Himmler. He eventually decides that he will remain in Lübeck but that Schellenberg should travel to Denmark rather than Sweden. With enormous relief, Schellenberg rushes off to pack.

Schellenberg's nervousness that he might be 'liquidated' is based on the fact that Himmler holds it a virtue to overcome any feelings of compassion which might prevent one from carrying out an execution. Addressing SS officials at a secret meeting in 1943, he explained, 'Most of you here know what it means when 100 corpses lie next to each other, when there are 500 or when there are 1,000. To have endured this and at the same time to have remained a decent person – with exceptions due to human weaknesses – has made us tough, and is a glorious chapter that has not and will not be spoken of.'

2.30am

In Villabassa in the Italian Alps, British MI6 agent Sigismund Payne-Best is sitting in his bedroom in the Hotel Bachmann waiting for news. Telephone contact has been made with German army units still fighting in the hills around Villabassa. Payne-Best had sent a message to the German area commander saying that he must come to their assistance – if the *Prominente* are executed by the SS, the Commander would be held responsible by the Allies when the war is won, for allowing such a blatant war crime to take place.

Waiting with Payne-Best is fellow prisoner General Alexander von Falkenhausen. Payne-Best hasn't told von Falkenhausen about the drunken warning from the SS guard, as the threat of execution will spread panic, and if people try to escape it will lead to reprisals. Payne-Best believes they should stay put and negotiate their way out of the crisis, hoping the German army Commander will arrive and take over. The Englishman knows full well that few of the SS guards have any enthusiasm for the mass execution due to take place later in the day.

General Alexander von Falkenhausen was the German army

Commander-in-Chief in Belgium until his implication in the 20th July 1944 plot to kill Hitler. The would-be assassin was Colonel Claus von Stauffenberg, an aristocratic army officer disillusioned by Nazi ideology and by his experiences on the Eastern Front, who planted a bomb in a briefcase in Hitler's headquarters in East Prussia. When it detonated, Hitler was blocked from its full blast by the heavy oak conference table. Four of the 24 people with him died of their injuries but Hitler, who had been leaning over the table at the moment of the explosion, suffered only splinters and small cuts and burns, singed hair and burst ear drums. He was well enough to meet Mussolini later that afternoon, and to show him the scene of his 'miraculous escape'.

Hundreds of German army officers like von Falkenhausen were arrested, suspected of being in on the conspiracy, and over 5,000 people were executed – not just army officers but also civilian opponents of the regime. Under an ancient German law known as Sippenhaft, members of the suspect's family could be arrested too. In the hotel with Payne-Best and von Falkenhausen are many relatives of those executed after the bomb plot.

At Rechlin airfield, Hanna Reitsch takes the controls of a tiny open-top aircraft and von Greim, again, squashes in beside her as they set off for Lübeck. They are now focused on the second part of the mission: to capture Heinrich Himmler. They have decided to head to Admiral Dönitz's headquarters in the hope that he will have information on Himmler's whereabouts.

In the Führerbunker the wedding celebrations continue. Adolf Hitler sits quietly while Eva knocks back the champagne. Generals Krebs and Burgdorf are on cognac.

General Krebs is the Army Chief of Staff, recently appointed on the grounds of his readiness to comply with the Führer's will. His predecessor, General Guderian, was sacked for disagreeing with what he regarded as Hitler's suicidal military decisions. Krebs is a much decorated, monocle-wearing infantry general, who joined the military in 1914 and never left. He is a fluent Russian speaker, the only Russian speaker in the bunker, having served as the military attaché in Moscow from 1936 to 1939.

General Burgdorf is more junior, a large and florid character, who is serving as Hitler's chief army adjutant. Following the attempted assassination of Hitler in July 1944, it was General Burgdorf who undertook the murder of Field Marshal Rommel. Rommel was believed to have had a peripheral involvement but Hitler knew that he could not put the country's favourite general on trial for treason. Burgdorf was sent to Rommel's family home on 14th October 1944 with instructions to give Rommel a choice: he would either be tried and executed for treason, or he would commit suicide and his family would be guaranteed immunity from prosecution. Burgdorf told Rommel that he had the poison on him. It would only take three seconds. The man known as the Desert Fox said goodbye to his wife Lucie and their 15-year-old son Manfred ('I shall be dead in half an hour...') and left the house with Burgdorf. They drove to a quiet country road, where Rommel took the poison. Hitler sent a message of condolence to Lucie.

Poor Neville Chamberlain believed that he could trust Hitler. He was wrong. But I don't think I'm wrong with Stalin.

Winston Churchill

About 3.00am

In Milan, two bodies are being dumped from a removal van onto the cobbles of the Piazzale Loreto. They are the mud-spattered remains of Italy's deposed dictator Benito Mussolini and his mistress Clara Petacci. He's wearing a grey-brown jacket, grey trousers with red and black stripes down the sides and black boots. A crowd swiftly gathers and people start pelting them with vegetables, spitting, kicking and urinating on the bodies; shots are fired into Mussolini's head. His eyes are still open. A woman fires five bullets into Mussolini's body shouting, 'Five shots for my five assassinated sons!' Piazzale Loreto has been chosen as the site to dump the bodies, as it was here that 15 executed partisans had been publicly displayed in August 1944.

On Friday 27th, Mussolini had been captured by Italian partisans. He had tried to disguise himself in the helmet and greatcoat of a German soldier and pretended to be asleep in the back of an army truck. He and Clara were taken to a partisan safe house in the hills. At four o'clock the following afternoon a man named Walter Audisio arrived, claiming to have come to rescue them. He was in fact a member of the Italian resistance. He drove them to a villa near the village of Giulino di Mezzagra above Lake Como. There Audisio read out a death sentence in the name of the Italian people and shot them both. One report claimed that Mussolini cowered in terror, another that he pulled open his coat and shouted, 'Aim for the heart!'

One hundred and fifty miles away, Allied trucks and jeeps of the 2nd New Zealand Division, part of the British Eighth Army, are driving through the dark streets of the northern Italian city of Padua. Men and women are running alongside shouting, '*Viva! Viva!*' Some are clapping, some are crying. The troops stop their vehicles in a small square in front of a church. Thirty-five-year-old Major Geoffrey Cox, a former *Daily Express* journalist turned intelligence officer, watches as groups of soldiers head into the nearby streets to deal with snipers. Desperately tired, Cox gets his bed roll out from his jeep and lies down in the back of a truck. The sound of rifle fire echoes around the square.

The New Zealanders are leading a charge to get to the large port of Trieste before Marshal Tito's Yugoslav Fourth Army. In their way is the German army and Fascists loyal to Mussolini. The Yugoslavs want Trieste as part of a new, larger Yugoslavia of which Tito is provisional prime minister. His country was invaded by the Axis powers in 1941, and since then the Allies have supported the Yugoslav resistance. But Trieste is important as a gateway to get supplies to Allied troops heading across the Alps and into Austria – plus, whoever controls the city, controls the northern Adriatic. Churchill is deeply concerned with the shape of Europe after the war. Two days earlier he sent a telegram to President Truman: 'The great thing is to be there before Tito's guerillas are in occupation. Therefore it does not seem to me there is a minute to wait. The actual status of Trieste can be determined at leisure. Possession is nine points of the law.'

Churchill also told Truman there will be 'great shock' when the US army withdraws from some of their zones of occupation in Germany and hands the territory over to the Russians, as agreed at the Yalta Conference. So if at the same time the northern Adriatic was occupied by Yugoslavs, 'who are the Russians' tools and beneficiaries', in Churchill's words, 'this shock will be emphasised in a most intense degree'.

The events of the last days of April 1945 had been shaped by the final conference between Churchill, Roosevelt and Stalin, held in early February at Yalta in the Crimea, with Stalin as host. Stalin arrived in the Crimea by train (he had a fear of flying), Roosevelt in the first presidential plane, nicknamed 'Sacred Cow', and Churchill also by plane, with plenty of whisky to fend off the typhus and lice he believed thrived in Yalta.

The Crimea had been occupied by the Germans, and the last Tzar's summer palace, where the conference took place, had been thoroughly looted, so furniture, linen and paintings had all been brought in by train from Moscow's best hotels – along with most of their staff. 'We could not have found a worse place for a meeting if we had spent ten years on research,' Churchill complained.

At the end of the first day things were not going well. Anthony Eden, the British Foreign Secretary, wrote that night, 'Stalin's attitude to small countries struck me as grim, not to say sinister.' He was right. Stalin's aim was to regain all the territory that had ever been under Russian rule, and as neighbours he wanted regimes that that could be controlled from Moscow. Stalin was convinced that Germany would rise again within 25 years and he wanted Poland as a buffer state under his influence. Roosevelt and Churchill wanted to ensure that any Polish government included Polish politicians who were in exile in London. Churchill especially needed a free Poland – after all, this was the reason that Britain had gone to war in the first place – 'the cause for which Britain drew the sword'. It was decided at Yalta that a Polish provisional government would be set up – the form of which would be decided by a commission. As for Germany, an agreement stated that the Allies 'shall possess supreme authority with respect to Germany. In the exercise of such authority they will take such steps, including the complete dismemberment of Germany as they deem requisite for future peace and security'.

On the last day of the conference, 11th February, the Big Three made the final changes to a statement of intent (Churchill objected to the word 'joint' as it reminded him of 'the Sunday family roast of mutton'.) Published the next day, the communiqué stated that the Declaration on Liberated Europe meant the establishment of order to enable 'the liberated peoples to destroy the last vestiges of Nazism and fascism and to create democratic institutions of their own choice'.

But Yalta had merely papered over the cracks. It was clear to most at the conference that the Soviets and the Western powers had very different plans for the future of Europe. 'The only bond of the victors is their common hate,' wrote Churchill.

About 3.15am/4.15am UK time

Flying from Rechlin airfield to Lübeck on the Baltic in a little two-seater, Hanna Reitsch and Luftwaffe chief Robert Ritter von Greim are under attack from Russian fighter planes which have control of the skies. Reitsch, who is one of the most skilled pilots of her generation, manages to dodge all attacks.

In the Hotel Bachmann in the Italian Alps, the news that British MI6 agent Captain Sigismund Payne-Best has been waiting for has arrived. General Vietinghof of the nearby German army garrison is sending a company of infantry to ensure the safety of the *Prominentes* from the SS. Vietinghof has promised to let the advancing Americans know that there are important prisoners in the Hotel Bachmann and in homes in Villabassa.

Relieved at the news, Payne-Best finally goes to bed.

> **You are free. We are the English army. Be calm. Food and medical help is on the way.**
>
> **Loudspeaker announcement to the inmates**
> **of Bergen-Belsen, 15th April 1945**

Twenty-one-year-old medical student Michael Hargrave is being woken up by an army cook in a transit camp outside Cirencester. It's bitterly cold and Michael has spent the night dressed in socks, trousers and sweater. He heads quickly to the washhouse, as he leaves for Germany in an hour.

A month ago, Michael saw a notice pinned to a board in Westminster Hospital asking for students to volunteer to help starving Dutch civilians. Yesterday afternoon Michael and 94 other volunteers were photographed by the press and then informed there had been a change of plan – they were not going to Holland at all, but to Bergen-Belsen concentration camp in north-western Germany.

The washhouse turns out to be a corrugated iron shed with no door and no glass in the windows. Michael has a very quick wash.

In Bergen-Belsen on the morning of the 15th April, Clara Greenbaum, her eight-year-old daughter Hannah and her three-year-old son Adam heard a strange rumbling sound. Leaving their hut they saw that the watchtowers were empty – in fact there were no guards anywhere. Thousands of emaciated prisoners stood facing the direction of the noise; many others lay on the ground dying. After a while, tanks with Union Flags flying from their turrets appeared, circled the camp twice and then stopped in front of the gates. Then about 500 soldiers arrived, gazed into the camp, and one by one were sick. Prisoners turned away in embarrassment. Clara and Hannah began to cry for the first time in three years. Then soldiers threw food over the fence and a tank smashed through the gates.

There to greet the British was the Commandant, Josef Kramer, a former unemployed electrician who had joined the SS in 1932. He stayed in the camp because he had been ordered to do so by his superiors.

Bergen-Belsen was built originally as a camp for well-connected, so-called 'exchange Jews', who could be swapped for German POWs. As the Russians advanced west, camps in Poland were evacuated by the Germans and the inmates forced to march on foot or sent in cattle trucks to camps in Germany. By early April,

Bergen-Belsen was hopelessly overcrowded. At the end of 1944 there were 15,257 inmates, by April there were 44,000.

In February there was a massive outbreak of typhus at Bergen-Belsen. It's believed that between 20,000 and 30,000 died. Two of the victims were 15-year-old Anne Frank and her sister Margot, who had hidden with their parents in a secret annexe in Amsterdam until they'd been discovered the previous August. The sisters were buried in a mass grave with 10,000 others just a few days before the British arrived.

One of the first correspondents to visit Belsen was the BBC's Richard Dimbleby. His colleague Wynford Vaughan-Thomas met him driving away from the camp. He looked like a changed man.

'You must go and see it, but you'll never wash the smell of it off your hands, never get the filth of it out of your mind. I've just made a decision… I must tell the exact truth, every detail of it, even if people don't believe me. This is an outrage… an outrage.'

A few hours later, Dimbleby recorded a 14-minute report describing the horrors of the camp.

Since July 1944 the BBC had been broadcasting details of what had been happening to Jews in camps such as Auschwitz thanks to reports smuggled out by the Polish resistance. Dimbleby's report was the first radio eyewitness account of the barbarism of the camps.

'I found a girl, she was a living skeleton… stretching out her stick of an arm and gasping something, it was: "English, English, medicine, medicine" and she was trying to cry but didn't have enough strength.'

One of Richard Dimbleby's last broadcasts from Germany will be from Hitler's study – sitting in his chair. Dimbleby came away with knives, forks and spoons with the initials A.H., which he would provide at dinner parties for people he didn't like.

4.00am

In the Führerbunker Traudl Junge finally finishes typing Hitler's testaments. The copies are taken through to the conference room for the witnesses to sign. Goebbels, Bormann and the generals Burgdorf and Krebs sign the three copies of the political testament as witnesses and Hitler's Luftwaffe adjutant Nicolaus von Below signs the will. Junge thinks how the bunker light makes everyone look grey and exhausted as she returns to the desk in the common room to put the papers in order.

Von Below has been with Hitler throughout the war, representing the Luftwaffe Commander Hermann Göring. He is honoured to be asked to sign Hitler's will. The last few days have been particularly tense as he has had to manoeuvre carefully to distance himself from his disgraced boss. Von Below is longing to find a way to leave the bunker. Only three weeks ago he travelled to the Baltic coast to say goodbye to his pregnant wife and three children. He had travelled back to Berlin in beautiful sunshine with great reluctance. He believes it unlikely that he will leave the capital alive.

'On behalf of my children, who are too young to speak for themselves, but who would unreservedly agree with this decision if they were old enough, I express an unalterable resolution not to leave the Reich capital...'

About 4.15am

Joseph Goebbels bursts in on Traudl Junge as she makes final corrections. He is weeping and shaking. He chokes out his words: 'The Führer wants me to leave Berlin, Frau Junge! He has ordered me to take a leading post in the new government. But I can't. I can't leave Berlin. I can't leave the Führer's side! I am *Gauleiter* of Berlin. My place is here. I can't see the point of carrying on living if the Führer is dead...'

Traudl Junge has never seen him so upset.

'He said to me, "Goebbels, I didn't expect YOU to disobey my last order as well!" I can't understand. The Führer has made so many decisions too late – why must he make this last decision too soon?'

Goebbels then asks her to take down his testament. She puts aside the documents she's been working on and picks up her shorthand pad and pencil. He starts dictating:

'For the first time in my life, I must categorically refuse to obey an order of the Führer. My wife and children join me in this refusal. Otherwise – quite apart from the fact that feelings of humanity and loyalty forbid us to abandon the Führer in his hour of greatest need – I should appear for the rest of my life as a dishonourable traitor and common scoundrel, and should lose my self-respect together with the respect of my fellow citizens.

'For this reason, together with my wife, and on behalf of my children, who are too young to speak for themselves, but who would unreservedly agree with this decision if they were old enough, I express an unalterable resolution not to leave the Reich capital, even if it falls, but rather, at the side of the Führer, to end a life which will have no further value to me if I cannot spend it in the service of the Führer, and by his side.'

Joseph Goebbels asks for three copies to be sent as addenda with Hitler's political and private testaments.

Traudl Junge starts typing and concentrates on typing as fast as she can without making errors. She is longing to go to bed. She has spent most of the last week looking after the Goebbels children, reading them fairy tales, playing forfeits. The thought of them brings a lump to her throat but she feels like an automaton. She keeps typing, trying to get these last three documents word perfect.

4.30am

Hanna Reitsch has commandeered a car at Lübeck airfield and is driving von Greim towards Admiral Dönitz's headquarters in Plön Castle near the Baltic. Robert Ritter von Greim is feeling very unwell. His leg wound is becoming increasingly painful as infection sets in. Every jolt of the car on the rutted road makes it worse. Their vehicle is under constant bombardment from Russian planes.

5.00am

Adolf and Eva Hitler retire to their bedrooms. In the past, she had complained that he only loved her when they were in bed together. He would prepare for sex with injections of bovine testosterone and she would take medication to stop her periods when she stayed with him. But those days are over. He gets himself ready for bed. He doesn't like help; he doesn't like to be touched. He washes carefully; he has always been fastidious about cleanliness. He changes into a white cotton nightshirt, and hangs his clothes carefully on a clothes horse. Liesl is waiting for Eva in her bedroom and helps her into an Italian blue silk nightgown. In the quiet of their beds they can hear the rumble of the Russian guns. The enemy are now only a few hundred yards from the bunker. The guns have been firing all night, but as dawn approaches the bombardment intensifies.

5.30am

Traudl Junge has finished typing Joseph Goebbels' testament. He almost tears the last sheet from her typewriter, checks and signs it and then retires to his room. Junge finds a spare camp bed and falls into an exhausted sleep as dawn is breaking over Berlin. Many buildings in the centre of the city are ablaze. The nearby Gestapo headquarters are under heavy artillery and howitzer attack. Following a massacre of the prisoners by the Gestapo guards on 23rd April, there are only seven inmates left inside.

Martin Bormann is in his room in the Reich Chancellery cellar. He needs very little sleep and keeps the same hours as the Führer, habitually staying up until the early hours. Tonight, before he settles down to sleep, he writes a diary entry:

'Sunday 29th April. The second day which has started with a hurricane of fire. During the night of 28th–29th April, the foreign press wrote about Himmler's offer of capitulation. The wedding of Hitler and Eva Braun. Führer dictates his political and private wills. Traitors Jodl, Himmler and the generals abandon us to the Bolsheviks. Hurricane fire again. According to the information of enemy, the Americans have broken into Munich.'

American intelligence scouts are indeed entering Munich as Bormann writes his diary.

5.50am

In Padua, New Zealander Major Geoffrey Cox wakes up in the back of his intelligence truck after only three hours' sleep. On a wall above him is a large map of Italy, with little flags showing the enemy divisions. The truck also contains captured German maps and scores of aerial photographs showing the German positions.

The sky is grey and Cox can still hear the sound of gunfire in the streets. He washes quickly, keen to find out what is going on as there is no time to be wasted if the Allies are to beat the Yugoslavs to Trieste. Cox's boss General Freyberg urged his officers, 'Press on at full speed, press on. Give them no rest!'

The Allies are being helped by Italian partisans in the north of Italy who are attempting to stop the retreating Germans destroying vital factories, railway lines and bridges. The partisans are a mixture of former Italian army units and bands of militia formed after the Germans occupied Italy following the armistice of 1943, when Italy left the Axis powers.

Propaganda broadcasts from Rome have given the partisans instructions on how they can help the Allied advancing armies, including guidance on pronouncing the word 'mine' to let their soldiers know where the Germans had laid minefields.

About 6.00am

After a night of travelling under fire, Reitsch and von Greim arrive at Plön Castle which has, for the last week, functioned as the headquarters of all German military forces in the north of Germany, under the command of Grand Admiral Karl Dönitz.

Robert Ritter von Greim is exhausted from the overnight journey but Hanna Reitsch is still exhilarated by the excitement of all their near misses and she gives Admiral Dönitz a passionate account of their mission and ferociously denounces Himmler. She passes on Hitler's order for Himmler's arrest. Dönitz explains that Himmler has the protection of a substantial SS escort battalion and can't easily be arrested.

Reitsch and von Greim will stay in Plön for a couple of days and Reitsch manages to have a brief interview with Himmler. She later claimed that she took the opportunity to convey her disgust at what she considered to be his treachery of the Führer but, given the presence of his SS guard, she was in no position to carry out the heroic arrest she dreamed of.

6.15am/7.15am UK time

The BBC Home Service is broadcasting a 15-minute programme called *The Daily Dozen – Exercises for Men and Women* based on a fitness programme for young recruits in the First World War.

'Have you taken leave of your senses, gentlemen, laughing so disrespectfully at the sovereign leader of your country?'

About 6.30am

A young officer, Bernd Freytag von Loringhoven, wakes his colleague Gerhard Boldt. The two men share a room in the upper bunker, where they sleep and work. Their job is to compile twice-daily reports on the military situation for the Führer's military conferences. Their room contains bunk beds, two desks and two telephones as well as a large map. Part of the room is divided off with a curtain, behind which their boss, General Krebs, sleeps. Von Loringhoven is bursting with news but he doesn't want Krebs to catch him gossiping, so as Boldt sits down to work, von Loringhoven looks up casually and whispers, 'Our Führer got married last night.'

Boldt looks so astonished that von Loringhoven can't suppress his amusement and the two of them collapse with laughter, stopped only by the voice of their boss, through the curtain: 'Have you taken leave of your senses, gentlemen, laughing so disrespectfully at the sovereign leader of your country?'

The two men fall silent and von Loringhoven waits until he hears Krebs get up and leave before telling Boldt all he has heard about the events of the night.

At Stalag VII-A at Moosburg outside Munich, British officer Major Elliott Viney is shaving. In the distance he can hear the sound of gunfire.

Viney has been a prisoner since May 1940 when he was captured after the attempt by the Bucks Battalion under his command to defend the town of Hazebrouck during the retreat to Dunkirk. (Later in 1945 Major Viney will be awarded the DSO for his leadership and bravery at Hazebrouck.)

Viney has only been in Moosburg for a fortnight. On 14th April he and other Allied officers were moved south from the POW camp at Eichstätt, just two days before it was liberated by the Americans. On the march, a squadron of USAAF Thunderbolts mistook the British khaki uniforms for Hungarian military uniforms (Hungary being a member of the Axis powers) and attacked. A number of Viney's friends were killed, and he only just escaped. Later that night when he unpacked his rucksack he found a large bullet from a Thunderbolt lodged in a shoe.

Viney has been up since before five as events in the camp are moving so fast. Last night the SS camp guards surrendered control to the prisoners, and some left. Now the prisoners are patrolling their own camp and manning the perimeter fence. Viney heads off to find some breakfast.

Let us not fail to grasp this supreme chance to establish a worldwide rule of reason – to create an enduring peace under the guidance of God.

President Truman, 25th April 1945

On the banks of the River Elbe, Russian and American troops are recovering after days of drinking and dancing.

On the morning of 25th April in Leckwitz, a hamlet in eastern Germany, an American officer named Albert Kotzebue saw a lone horseman he couldn't identify ride into a courtyard; he and his men followed in their jeeps. The man turned out to be a Soviet cavalryman, Aitkalia Alibekov, on a scouting mission. It was 11.30am. The two mighty armies had met for the first time. Germany was cut in two.

Alibekov led Kotzebue and his men to the River Elbe, where they waded knee-deep through bodies of dead Germans to get to the other side. There they met other Russians, and formal salutes were soon replaced by pats on the back and toasts from the Russians to 'our great leaders – Stalin and Roosevelt' (they didn't realise that Roosevelt had died a fortnight before and been replaced by Vice President Harry Truman). Over the next few days the men swapped cigarettes, danced and got drunk. There were celebrations in Times Square, and in Moscow 324 guns fired 24 salvos in salute.

A few hours later an historic conference opened in San Francisco to determine the shape a new international peace organisation called the United Nations should take.

One thousand delegates from all over the world were there. A US delegate wrote to his wife that San Francisco was 'dazzling... there are rich hotels teeming with the diplomatic corps of the world

– food beyond description – wines, liquors, cars for one's beck and call – free movies...' It was a world away from the squalor of the battlefields of Europe and the Far East. On flags and on the badges worn by the delegates was a new emblem designed by the graphic artists of the Office of Strategic Services (a forerunner of the CIA) showing a world map set against a blue backdrop, with the US as host nation at its heart. Later the map will be tilted to have the international dateline at its centre.

In San Francisco and on the Elbe, all is not as harmonious as it seems. Russian soldiers in Germany mixing with their Allies have been told to 'take no initiative in organising friendly meetings... give no information about operational plans or unit objectives'. In San Francisco Bay the Russians have an 'entertainment' ship called the Smolny, *purportedly full of caviar and vodka, but in reality it was fitted out with spying equipment and a secure phone line to send messages back to Moscow.*

On 28th April, RAF pilot Eric Lapham, who'd recently left a prisoner-of-war camp in Germany after the guards had fled (the last guard meekly handed over the keys to the gate after a POW bravely walked up to him and stuck his hand out for them), came across some Russian soldiers who spoke English. They talked about the Russian–American meeting at the Elbe and then Lapham asked them where they thought their advance would end. 'We were rather shattered when they said "the English Channel"', he recalled.

Our main enemy is America. But the basic thrust must not be delivered against America itself.

Joseph Stalin

Stalin is paranoid that he will be betrayed – and with good reason. On 22nd June 1941 German forces invaded Russia, breaking their non-aggression pact. Stalin was so shocked he said that someone should 'urgently contact Berlin' as Hitler surely didn't know about the attack.

This has made him deeply suspicious of his Allies. He is convinced that the US and Britain would like to secure a separate peace with Germany, and then all three countries would turn on Russia. Until Stalin received a telegram from Churchill on 5th June 1944 ('tonight we go...'), he had been unconvinced that the Second Front – the invasion of northern Europe led by General Eisenhower – would actually take place. Russia has suffered greatly during its four-year battle with Germany. It's estimated that ten million Russian soldiers died in action in the Second World War, representing 65% of all Allied military deaths – the proportion of British and US military deaths was 2% each; a further three million Russians died after they became prisoners of war, and seven million Russian civilians were killed.

Stalin is after revenge, and he wants to get to Berlin first, capture Hitler and put him on trial.

At the end of March 1945, General Eisenhower sent a personal message to Stalin, reassuring him that his armies would not march on Berlin. Churchill was furious that Eisenhower could have made such a unilateral decision – he was convinced that Berlin should not fall into Russian hands (even though it was well within the agreed Russian zone of occupation).

General Patton confronted Eisenhower: 'We had better take Berlin and quick.'

'George, why would anyone want it?'

'I think history will answer that for you.'

7.00am

In a square on the outskirts of Padua, New Zealand soldiers are shaving, their mirrors placed on the side of their tanks. Geoffrey Cox and the other intelligence officers are having a civilised breakfast round a table covered in a white cloth. Women on their way to early Sunday mass stop and stare at the scene.

An Italian man runs up to the officers claiming that a British soldier has looted his flat and taken his radio.

'We fight for you, and then you do this. It is not right!'

'You fight for us?' Cox replies, 'Who the hell do you think we are fighting for here in Italy?'

There has been a great deal of looting throughout the war. In the early years of their conquests in Europe the Germans practised it on a massive scale, stripping factories of their machinery, and museums and art galleries of their treasures and shipping them back home. Now the looting is more opportunistic. British tank crews are reversing their tanks through German warehouse doors and stealing the contents; Russian soldiers are grabbing anything of value they find, from watches to cloth, and sending it back home. They are allowed to send a parcel a month. Many exceed their quota.

Red Army officer Akim Popovichenko wrote to his wife a few days ago, 'Today at last I have succeeded in sending you parcels of valuable items... so many silk and wool fabrics, I can't remember how many metres... there are silk stockings for you, I think about eight pairs, all new of course, then two silk ladies' blouses... you would be the richest woman in Smela. I mean that seriously.'

Daily Express journalist Alan Moorehead, travelling with British troops in Germany, watched a wine warehouse in the village of Steyerberg being looted. Villagers and refugees helped themselves to bottles of the finest wine he had ever seen – a child carried a case of Château Yquem; his parents used a wheelbarrow to carry their haul. Others struggled to hold onto large magnums, jeroboams and rehoboams of Rothschild Château Lafite 1891. Many were dropped and smashed.

Last weekend the BBC's Wynford Vaughan-Thomas told his radio listeners about the former slave labourers he'd seen take tractors, bicycles, lorries, even eggs and chickens from the farms where they'd been forced to work. Vaughan-Thomas concluded, 'Yes, the Germans are in for a grim winter. But then, they might have thought of that before they based their agriculture on slave labour.'

In nine days' time, on VE Day, the world will discover the full extent of the art treasures the Nazis have stolen. In a salt mine at Altaussee in the Austrian Alps, American soldiers will come across a vast network of caves transformed into an underground art gallery, and will be closely followed by a team of experts known as the Monuments Men who will catalogue what has been found. The items hidden away from the threat of Allied bombers include 6,577 paintings, 2,300 drawings and watercolours, 954 prints, 137 pieces of sculpture and 181 cases of books.

Also on VE day, in another salt mine, this time in Weimar in Germany, another team of Monuments Men led by sculptor Walter Hancock, will make an even more bizarre discovery. In a hidden chamber in the mine there are four large caskets. On each is a piece of Scotch tape on which has been scribbled in red crayon the name of the body inside: 'Feldmarschall von Hindenberg', 'Frau von Hindenberg', 'Friedrich Wilhelm, der Soldaten König', and finally the king whose portrait Hitler has hanging up in the bunker, 'Friedrich der Grosse' – Frederick the Great. Slave labourers who've worked in the caves will tell Hancock that in early April the German army brought the caskets to the mine, 'to preserve the most potent symbols of the German military tradition around which future generations might rally'.

The people of Berlin emerge from their shelters in ruins and overcrowded underground bunkers to search for food. sixteen-year-old Armin Lehmann, who is working as a Hitler Youth courier, is horrified by the desperation he has witnessed in recent days. He is haunted by the high-pitched sound of a squealing horse which had been injured by shrapnel. Two men were hacking at its flesh with a knife and a saw. They didn't have the ammunition to kill it first.

The Russian journalist Vasily Grossman, who has accompanied the Soviet 3rd Shock Army is surprised to find the gardens and allotments of Berlin's suburbs full of blossom on this spring morning. He notes, 'A great thunder of artillery in the sky. In the moments of silence one can hear the birds.'

Forty-one-year-old journalist George Orwell is spending a second morning billeted with a German family in the suburbs of Stuttgart, as all the hotels in the city are closed. His only possessions are a typewriter and a large suitcase. Orwell is travelling with the US Third Army as a correspondent for the *Observer* newspaper, and is dressed in the regulation British army reporter's uniform. Yesterday Orwell filed a piece for this morning's paper about the widespread looting by former camp inmates who have got hold of trucks and cars, and with newly acquired rifles are 'letting fly at pieces of driftwood in the stream'.

The German family with whom Orwell has been staying has told him they are keen for the British and Americans to occupy as much of Germany as possible; they dislike the French and fear the Russians. They, and many other Germans Orwell has spoken to, don't believe that the Allies are in agreement about their aims for Germany. Everywhere Orwell goes the Allies hoist only their own flag in the zones they're occupying. The headline above his piece in this morning's *Observer* reads: 'THE

GERMANS STILL DOUBT OUR UNITY. THE FLAGS DO NOT HELP.'

Orwell has been writing for the Observer *since 1942. They had wanted him to report from North Africa in 1943, but he failed the medical the army requires journalists to take. It's believed that Orwell made it to Germany only thanks to the* Observer's *owners, the Astor family, exploiting their many contacts in the government.*

Just a month ago Orwell's wife Eileen died during a routine operation to remove a growth in her womb. Last summer they adopted a baby boy called Richard; he's being looked after by a friend's wife. Orwell decided to return to Europe, because, as he explained to a friend, 'perhaps after a few weeks of bumping about in jeeps etc. I shall feel better.' Orwell's reports for the Observer *are bleak, reflecting his grief and also the fact that he is ill with pneumonia; ill enough to have drawn up a document at the end of March entitled 'Notes for My Literary Executor' – a list of works he wanted republished and those he did not. Orwell sent it to his wife to sign, but by then she was already dead.*

George Orwell is not yet known as a writer. His first book Homage to Catalonia *sold only 700 copies, but he has great faith in a short 'fairy tale' that he's just finished that he knows will be controversial.* Animal Farm *is a satire on the Russian Revolution and tyranny in general. Many publishers in the UK and the US have turned it down as the Soviet Union is a war ally, but Secker and Warburg have taken it on and plan to publish it when more paper, which is severely rationed, is available. They may also be waiting for Hitler to be defeated and for the end of the alliance with Stalin. The manuscript that Secker and Warburg are working with is crumpled and dirty – it is in Orwell's words 'blitzed' after a V1 exploded near their London flat in June 1944 and brought the ceiling down.*

Orwell has taken advantage of the delay, and even as late as last month he's been tinkering with the proofs, asking to change the scene in which the windmill blows up, so that 'all the animals including Napoleon flung themselves on their faces' becomes 'all the animals except Napoleon'. Napoleon – 'Our Leader, Comrade Napoleon' – is a pig who rules Animal Farm and is based on Stalin. Orwell explained to his publisher that this change was to be fair to Stalin who had chosen to stay in Moscow during the German invasion rather than flee.

Orwell has with him in Stuttgart a Colt .32 pistol, lent by the American writer Ernest Hemingway. In Barcelona in 1937, Stalin's agents almost had Orwell imprisoned. This has left him paranoid that they'll attack him again.

7.15am/8.15am UK time

On the BBC Forces Programme they are playing 'Morning Star' by Frank Sinatra.

In Munich, 47-year-old teacher Anni Antonie Schmöger and her sister are at seven o'clock mass. They've decided to come to an early service in case there is an air raid later. On the way to church, Anni was disappointed to see that some of her neighbours had white flags hanging outside their houses. She can't bear to think that Americans will soon be marching through her city.

Suddenly air raid sirens sound and the congregation hear the sound of bombs exploding close by. Everyone runs for the door, including Anni and her sister. Then they change their mind and turn back - they haven't yet had communion.

Everywhere regimental staffs without regiments and division staffs without divisions are looking for

picturesque boltholes. They are unemployed now...
sleeping late, breathing in the mountain air... destroy-
ing ambiguous documents, discussing the situation,
coordinating future answers to awkward questions...

Author Erich Kästner, April 1945

7.30am

Twenty-year-old German Lieutenant Claus Sellier, wearing
only his underwear, is looking out of the window of the Hotel
Gasthaus Zum Brau in Lofer, Austria. He's watching orderlies
putting luggage in the back of jeeps parked in a row along the
street. Standing nearby are a group of sombre-looking officers;
they shake hands and one by one drive off. Sellier and his
colleague and friend Fritz (writing in later life, Claus Sellier
never mentions Fritz's surname) are now the only guests left in
the hotel.

Both men are in the 79th Mountain Artillery Regiment and were
recently promoted, along with all their fellow cadets, to mark
Hitler's birthday on the 20th April. That same day, Claus and Fritz
were summoned to the office of a distraught-looking Colonel Rauch,
who was in charge of their artillery training school in Rokycany,
German-occupied Czechoslovakia. Rokycany was surrounded by
Allied forces and the telephone lines were down. Colonel Rauch
gave Claus and Fritz a mission to deliver two packages – one to army
regional headquarters, which the colonel thought was possibly in
the vicinity of Berchtesgaden in Bavaria, and a second to army
provision headquarters in Traunstein, Bavaria. Claus suspected they
contained requests for urgent supplies. Rauch's collar was unbut-
toned and his face was flushed.

'I selected you because you have excellent records, and you
are from Bavaria. You must get there! Those documents are very

important. *Guard them with your lives! I'm relying on you.'* He gazed at a map. *'It won't be easy – it looks like we're cut off.'*

The two young lieutenants were flattered. When Claus thought about the headquarters, he envisaged the sort of place he'd seen in the newsreels – generals standing around a table, moving divisions across an enormous map. He pictured the oak table that saved the life of the *Führer* when Count Claus von Stauffenberg's bomb had exploded under it.

'I will be standing near it when I present these important documents,' Claus thought at the time.

The reality is somewhat different. Claus never imagined that the army regional headquarters would be in a hotel. When they arrived on foot last night, after an exhausting four-day journey, they handed over the first package to the major on duty. He'd been more interested in reading his magazine than acknowledging the new arrivals. The major glanced at their package and then threw it over his shoulder; it landed on the floor among other papers and envelopes. Claus was furious that they'd risked their lives only for the document to be discarded.

'I guess you didn't know that the army headquarters was dissolved today?' the major said.

'Dissolved? Do you mean the war is over?!' Claus said.

'No, I didn't say that. I said that this headquarters is no longer in existence, as of today. As far as I know the war continues.'

That evening, Claus and Fritz had eaten in the hotel, whilst a group of generals, told jokes and drank plenty of wine. No one returned the young men's greeting of Heil Hitler.

Claus walks away from the hotel window and starts to put on his uniform.

'My vision grew a little misty. Perhaps it was the rain on the Perspex...'

8.00am/9.00am UK time

In the corridor dining room of the upper bunker three young officers, Lorenz, Zander and Johannmeier, are having breakfast. They have been given the mission of delivering the three copies of Hitler's and Goebbels' testaments: one to Grand Admiral Dönitz, whom Hitler names in the political testament as his successor as Chancellor of Germany; one to Field Marshal Schörner, named as the new head of the army, and the final copy to the Nazi Party headquarters in Munich. A carbon copy has been kept for the bunker.

The three officers help themselves to food from a stacked trolley. There is fresh bread from Berlin's only surviving bakery, plus salami, roast beef, pickles and cheese from the vast stores in the Reich Chancellery cellars. The couriers eat as much as they can and stuff their pockets. Only Wilhelm Zander is gloomy. The 34-year-old has begged to be excused from this mission. He wants to die in the bunker. If this is the end for Nazism he can see no reason to carry on.

A couple of miles away, in a neighbour's Berlin flat, 34-year-old journalist Marta Hillers has just finished a breakfast of ersatz coffee and bread and butter when a group of Russian soldiers stride in. Her neighbour keeps the front door unlocked to avoid having it smashed. They are used to invasions of boorish Russian soldiers but one of today's intruders seems different. Marta Hillers described him briefly in her diary which was published anonymously after the war: 'Narrow forehead, icy blue eyes, quiet and intelligent.' His name is Andrei, and he is a school teacher by profession. He tells her that it isn't Hitler who is to blame for the war, but the capitalist system which created him. 'The conversation did me a lot of good... simply because one of them treated me as an equal, without once touching me, not even with his eyes.'

Most days, since the Russians arrived, Marta Hillers has been raped. The previous afternoon two grey-haired Russian soldiers barged in. One of them stood guard as the other threw Hillers onto a bed. He smelled of brandy and horses. He raped her and then forced open her jaws and 'with great deliberation he drops a gob of gathered spit into my mouth'. The assault over, he got up to go and thumped down a crumpled pack of Russian cigarettes on the bedside table. 'Only a few left,' Hillers noted. 'My pay.'

Stalin refused to punish Russian soldiers who treated women brutally. He explained his position to Milovan Đilas, the Yugoslav communist: 'Imagine a man who has fought... over a thousand kilometres of his own devastated land, across the dead bodies of his comrades and dearest ones. How can such a man react normally? And what is so awful about having fun with a woman after such horrors?'

In the cellar of her grandparents' large house in Oosterbeek near Arnhem in the Netherlands, 15-year-old Audrey Hepburn-Ruston is hiding with her mother Ella. She has not been outside since the beginning of March when she narrowly escaped a round-up by Nazis looking for young women to staff Wehrmacht kitchens. Her family has suffered a great deal – her older brother has been taken off to a German labour camp and her uncle has been shot.

Before the German invasion, Audrey was training to be a ballerina and she has taken part in secret performances to raise money for the Dutch resistance. But Audrey, who is using the name Edda van Heemstra, because English-sounding names are too dangerous, is now too ill to dance. She and her mother Ella are malnourished – their diet consists of tulips and turnips.

'Tulip bulbs. It sounds terrible,' Audrey Hepburn recalled later. 'You don't just eat the bulb. Tulip bulbs actually make a fine flour that is rather luxurious and can be used for making cakes and cookies.' Nonetheless, Audrey is suffering from respiratory problems, acute anaemia and oedema caused by malnourishment. The oedema will leave stretch marks on her ankles for the rest of her life.

Audrey passes the time in the cellar doing puzzles and drawings by the light of a lantern.

The Allies have already recaptured parts of Holland, but there are still about 200,000 Germans holding out in the north of the country, including in the cities of Amsterdam and Rotterdam. General Eisenhower has a dilemma – the manpower needed to defeat the German army in Holland will delay the Allied victory. '[The] most rapid means of ensuring liberation and restoration of Holland may well be the rapid completion of our main operations,' he wrote. This is no comfort to the thousands of Dutch who are starving. British intelligence has learned that there has not been a live birth in occupied Holland for nine months due to the malnutrition of the mothers. In a desperate search for firewood, the citizens of Amsterdam have cut down all the city's trees, removed the sleepers from under the tramlines and stolen floorboards and bookshelves from the empty houses of deported Jews and labourers.

General Eisenhower has made sure the Allies are prepared for an airdrop of food – stores are ready to feed a million people every 24 hours, and the RAF and USAAF are well rehearsed. What is needed is a safeguard from the Germans that their planes won't be attacked as they carry out the food drop. Yesterday, in a small school called St Josef's in the village of Achterveld just inside Allied lines, the Allied representatives, led by Major-General Sir Francis de Guingand, met with the German delegation, led by Ernst Schwebel – 'one of the most revolting men I have ever seen,' de Guingand wrote later. At the meeting the Germans agreed to the creation of safe air zones where Allied planes could fly without being attacked.

What has been dubbed Operation Manna is under way. Two RAF Lancasters are now lifting off from their base in Lincolnshire with eight specially built panniers in their bomb bays, containing tea, sugar, dried eggs, tinned meat and chocolate. The crews in the air and those getting ready to fly are apprehensive because the Germans have so far only given a verbal agreement to safe air zones. Flight Sergeant Bill Porter of 115 Squadron recalled, 'As we crossed the Dutch coast on 29th April we could see the German gunners standing by their guns, but the barrels were horizontal.'

Lancaster pilot Robert Wannop kept a war journal and recalled his first flight, just 500 feet off the ground. 'Children ran out of school waving excitedly – one old man stopped at a crossroads and shook his umbrella... Nobody spoke in the aircraft. It wasn't the time for words. My vision grew a little misty. Perhaps it was the rain on the Perspex, perhaps it wasn't. One building was painted with huge white letters "THANK YOU RAF". Those brave people who had so often risked their lives to save an RAF aircrew and return him safely to England. Who had spied for us and done countless other deeds that may never be revealed. They were thanking us for a little food. I felt very humble.'

Two days after the Yalta Conference, on 13th February, Robert Wannop had been part of a massive RAF and USAAF bombing raid on the historic city of Dresden. The orders given to him and other RAF pilots were to 'hit the enemy where he will feel it most, behind an already partially collapsed front... and incidentally to show the Russians when they arrive what Bomber Command can do'. Wannop wrote a few days later, 'Above it all we sat sombre and impassive, each man concentrating on the job in hand. The whole city was ablaze from end to end. It was like looking at a sea of liquid flames, inspiring in its intensity. It was so bright at bombing height that we could easily have read a newspaper.' The firestorm killed at least 25,000 people. It melted the road surfaces and burned people to cinders.

At RAF Witchford the Lancaster crews of 115 Squadron are being briefed about their mission. It is a relief for them to be dropping food rather than bombs.

Eighteen-year-old Dutch girl Arie de Jong wrote later, 'There are no words to describe the emotions experienced on that Sunday afternoon. More than 300 four-engined Lancasters, flying exceptionally low, suddenly filled the horizon. I saw [one] aircraft tacking between church steeples...'

At the end of April and the beginning of May, hundreds of tonnes of food will be dropped over Holland. Some crews tie home made parachutes to the food parcels sent from their families at home and drop them to the starving people below. In among one consignment containing bags of flour and chocolate an airman left a note:

'To the Dutch people.

'Don't worry about the war with Germany. It is nearly over. These trips for us are a change from bombing. We will often be bringing new food supplies. Keep your chins up. All the best.

'An RAF man.'

A few Dutch civilians wear what the USAAF have nicknamed 'happiness hats' – brightly coloured headgear made from the parachute silk from downed Allied airmen; they are so bright they can be seen by the low-flying aircraft. The parachutes had been hidden but now are being worn proudly as a sign that they had helped the Allied cause. The crew of one USAAF bomber were flashed by a woman wearing a 'happiness skirt' – and no underwear.

8.15am

Lieutenant Claus Sellier is standing in the lobby of the Hotel Gasthaus Zum Brau, which until yesterday was the temporary German army headquarters for the region. He is now dressed in the full uniform of a member of the 79th Mountain Artillery Regiment. On his chest are medals that he won fighting the Russians in Hungary. Claus looks over the receptionist's desk and sees that the package he brought yesterday is still lying on the floor, unopened. Claus wonders if he should go round and open the package and check whether it contains what he assumes – a request for urgent supplies from his commanding officer. Instead he gives it a kick, then makes the sign of the cross over it. He's done all he can to complete the first part of the mission – although Claus can see that no one here is interested. In his room is the second package that must be delivered soon.

About 8.30am/9.30am UK time

In a large detached house named Burleigh, in a village outside Coventry, the telephone is ringing. Mrs Clara Milburn answers; it's her friend Mrs Greenslade.

'Aren't you excited?' she begins and explains that she's seen a story in yesterday's *Daily Telegraph* that POWs from Oflag VII-B have been liberated. Clara Milburn's son Alan has been a prisoner in Germany since Dunkirk. Mrs Greenslade means well, but Alan is in Stalag VII-B not Oflag VII-B.

Alan has written regularly over the years; the last letter Clara and her husband Jack received was on 23rd March – it had taken over two months to reach them. Alan wrote about his working party doing gardening in the local town and how cold the weather's been – 'the old ears and fingers get nipped first thing'. Seven other men from the 7th Battalion Royal Warwickshire Regiment were captured with him; three have been moved to other camps.

Last Wednesday a young man named Jack Mercer came to see the Milburns. He had been in Stalag VII-B with Alan up until 18 months ago, but then had been moved to another camp by the Germans. Jack's camp was liberated by the Americans and he'd got home five days ago. Clara and her husband appreciated the young man's visit, especially as he'd cycled 60 miles from Stoke to see them.

Later today Clara will get out an old exercise book on the first page of which she has written 'Burleigh in Wartime', and she will write up the latest war news: '...Berlin is being hammered street by street and house by house. Thousands of Germans are killed each day and their sufferings must be ghastly, but how unnecessarily they have made others suffer – and are not sorry.' Clara has kept this diary since the day Alan was called up in 1939.

Clara is not alone in keeping a diary; hundreds of others around the country are doing the same thing, feeling that they want a record of these momentous days. Many, like Clara, are taking cuttings from newspapers to stick alongside their diary entries.

At Stalag VII-A at Moosburg, British Major Elliott Viney has finished his breakfast and is watching two USAAF P-51 Mustangs fly low over the camp. They perform a victory roll and the men clap and cheer like mad. They can hear the sound of gunfire nearby. They know that liberation is close at hand.

Also watching and cheering the planes is a former P-51 pilot – 24-year-old Flight Lieutenant Alexander Jefferson is enjoying his first evening of freedom for eight months. In August 1944 Jefferson was shot down just outside Toulon while attacking a radar installation, and he was captured and taken first to a POW camp in Poland, and then, as the Russians advanced, moved with thousands of others to Moosburg.

Alexander Jefferson is one of the USAAF's first black pilots. When the US entered the war in December 1941, black people were not allowed to fly planes. In 1943 Jefferson became part of the Tuskegee Institute Experiment, which was set up to determine if black people could, in fact, be pilots. Shortly after, he was assigned to the 332nd 'Red Tail' Fighter group; the Germans soon came to respect these 'Schwarze Vogelmenschen' or 'Black Birdmen' as skilled bomber escorts.

Jefferson will eventually sail home on the liner Queen Mary *two months after being liberated. Years later he recalled the welcome he received: 'Having been treated in Nazi capture like every other Allied officer, I walked down the gangplank towards a white US army sergeant on the dock, who informed us "Whites to the right, niggers to the left."'*

About 9.00am/10.00am UK time

Medical student Michael Hargrave is waiting on the runway at Down Ampney aerodrome by the Dakota transport plane that's due to take him and other volunteers to Germany to help the sick at Bergen-Belsen concentration camp. Overnight snow has been brushed from the wings by the ground crew, the student's luggage is on board and Hargrave is drying his wet gloves on the tail of the plane.

In central Berlin there's a sudden lull in the sound of artillery fire. Several Hitler Youth runners arrive in Boldt and von Loringhoven's office in the upper bunker to report that the Russians are advancing with tanks and infantry towards the Reich Chancellery buildings. For days Boldt and von Loringhoven have been trying to work out how they can get themselves sent out on a combat mission. They have decided that this is their best hope of survival. It is clear that time is running out. Boldt feels sick with tension. The silence of the guns unnerves him.

On the outskirts of Berlin, Yelena Rzhevskaya is attempting to interrogate a 'tongue' – as the Russians call their informants – a 15-year-old Hitler Youth with 'bloodshot eyes and cracked lips'. Rzhevskaya is with the Russian 3rd Shock Army's SMERSH intelligence detachment. She's a German speaker working as an intelligence interpreter. The detachment has just received instructions to make their way to the government district and head for the Reich Chancellery. Their orders are to take Hitler alive, but Rzhevskaya is confused and frustrated as information is 'scarce and self-contradictory and unreliable'. They aren't even sure that Hitler is in Berlin. The 'tongue' isn't talking and Rzhevskaya concludes that he knows nothing: 'He is sitting here looking around but not understanding anything. Just a boy.'

Claus Sellier and his fellow Mountain Artillery lieutenant Fritz have met for breakfast at the Hotel Gasthaus Zum Brau, the one-time regional army headquarters. They are enjoying hot coffee and fresh rolls, but their mood is sombre. Claus is thinking of his three best friends at school – the group of them had been nicknamed the Four Musketeers. Now the others are dead – two died in Russia, one was shot down over the Atlantic.

'What do you think we should do now?' he says to Fritz.

'We'll go to Traunstein and deliver the last package,' Fritz replies, then adds bitterly, 'Do you think Hitler knows that his generals have jumped ship? What are we going to tell Hitler if he calls here? "Yes, Sir, *Mein Führer Hitler.* No, sir, *Mein Führer!* Everybody at your headquarters has gone. It's over, sir! You should go too!"'

The two men laugh, and then head to their rooms to pack.

'S-3 to all battalions. Upon capture of Dachau, post airtight guard and allow no one to enter or leave.'

9.15am

Corporal Bert Ruffle of the Rifle Brigade has been a POW since he was captured at Dunkirk on 26th May 1940. He's a prisoner in Stalag IV-C, an all-British camp near Wistritz in the Sudetenland, and like hundreds of others, Ruffle is forced to work constructing the *Sudentenlandische-Treibstoff-Werke* – an oil refinery. The refinery has taken four years to build and is almost ready to start production. Ruffle never works very hard as he doesn't see why he should aid the German war effort.

Normally they're woken up by a guard bursting into their hut at 4am, but today Ruffle and his friend Frank Talbot of the Queen Victoria Rifles have a more pleasant job. They have been selected to go to the nearby town of Brüx to collect some building material for one of the foremen at the refinery. From the back of their lorry, they can see that the town has been bombed heavily by the Allies.

Ruffle is glad of any respite from the tough oil refinery work. Over the past few weeks their food ration has dropped – a loaf of bread a day now has to feed eight men rather than six. Last weekend was his 35th birthday and to mark the occasion he made himself a cake out of flour, burned barley 'coffee' grounds, potatoes and a small amount of sugar. 'You never saw such a conglomeration in all your life but we ate it,' Ruffle wrote in the diary he's been keeping since January.

Like many of the other POWs, Ruffle is starting to get dizzy spells and is seeing spots in front of his eyes. Their health suffered in the numerous marches they were forced to take as the Germans moved them away from the advancing Russians; one trek in the January snow and mud lasted over six weeks. On the march Ruffle witnessed many scenes of brutality – a British POW killed for trying to grab a potato from the side of the road; Russian prisoners shot one by one as they marched.

Ruffle wrote that evening, 'What would happen was a guard would snatch a prisoner's hat and then throw it away. The prisoner was told to fetch it and, as he left the column to retrieve it, he was shot. It was nothing for a guard to give a prisoner a push and then shoot him as he staggered. All told, there must have been about hundred Russians who would not see Russia again.'

9.22am

Twenty-eight-year-old Lieutenant Colonel Felix L. Sparks is on an important mission. The infantry and tanks of his regiment – the US 157th Infantry of the 45th Infantry Division – have been given the task of taking part in the capture of Munich, the capital of Bavaria and the home of Nazism, and then to push on to destroy Hitler's mountain residence – the Berghof, outside Berchtesgaden. They have been making good progress, covering on average 50 miles a day, and they're now only 30 miles from Munich.

Sparks' tanks are full of fuel, German opposition is light (little more than a few roadblocks), so Sparks is confident that the city will soon fall.

A message is radioed to his jeep from headquarters. 'S-3 to all battalions. Upon capture of Dachau, post airtight guard and allow no one to enter or leave.'

Sparks hears it with fury. Capturing and taking over a concentration camp is going to slow him down – but he knows he has no choice. Yesterday he and other commanders were told that Dachau would be in their zone of action the next day, and that it was a 'politically sensitive area'. This morning, Sparks divided his 56 tanks into two units and told them to go either side of the concentration camp and then to proceed to the town of Dachau, and reach Munich by nightfall.

On 10th July 1943, Sparks landed with the 157th Infantry as part of the Allied invasion of Sicily. It is now day 511 of their long, hard campaign. They fought through Italy to Rome; then sailed to the South of France, fighting across the Alps and into Germany. Six days ago they were in Nuremberg, where in a battle by the opera house, Sparks was forced to abandon his jeep, which had in it letters from his wife Mary and photographs of his year-old son Kirk. Now the only pictures he has of them are stuck on the butt of his Colt .45 revolver.

'I was looking for pictures, not prisoners...'

9.30am

The bodies of Mussolini and his girlfriend Clara Petacci are hanging upside down from meat hooks outside a petrol station on a corner of the Milan square where they had been dumped earlier. As the square filled up, it was hard to prevent the crowd from trampling the bodies, so in an attempt to calm the onlookers, the bodies were strung up. Their names are on placards pinned to their feet.

Milton Bracker, a reporter for the *New York Times*, is pushed towards the bodies by the ecstatic Milanese, into what he would call later 'the circle of death'. The crowd think Bracker's driver, Private Kenneth Koplin, is an American colonel on an official mission to see the bodies, and push him from his jeep to take a close look. Koplin feels sick and can't wait to get away.

In the crowd, taking one of his last photographs of the 600-day Allied war in Italy is a young second lieutenant working for the British Army Film and Photo Unit. Twenty-four-year-old Alan Whicker has seen plenty of fighting – including the Allied amphibious landings at Anzio in January 1944 and the liberation of Rome the following June (where he attended a press conference with Pope Pius XII where US photographers were shouting 'Hold it, Pope!').

On 25th April he and his team of cameramen arrived in Milan, ahead of the advancing Americans, Whicker having swapped his jeep for a large Fiat limousine. They were told by Italian partisans that the SS holding out in the city would only surrender to an Allied soldier. Whicker wrote later, 'I was looking for pictures, not prisoners, but allowed myself to be led towards the enemy stronghold.' There, an SS general, clearly disappointed at Whicker's low rank, nevertheless clicked his heels and handed over his revolver.

Now, four days later, Whicker is in front of the Milan petrol station taking pictures as the mob spit and scream at the bodies of Mussolini and Clara Petacci. He too is appalled at the scene. 'It was not, at that moment, a very splendid victory,' he wrote later.

Alan Whicker's day is not yet over. He has a traitor to catch.

The Italy section of the British Army Film and Photo Unit took over 200,000 still pictures during the Italian campaign, and over half a million feet of film. It came at a high price. Eight of the 40 officer and sergeant cameramen were killed and 13 seriously wounded.

10.00am

A Hitler Youth runner appears in von Loringhoven and Boldt's office in the upper bunker to report that the Russian tanks are now about 500 metres from the Reich Chancellery.

In Padua, New Zealand senior intelligence officer Geoffrey Cox is watching a Sherman tank roar up to his command post. On the front is John Shirley, one of the finest radio experts in the division.

John Shirley has proved to be invaluable to Geoffrey Cox's intelligence team. It's clear from the interrogations of German prisoners that they have considerable knowledge of Allied troop movements, and Shirley has helped establish that they've been using First World War techniques to eavesdrop. The Germans have been laying their own telephone lines alongside the Allies', and so have picked up, thanks to the physics of induction, what was being said.

In Padua, through interrogations and examining captured files, it was also discovered that during the famous battle of Monte Cassino in 1944, the Germans had employed another ingenious method to get information. At one point Allied telephone cables had been laid along a railway embankment that ran towards German positions. The rails worked as reliable conductors, so all the Germans had to do was attach listening equipment to them to discover vital intelligence.

Further back on the Sherman tank, holding white flags in one hand and holding on with the other, are four German officers. Cox orders the men to be put in a disused office building with other German POWs. Prisoners are becoming a real problem; that morning the Italian partisans captured 5,000, and the Allies can't spare men to guard them.

Cox arrives to speak to the four officers and arrange for their transfer south. They give him the Nazi salute. One of them, a general, asks if he can take with him a basket filled with bottles of cognac. But Cox is in no mood to be helpful, having heard the general's aide de camp and other officers making comments about their Maori guard, calling him a '*Neger*'.

Cox picks up the basket of cognac and hands it over instead to the guard.

Like many Allied soldiers, Geoffrey Cox's attitude to the Germans has hardened since the publication a few days ago of photographs from Bergen-Belsen in the forces' newspaper Union Jack. *He has seen death both as a correspondent and as a soldier, but those pictures shocked him – and his men. Cox wrote later, 'To the troops who saw them now, as they jolted forward in the back of their three-tonners… they were one more stimulus to an aggressiveness that was already a flood tide.'*

Two days ago, Cox ripped out a picture of Belsen from Union Jack *and gave it to his interrogator Mickey Heyden.*

'Stick this up in your truck when you're interrogating and see what they say about it…'

'I will – but I know in advance what they will say – "Gräuelpropaganda" [atrocity propaganda].'

A short while later, Cox went to see several hundred captured German soldiers. Taken with them were four Russian women, who the Germans claimed were hospital workers, but Cox could see that was a lie. All the women were crying; one was staring at the

Germans with total hatred. A Kiwi guard offered them some chocolate cake, but they were too frightened to take it.

As he watched them, a prisoner in his late thirties came up to Cox and said he was a lecturer in English from Hanover. Cox was too tired to fully interrogate the officer, so he decided to see where the man's sympathies lay.

'I have always loved England,' the German said. 'I have made this war with a very heavy heart. Many Germans have made this war with a heavy heart.'

Cox showed him the pictures of Belsen, saying, 'Enough Germans had light enough hearts to accomplish this.'

The man looked at the pictures but was clearly unconvinced. Cox pointed out the Russian women.

'Do you feel no shame about that sort of thing? Does it not seem evil to you to take girls like that and drag them from their homes to be used as slaves?'

'It is ugly. But it is one of those things which come from war.' Then the German officer said, 'May I ask you one question? What will happen to us?'

The way the captured soldiers looked at the women had enraged Cox, and he thought of all the atrocities he'd seen in Italy, including just this past Sunday – the bodies of men who'd been dragged out of mass, put up against the church wall and shot.

'You will be handed over to the Russians to rebuild some of what you have destroyed,' Cox lied. The man looked terrified, and as Cox walked away he heard the prisoners start whispering, '...den Russen übergeben!' and he took some satisfaction that he'd scared them.

Lieutenant Claus Sellier and his friend Fritz are walking out of the Austrian town of Lofer and heading for the German border and the army provision headquarters in Traunstein to deliver their final package – what Sellier suspects is a request for urgent supplies for their beleaguered training camp. Claus feels free and strangely elated, since the generals have all disappeared. They come across three German soldiers – one has a bandaged foot and is being helped by the others.

'Where are you going?' Claus asks the wounded soldier.

'Home to Berlin...'

'But that's 1,000 kilometres! And you're limping – how will you get there?'

'What else can we do? We were told to leave the hospital and so we're going home. I don't care how far it is. Anyway – do we have a choice?'

'But there's a big battle round Berlin... Aren't you scared?'

The soldier shows Claus a letter from a doctor. It says, 'Released from the hospital. Do the best you can! We need the beds for the next bunch of wounded soldiers that comes in.'

'I'm going home. I have a bed there – I hope.'

The soldiers go their separate ways.

10.30am

In his bedroom office in the upper bunker, the monocled General Krebs is on the telephone to army headquarters in Berlin. He is told that the German defence is collapsing on all fronts. Then the line suddenly goes dead. The air balloon which supports the radio-telephone communications has been shot down. All telephone communication between Berlin and the outside world has ended.

Almost immediately a Hitler Youth runner arrives with news of a report that General Wenck's 12th Army is still holding out south-west of Berlin. Officers Boldt and von Loringhoven exchange glances. This could be the escape opportunity that they have been waiting for. They need to convince General Krebs that they can do most good by breaking out and fighting with Wenck. They know that if there is any suspicion that they are trying to flee, they will be executed.

Sixteen-year-old Armin Lehmann is one to the Hitler Youth runners. Once the telephone line goes down he finds himself making several trips a day across Berlin's central street, Wilhelmstrasse, taking messages between army headquarters and the Führerbunker. He recalled these last days in a memoir published in 2003:

'It was a nightmare.

'It was a game of Russian Roulette and those who stepped out from cover were taking their life in their hands. At best they would get a mouthful of the constant cloud of phosphorus smoke and poisonous petrol from the incendiaries; at worst they would be sliced down by a Russian rocket. By then Wilhelmstrasse stank with the smell of scorched bodies... It was a particularly nauseating, sickly sweet smell... If a katyusha strike hit anywhere near where one was, it often produced sudden blindness and a terrible disorientation. That was the most dangerous moment. One had to find one's feet straightaway otherwise the next strike could be for you... The crossing had become an open air burial pit.'

In the last four or five days of the Battle of Berlin, 20 of Lehmann's fellow Hitler Youth runners were killed in Wilhelmstrasse. Young boys who refused orders were strung up as an example to others. Only a couple of days ago Lehmann was briefly arrested for staring at the body of a young boy, 'he cannot have been more than 13', who had been hanged from a post with a length of clothes line. He was missing an ear and wearing a Home Guard uniform which was much too big for him. Lehmann had heard rumours that children were being hanged for cowardice, but this was the first evidence he had seen of it.

11.00am/3.00am PWT (Pacific War Time)

John F. Kennedy is fast asleep in the Palace Hotel in San Francisco. The 26-year-old future President of the United States is working as a journalist for the *Chicago Herald-American*, reporting on the international conference to decide the shape of the United Nations that convened four days before. Kennedy's newspaper byline says he gives 'the point of view of the ordinary GI.' Kennedy served as a commander of a motor torpedo boat that in August 1943 was rammed by a Japanese destroyer. His dramatic rescue of his crew has turned him into a war hero.

Last night, Kennedy filed the first of his dispatches for the *Chicago Herald-American* (for which he is paid $250). It began: 'There is an impression that this is the conference to end wars and introduce peace on earth and good-will towards nations – excluding of course Germany and Japan. Well, it's not going to do that.'

Kennedy is sceptical because he knows what is going on behind the scenes. He is incredibly well connected thanks to his father Joe, who was US Ambassador to London between 1938 and 1940. No ordinary journalist, JFK has dined with Averell Harriman the US Ambassador to Moscow, Chip Bohlen, a special assistant to the Secretary of State, and Anthony Eden, the leader of the British delegation and future Prime Minister. Already a womaniser, at one event JFK stole Eden's attractive dance partner.

John F. Kennedy is not a well man – he is thin and drawn. He suffers from Addison's disease and almost continual back pain. Betty Spalding, a friend staying in the same hotel, recalled that 'he wasn't his usual joyful self – he spent a lot of time in bed'. In JFK's hotel room is a back brace that he uses to keep his spine straight.

He will use the brace for the rest of his life. It will be one of the reasons why he dies in Dallas in November 1963. Instead of falling after being hit by Lee Harvey Oswald's second bullet, the brace keeps him upright and an easy target for the third.

Kennedy is one of 600 accredited journalists at the UN Conference whose number bizarrely includes actors Orson Welles, Rita Hayworth and Lana Turner. San Francisco is the place to be.

Charles Ritchie is part of the Canadian delegation, and is finding the conference and San Francisco fascinating. Before he went to bed he wrote in his diary, 'The sun shines perpetually, the streets are thronged, there are American sailors everywhere with their girls and this somehow adds to the musical comedy atmosphere. You expect them at any moment to break into song and dance... This seems a technicolor world glossy with self-assurance.'

Across town, in a restaurant called Fosters, journalists Alistair Cooke and Tony Wigan are eating a meal of two eggs over easy, sausages, pancakes and syrup. They arrived in San Francisco the same day as Kennedy; Wigan is a correspondent for the BBC, 37-year-old Cooke a reporter for the *Manchester Guardian*, although he also is one of three regular contributors to the BBC radio programme *American Commentary*. In his *American Commentary* on 25th April, Cooke summed up what was going on in the UN talks for his listeners in Britain: 'What this conference is about is to see if we can become good citizens of one world, before we become its victims.'

The men have already got into an exhausting routine. To keep tabs on the meetings of the 46 nations represented at the talks, as well the discussions about the role of the Security Council and the General Assembly, they find themselves having to cross town all day. Having spoken to the key chairmen in each committee around 6pm, Cooke then writes his daily piece for the *Manchester Guardian*. Then the two men broadcast live on the BBC, and because of the time difference, don't finish until 2am. They'll be in bed in a couple of hours' time.

Another key part of Cooke's day is telephoning and writing to the woman for whom he has recently left his wife – a war widow named Jane Hawks. Exactly a year later they will be in San Francisco on their honeymoon.

Cooke has filed his piece for Monday's *Manchester Guardian*. It includes the remarkable moment at about 2pm the previous afternoon when, in the middle of a very dull speech at the conference, a delegate from Honduras held up a newspaper with a large headline printed in red saying 'Nazis Quit'. The delegate was then surrounded by photographers glad of something interesting to shoot. Cooke wrote, 'Mr Vyacheslav Molotov [the Russian Foreign Minister] rose and smiled and bowed in what seemed like an acknowledgement of the longed-for news. He motioned the delegates to sit, and the translation that nobody now listened to droned on.' President Truman issued a statement an hour later denying the 'Nazis quit' rumour.

For seven weeks Cooke and Wigan reported from the conference. The Manchester Guardian *paid Cooke five cents a word – he made $2,025 by the time the conference disbanded. Cooke filed his last* American Commentary *in August 1945, and soon after he started a weekly* American Letter, *that in 1950 became* Letter from America. *It ran for almost 60 years.*

'Molotov' is an alias derived from the Russian word for hammer. The Minister is tough and uncompromising, and in Churchill's words 'a man of outstanding ability and cold-blooded ruthlessness'. Molotov carries out Stalin's wishes to the letter, especially as he knows that the Russian leader is suspicious of his Jewish wife Polina who has a brother living in the United States. Stalin has arrested the wives of colleagues in the past.

The dour-looking Molotov has a softer side. While in San Francisco he is writing to Polina almost every day. One letter began: 'Polinka, darling, my love! I'm overcome with impatience and desire for your closeness and caresses...'

About halfway between the concentration camps in Buchenwald and Theresienstadt, an Allied air raid drops bombs close to a long line of Jewish prisoners who are on a forced march away from the advancing Russians. Many of the prisoners use the distraction this causes to try to escape. About 1,000 are caught and shot, about 1,700 continue, but many are too weak and sick to even attempt to run in the first place. When they arrive at Theresienstadt on 7th May there are only 500 survivors.

'No one can imagine what he demands of me...'

Hitler's valet Heinz Linge knocks on Hitler's bedroom door. For the last six years it has been Linge's job to time the Führer getting dressed. Linge holds a stopwatch and when Hitler shouts 'Los!' he sets it going and the dressing race begins. In the early days the faster he got dressed, the better the Führer's mood, but as he has become more disabled the game has become more of a rarity. This morning Hitler has completed the race before it has even begun. He is lying on his bed fully clothed. Except for his tie. There is a special ritual for the tie. Hitler stands in front of the mirror with his eyes closed.

'Los.'

As Linge does up the tie, Hitler counts the seconds. '*Fertig!*' Hitler opens his eyes and checks the tie in the mirror.

Hitler's barber, August Wollenhaupt, knocks and comes in to the bedroom. The Führer has already shaved himself, but Wollenhaupt attends to the hair and moustache which require fortnightly trimming. The moustache is designed to cover his unusually large nostrils. The style has come from America, where it is known as the toothbrush moustache. Both Charlie Chaplin and Walt Disney sport them. In Bavaria it is known as a *Rotzbremse*, 'snot break'. Putzi Hanfstaengl, who knew Hitler from the beer halls of Munich in the 1920s, told him he should grow it right across the top of his mouth, 'Look at the portraits of Holbein and Van Dyck; the old masters would never have dreamed of such an ugly fashion.' Hitler replied, 'Don't worry about my moustache. If it's not the fashion now, if will be later, because I wear it.' By April 1945 its brief period of popularity is very much over.

In the past the barber's work has also been timed, in a good-humoured way. Wollenhaupt likes the Führer, finds him 'genial', softly spoken and appreciates the fact that he always asks after his family, and is interested to hear the word on the street.

Hitler's bedroom is small and simply furnished. The only ornaments are two framed photographs beside the bed. One is of Hitler's mother Klara who died when he was 17. The other is of his first and long-term driver, Emil Maurice.

Maurice was an early member of the Nazi Party. He was impris-oned with Hitler in 1923 in Landsberg Prison where Hitler dictated part of the first draft of Mein Kampf *to him. The two men remained close, working and holidaying together until a dramatic falling-out in 1931.*

For the six years up to 1931 Hitler had been living with his half-sister and her daughter, Geli Raubal, in Munich. Geli Raubal, now

23, was his constant companion. They went to shows, concerts, restaurants, picnics in the countryside and even clothes shopping together. Rumours about the nature of their relationship were widespread. However, Raubal and Maurice were secretly having an affair and when Hitler discovered this he flew into one of his infamous rages. Maurice feared for his life as Hitler threatened him with a gun and chased him around the house, cracking his hippo-potamus hide riding whip. Maurice lost his job and later sued Hitler for unpaid wages, with partial success.

Hitler then introduced strict rules forbidding Geli Raubal from going out of the house without him, unless she had a chaperone. 'My uncle is a monster. No one can imagine what he demands of me...' she protested, a complaint which her friends interpreted in different ways.

On 18th September 1931 Hitler and Raubal had a violent argument shortly before he left for Nuremberg. The following morning she was found dead of a gunshot wound in Hitler's apartment. The gun that fired the fatal shot was Hitler's. The official verdict was suicide but Hitler was forced to issue a statement denying any involvement.

Having left Hitler's service as his personal driver, Maurice joined the SS. There were rumours that Maurice worked for Hitler as an assassin. In 1935, following the introduction of the racial purity laws, Himmler wanted to expel Maurice from the SS because of his Jewish great-grandparents. However, Hitler intervened and Maurice was given the official status of 'Honorary Aryan'. He seems to have paid Maurice a sinecure for the rest of his life, and chose his picture as one of the few personal items he took into the bunker.

Linge administers cocaine drops to Hitler's right eye, which has been causing intense pain for the last few days, and has been problematic in bright light for many years. He also gives Hitler a packet of pastilles to suck throughout the day. These are Dr

Koester's Anti-Gas Pills, which Hitler takes for his stomach cramps and flatulence. They contain a mix of two deadly poisons: strychnine and atropine (belladonna). Linge always carries spare pastilles, and spare reading glasses. Although Hitler never wears glasses in public, at meetings, Linge later recalled, 'he would toy with them in his hands which often resulted in them getting broken when he got tense'.

A week ago Hitler had furiously dismissed Theodor Morell, his personal doctor, accusing him of trying to sedate him with morphine in order to whisk him out of the capital. Morell had, at the earliest opportunity, flown out of the bunker himself and was now in Obersalzberg with Eva's family. He left behind a cabinet of medicines and medical equipment including glucose and amphetamine injections, which he had used daily to boost the Führer's energy. At one point Hitler was taking 28 different pills and injections every day. Morell had been treating Hitler for nine years and, until his unexpected dismissal, Hitler would hear no criticism of him. He recommended Morell to all the senior Nazis, most of whom suffered from symptoms of stress, but Himmler, Göring and Speer all privately regarded the nervous, overweight doctor as a quack. Hitler himself was a hypochondriac but, as well as numerous stress-related conditions, was now suffering from a heart problem and Parkinson's disease.

Hitler sends Linge to bring Wulf, his favourite of the puppies born to his Alsatian Blondi in the bunker. As was evident in the First World War when his only friend was a terrier he called Foxl, Hitler is a great dog lover. He is particularly attached to Blondi, whom he believes to be exceptionally clever and sophisticated. In an interview given by Traudl Junge towards the end of her life, Hitler's secretary remembered that Blondi could provide Hitler with a whole evening's entertainment. She barks on command, and when he gives the order to 'sing' she produces a howl. Hitler is most proud of the fact that if he then instructs her to 'sing like Zarah Leander' – the Swedish singer of a popular song called '*Wunderbar*', famed for her deep voice – Blondi gives a special deep howl. Hitler boasts about Blondi endlessly, telling everyone that she obeys his every word.

11.05am

General Krebs asks von Loringhoven and Boldt, the two officers who are planning their exit from the bunker, to update him on the morning's runner reports in preparation for the midday situation conference with the Führer. They are ready with their maps and papers. Boldt points out the streets where the German forces are making strenuous efforts to hold back the Russians. The other news of the morning has been confusing and contradictory except for the report that Wenck's 12th Army is southwest of the capital.

Von Loringhoven takes his chance.

'General, would it be useful if Boldt and I were to make speedy contact with General Wenck? We could give him the true picture of the situation in Berlin and in the Reich Chancellery. We could urge him to break through to the city as soon as possible and could indeed guide him on the best route for his attack.'

Boldt nods. 'There is very little left for us to do here in the bunker now that the telecommunications are down.'

Krebs hesitates. He is not sure what the Führer will make of the plan. General Burgdorf suddenly appears. He's come to see if Krebs wants a drink. Burgdorf is much more enthusiastic about the officers' proposal than Krebs. He wants his adjutant Rudolf Weiss to go with them. Martin Bormann then comes in; he's also wondering about a drink.

Generals Krebs and Burgdorf form what von Loringhoven calls a triumvirate of drinkers with Martin Bormann. The three men are spending most of their time sitting in the bunker corridors drinking schnapps. From time to time they cruise over to the Reich Chancellery where a kind of mass hysteria, fuelled by the endless supply of alcohol in the cellars, has led to a relaxing of sexual inhibitions. The young women in the Reich Chancellery are seen as fair game.

Bormann's philandering has the support of his wife Gerda, the mother of his ten children. Just over a year ago he wrote to her with the proud news that he had succeeded in seducing the actress Manja Behrens. Gerda wrote straight back with her congratulations and offering to welcome Manja into their household. She goes on to suggest that, given the terrible decline in the production of Aryan children as a result of the war, they should arrange a system of motherhood by shifts 'so that you always have a wife who is usable'.

Burgdorf explains to Martin Bormann the idea of sending the three officers to General Wenck and, to the astonishment of Boldt and von Loringhoven, Bormann also likes the plan. Krebs is finally persuaded. Now the Führer must be convinced.

General Walther Wenck is attempting to break through the Russian encirclement of Berlin from the south and has obeyed Hitler's recent orders to disengage from fighting the Americans in the west in order to fight the Soviet troops. However, his motives are secretly at odds with the Führer's. Wenck no longer believes that it is possible to defend the capital. His aim is to try and create a corridor through which civilians and soldiers can make their escape. A week ago he addressed his young soldiers and explained their mission: 'It's not about Berlin any more, it's not about the Reich any more'. Their aim is to save lives.

About 11.15am

'Identification please!'

A young SS officer has stopped his truck behind Claus Sellier and his friend Fritz and shouts at them from the cab. The two men are instantly irritated by the officer's attitude. Fritz shows his papers and says, 'I'm glad you showed up, you can take us to Traunstein.'

'Sorry, I can't take you, I've no room.' The SS officer points to the men in the back of the truck. 'My orders are to take these soldiers to a position where they can defend the road.'

Fritz angrily pulls out a notebook and pen from his jacket pocket, saying, 'What is your name? State your rank and your unit number! Did you never read military regulations? It says you are supposed to help an officer who has an important mission, under any circumstances. Do I understand correctly that you're refusing to take us?'

Stunned, the SS officer gets quickly out of the cab and salutes them.

'*Heil Hitler*!'

Claus and Fritz return the salute but with little enthusiasm, and follow the officer up into the cab. As they set off, Fritz takes his time writing the SS officer's name in his book. Seeing this, the officer tries to impress his new passengers and make amends.

'We're setting roadblocks to check on soldiers who are wandering around. Some of the bastards seem to think the war is over already. We take them prisoners. Then they will be investigated for treason and court-martialled.'

Claus is hoping that the SS officer has missed the three soldiers they passed an hour earlier. He has had enough of the officer's attitude and just wants to get away. Claus asks if they can be dropped off in the next village. They jump out of the cab, and before the truck pulls off, Claus shakes hands with all the soldiers in the back, wishing he could tell them that the war is lost and they shouldn't believe what the SS officer is telling them.

Meanwhile Fritz makes a show of ripping up the page with the SS officer's details, saying, 'I won't report you this time.'

Two days later, from the safety of a forest, Fritz will watch as the same SS officer, together with other SS men, stops wounded German soldiers at a checkpoint. The officer takes the men's papers and, without reading them, rips them up. The soldiers are then tied with their hands behind their backs, and signs are put around their necks that read: 'I'm a coward. I don't want to fight.' One by one they are hanged from a tree as the SS men shout 'Cowards!' at them. Some of the soldiers carrying out the executions are as young as 15. Witnessing this, Fritz will look at the Hitler Youth badge he's had since school, and for the first time feel ashamed of it. He sits in the forest and weeps.

'Tonight you will hear an Englishman who is speaking to you at his own request and of his own free will...'

Second Lieutenant Alan Whicker of the British Army Film and Photo Unit is in a radio station in Milan, and through a translator, is asking for an appeal to be sent out for the whereabouts of John Amery – a notorious traitor who has been broadcasting Fascist propaganda since 1942. John Amery is no ordinary traitor – he is the son of the British Cabinet Minister Leo Amery. Whicker knows that the partisans have captured him; he just doesn't know where he's being kept.

Thirty-three-year-old John Amery is in fact only a short distance from Whicker, in the Milan city jail. He is unshaven and wearing a Fascist black shirt.

Amery is a complicated man and possibly mentally ill. He had a privileged childhood, brought up in the family home on Eaton Square in London and educated at Harrow. His housemaster described Amery as 'without doubt the most difficult boy I have ever tried to manage... he seemed unable in those days to distinguish right from wrong. He seemed to think he could be a law unto himself.'

In his early twenties Amery travelled and worked around Europe with his wife Una, a former prostitute. By the time Churchill brought his old friend Leo Amery into his wartime Cabinet in May 1940 and gave him responsibility for India, John was a virulent anti-communist and anti-Semite (which was strange considering he is part Jewish).

In March 1942, now living in the French Alps, John Amery wrote a letter to a French newspaper criticising an RAF bombing raid on the Renault factory in Paris, in which 623 civilians were killed. He said that a number of his countrymen agreed with his views. MI5 swiftly picked up on the letter, and an official noted in Amery's file that the letter's contents should deter Amery from returning to England. 'Or if he does, he should be assured of a reception at the hands of a firing squad.' At the same time the German Foreign Office in Berlin also got to hear of this outspoken British Cabinet Minister's son.

In November 1942, the Reichs-Rundfunk-Gesellschaft *(Reich Broadcasting Company) introduced a new voice to its* Germany Calling *programme: 'Tonight you will hear an Englishman who is speaking to you at his own request and of his own free will...'*

Amery spoke about how Britain's alliance with Russia would lead to communism in Britain; how all the newspapers in London are Jewish-controlled, and in a passage that was probably written by the Propaganda Ministry, he claimed Germany didn't want to rob Britain of her Empire: 'There is more than enough room in the world for Germany and Britain.'

On 20th April 1943 he visited a POW camp in an attempt to recruit British soldiers to join a British Legion of St George to fight the Russians. He had even designed some posters showing a Tommy marching with the German army, with the caption: 'Our Flag Is Going Forward Too.' Amery was hissed and booed.

Amery was becoming an embarrassment to the German Propaganda Ministry. He was frequently drunk and his broadcasts had little impact. Then Amery's second wife Jeanine (whom he had bigamously married, and was also a prostitute) died after an apparent overdose.

In September 1943 he moved to Italy and met with Mussolini, who had been installed by the Germans as the leader of the Italian Social Republic in the north of the country, which they controlled. Amery began broadcasting on the state-controlled network. On 25th April 1945 he was arrested by the partisans in Milan and placed in the city's jail.

With Amery in jail is his third wife Michelle, whom he met on a train only days after his second wife's funeral. Like his two other wives, she is also a prostitute. They nervously await their fate. After the death of Mussolini and his mistress, they know the partisans are capable of anything.

11.30am

In the Italian Alpine village of Villabassa, the SS guards who have been holding British Secret Service agent Captain Sigismund Payne-Best and the other *Prominente* prisoners are staring at two machine guns belonging to a small unit of German army infantry. The infantry have arrived to protect the

Prominente from the SS who have orders to execute the prisoners today. Thanks to the efforts of Payne-Best, the German army Commander knows that if they are killed, the Allies, now only a few miles away, will hold them responsible.

The SS start talking among themselves about what they should do. Payne-Best walks up to Lieutenant Bader, the SS officer in charge. The two men have met before – Bader is a member of a Gestapo execution squad which moved round the various concentration camps where Payne-Best was being held.

'Throw down your arms or else those machine guns will go off,' Payne-Best says. To his amazement Bader and the SS troops do what they're told and drop their sub-machine guns on the ground. Watching the scene have been a number of Italian civilians, who immediately snatch up the weapons. Bader pleads with Payne-Best to use his influence to let him have some petrol so he and his men can leave Villabassa.

But the SS truck never leaves the square. Denied petrol, Bader and his men decide to walk to the town of Bozen about 60 miles away. En route they are attacked by Italian partisans and a number of them are hanged from telegraph poles by the road. In their abandoned truck in Villabassa are 300 Red Cross parcels intended for prisoners in Dachau, which the SS had stolen.

'Sometimes I think, with horror, that in her heart that child saw through the pretence of the grown-ups.'

11.45am

Underneath the Reich Chancellery in Berlin, the six children of Joseph and Magda Goebbels are playing in the corridor of the upper bunker. Most of them are excited to be there. They call the bunker a 'cave'. They feel completely safe from the bombs as they wait for the victory their parents have promised. They have made friends with some of the people working here. Misch, the gentle giant at the switchboard, is a particular favourite and they have made up a rhyme about him which the four-year-old, Heide, sings every time they see him: '*Misch, Misch du bist ein Fisch!*'

In the words of Hitler's secretary Traudl Junge, who has been helping to look after them, 'They were charming, well brought-up, natural-mannered children. They knew nothing of the fate awaiting them, and the adults did all they could to keep them unaware of it... Only the oldest, Helga, sometimes had a sad, knowing expression in her big brown eyes. She was the quietest, and sometimes I think, with horror, that in her heart that child saw through the pretence of the grown-ups.'

11.50am

The three couriers of Hitler's testaments, Lorenz, Zander and Johannmeier, finally leave the bunker. They have stuffed their pockets with food from the breakfast trolley but have no money or papers. All morning they have been discussing possible routes. They will travel together until they get past the Russian encirclement. Johannmeier is instructed to then make his way to General Schörner in Czechoslovakia; Zander is to head for Admiral Dönitz's headquarters in Plön and Lorenz is to go with him with the ultimate aim of flying to Munich to the Nazi Party headquarters. If any of the couriers fail to get to their destination their orders are to aim for British and American territory, which is now about 50 kilometres to the west. There is a strong belief in Germany that the Allies treat prisoners better than the Russians do. At least there is no Siberia in the west.

They leave through the underground garages below the Reich Chancellery building. Johannmeier leads the way along Hermann-Göringstrasse, with the help of a young soldier called Hummerich. They check each road crossing is safe from snipers and beckon Lorenz and Zander with hand signals. The wide street is lined with ruined houses and the road is blocked by debris.

Midday/7.00am EWT (*Eastern War Time*)

Lieutenant Colonel Felix L. Sparks has given the task of liberating Dachau concentration camp to I Company – a reserve unit. The rest of his regiment is heading towards Munich to take part in the capture of the city as planned. Sparks has been told that the concentration camp is a 'politically sensitive area', so he is travelling with I Company in his jeep. They are now only about a mile east of Dachau.

'I don't know what the hell we're running into,' Sparks told I Company Commander Lieutenant Bill Walsh, 'I'll give you an extra machine gun platoon. A heavy weapons company will go with you.' Twenty-five-year-old Walsh knows nothing about concentration camps. He assumes they are POW camps, full of Allied soldiers. He'd once seen a POW camp in New York State full of German prisoners; he guesses it might look like that.

Unaware that they've narrowly escaped being executed by the SS, 120 of the *Prominente* prisoners are assembled in the dining room of the Hotel Bachmann. Standing on one of the tables are British secret agent Captain Payne-Best and fellow prisoner Colonel Bogislav von Bonin. They tell the expectant prisoners – von Bonin in German and then Payne-Best in English and

French – that they are free. But they add that they must stay close to their hotels as it is rumoured that there are still armed SS men around, and the war is not yet over.

Payne-Best tells them that they are all to be taken by the local partisans to the safety of a hotel higher in the Alps. It can be accessed only via a single-track road that is easily guarded; there they will wait for the Allies to arrive.

Payne-Best discovers something strange. He can speak French without difficulty, but English is an effort. During his five and a half years of imprisonment he has tried to speak only German and so it's hard to recall the correct English words and phrases. Also, for some reason his false teeth made by the Sachsenhausen dentist make speaking English hard – but are no trouble when he is speaking in French and German.

President Truman is sitting at his desk in Blair House, a large Georgian property just over the road from the White House. His study is quiet – no one else is up. Truman, his wife Bess and their daughter Margaret moved here a couple of days after the death of President Roosevelt on 12th April; they plan to move into the White House once the redecoration and cleaning they've ordered has finished. (In fact it will soon be discovered that the building is structurally unsound, and so the Trumans don't move in until 1952). The President is writing a letter to his mother and sister, who live in Missouri; he conscientiously writes to them every week. The new President is finding the intrusion of the press into his family life especially irksome.

'Dear Mamma and Mary,

'I hope you haven't been bothered too much. It is a terrible – and I mean terrible – nuisance to be kin to the President of the United States. Reporters have been haunting every relative I ever heard of... A guard has to go with Bess and Margaret everywhere they go – and they don't like it. They spend a lot of time trying to beat the game, but it can't be done. In a country as big as this one there are necessarily a lot of nuts and people with peculiar ideas...'

Although Truman doesn't like press intrusion, he tolerates the weekly press conferences, even when the questions are wide-ranging (in his first press conference he was asked about the new Polish government but also his views on the disposal of synthetic rubber plants).

After leaving his farm to fight in the First World War, Truman opened a haberdashery in Kansas that soon went bust. That and his inexperience in foreign affairs has led to a certain amount of snobbery about him in Washington. Alistair Cooke was at that first press conference, and before they went in, the other reporters were saying they ought to be gentle with Truman, as he would probably 'fumble it'. They were in for a surprise. Cooke said later, 'We staggered out after taking a drubbing from a sergeant-major. He always knew what he wanted. He might have failed as a haberdasher, but he plainly had no intention of failing as a president.'

Roosevelt's death, despite his long-term health problems, came as a shock to the nation – and to the Vice President. Truman wrote later, 'I had hurried to the White House to see the President, and when I arrived, I discovered I was the President...' He had only been Vice President for 82 days.

On 25th April the United States Secretary of War Henry L. Stimson came to see President Truman to tell him something that had been kept secret from him as Vice President – that the war with Japan could soon be over.

'Within four months, we shall in all probability have completed the most terrible weapon known in human history, one bomb of which could destroy a whole city.'

On 29th July Truman will authorise the dropping of the atomic bomb on the Japanese city of Hiroshima.

During his term as Vice President, Truman met with Roosevelt privately only twice. He knew very little about what had been decided at Yalta, in fact, he wrote later, the President never spoke to him about 'the war, about foreign affairs or what he had in mind for peace after the war'. But Truman is a shrewd man and a keen student of history – he has examined the lives of many great war leaders, from Hannibal to Robert E. Lee. Truman once boasted he'd read every book in his home-town library.

12.15pm/1.15pm UK time

Intelligence officer Major Geoffrey Cox is getting ready to move out of Padua. Around him, other members of the 2nd New Zealand Division are loading up their trucks. News has arrived that the route to Venice, 30 miles away, is almost secure. The plan to capture the city is codenamed Operation Merlin.

For the past few days the New Zealanders have driven through villages where girls have thrown flowers and blossom as they passed. It is a small reward for the tough slog through Italy in the past few months. They feel that they are the forgotten army – their battles rarely knock news of the advances in northern Europe from the front pages. Some of the jeeps of the 2nd New Zealand Division have 'D-Day Dodgers' scrawled on the side in chalk – the unfair nickname that some have given them back home.

Most of the troops in the Italian campaign feel unfairly maligned. On 3rd May 1945 Major Neil Margerison will write to his fiancée from Italy, 'People in England don't understand the conditions which have prevailed in Italy. They think that we have been disgustingly slow about the job, and that any propaganda regarding the difficult terrain and terrible weather are an official excuse for our procrastinations.... Chaps serving in Italy are "good time boys" or "D.D.D.s" (D-Day Dodgers). Chaps who

*have returned from overseas service in the Med. (4½ years) take
a back place to the chaps who are serving in France and receiving
leave every six months...'*

On the BBC Home Service, Lieutenant J. Trenaman is
presenting one of a series of 15-minute programmes called
Teaching Soldiers to Read.

*The BBC has a policy both on the Home Service and on the
Forces Programme to educate and inform servicemen, as well as
to provide entertainment. One such innovation is a round-table
discussion called* The Brains Trust *(its name taken from Roosevelt's
nickname for his circle of advisors) that tackles such varied questions as 'What is democracy?' and 'What is a sneeze?' It began in
1940 on the Forces Programme but proved so popular it's repeated
on the Home Service. By 1945 it has an audience of 12 million. One
factory worker wrote in his diary: 'The favourite topic on Mondays
seems to be the previous day's* Brains Trust. *Hardly anyone ever
confesses that he didn't hear it, or if they do, take care to give
adequate reason for so doing.'*

'Give my regards to Wenck. Tell him to hurry or it will be too late.'

12.30pm/8.30pm Okinawa time

'Mein Führer,' General Krebs begins, 'there are three young
officers who are keen to try and break out of Berlin and make
contact with General Wenck so that they can update him on
the situation here and support the speedy attack of the 12th
Army on the capital.'

There is a silence of several seconds before Hitler replies. He seems weary. It has been a difficult situation conference. All the reports are extremely discouraging.

'Who are these officers?'

Krebs gives him their names.

'Who are Boldt, Weiss and von Loringhoven? Send them in.'

Standing at the back of the conference room, the Luftwaffe adjutant Nicolaus von Below listens carefully to what follows. Like these young officers he is desperate to find a way to survive. With the telephone lines down he has no means of contacting his pregnant wife and children on the Baltic coast.

The three officers file in and von Loringhoven sets out the plan. He is surprised how calm the Führer seems. He points out their possible route options on the large map laid out on the table. The second option involves travelling down the River Havel. Hitler immediately prefers it.

Von Loringhoven elaborates, 'Once we reach Pichelsdorf Bridge we will take a rowing boat and row up the River Havel, between the Russian lines as far as Wannsee Lake.'

Hitler interrupts, 'Bormann, supply these officers with a motor boat, otherwise they will never get through.'

Boldt feels a rush of panic. If the mission depends on Bormann obtaining a motor boat in the current circumstances it will never take place. But no one is supposed to contradict the Führer. Boldt has to risk it: '*Mein Führer*, we will get hold of a motor boat ourselves and deaden the noise. I'm convinced that we will get through.'

Hitler slowly stands up again. He shakes the three officers by the hand. 'Give my regards to Wenck. Tell him to hurry or it will be too late.'

On the island of Okinawa, the commander of the Japanese forces General Mitsuru Ushijima has called his staff together in a spacious cave 100 feet beneath ancient Shuri Castle, the headquarters of his 32nd Army. On 1st April, Easter Sunday, US forces launched a massive amphibious assault on the south of the island – 1,200 vessels landed over 170,000 soldiers. General Ushijima has 77,000 Japanese and 24,000 Okinawan auxiliaries to fight them, and so far, in slow, bloody battles reminiscent of the First World War, they have succeeded in holding the Americans back.

General Ushijima's Chief of Staff General Cho is holding forth: 'We must mount a massive counter-attack while we still have the strength! In a few weeks attrition will have eaten away at our forces, and we will be too weak to take the offensive. We must strike now and destroy the Americans, even at the risk of losing our whole army!'

General Cho is famous for his hard drinking and his extreme views. In the 1930s he advocated holding the Emperor at knife-point until he introduced military rule in Japan. Facing Cho at the meeting is the man responsible for the strategy for the defence of Okinawa, Colonel Yahara. He guessed exactly where the Americans would land and had prepared an impressive line of defensive fortifications, with Shuri Castle at its centre. He has no time for Cho's fiery rhetoric.

'The Americans have suffered great losses... but it would be folly to attack, because to break through the American lines on the high ground would demand much greater forces than we possess. Therefore, the army must continue its current operations, calmy recognising its final destiny, for annihilation is inevitable, no matter what is done.'

Cho is unimpressed and starts to outline an audacious plan.

12.35pm

The Sherman tanks of the US 14th Armoured Division are crashing through the ten-foot-high wire fence of Stalag VII-A at Moosburg outside Munich. The tanks are immediately swamped by emotional POWs. An American Air Corps lieutenant kisses a Sherman, saying, 'God damn, do I love the ground forces!' A bearded paratrooper climbs onto a tank and kisses its crew commander, tears running down his cheeks. 'You damned bloody Yanks, I love you!' a tall Australian shouts, throwing his arms around a shocked jeep driver. One member of a tank crew recognises his brother among the POWs. British Major Elliott Viney – a prisoner for nearly five years – writes in his diary, 'AMERICANS HERE.'

Another British officer wrote optimistically in his diary later that day, 'God bless the bastards... after five years, free at last. May be home next Sunday.'

A few hours later General George Patton will arrive and point to the swastika flying from the camp's flagpole, and yell: 'I want that son-of-bitch cut down, and the man that cuts it down, I want him to wipe his ass with it!'

In the last few weeks conditions in the camp, built for only 10,000, have become extremely harsh. There are now 80,000 prisoners in Moosburg. A long trench had been dug as a latrine and hundreds were suffering from dysentery. Most of the guards have fled.

In the five years since the British POWs like Elliott Viney and Bert Ruffle were captured, there have been many changes to the Allied armies. One group of RAF prisoners failed to recognise the uniform of their British liberators, and had hidden in a tree for hours until they heard their accents. Elsewhere, reporter Alan Moorehead overheard a POW say in awe, 'So that's what a jeep looks like!'

About 12.45pm

Bert Ruffle and Frank Talbot have finished the job in Brüx. Instead of the usual work building the oil refinery, they were sent with a camp guard to pick up some materials for one of the refinery foremen. Next to them in the truck, under a tarpaulin, is a crate of beer they discovered in Brüx – they are taking some surreptitious swigs. The guard spots them, but says nothing. The men offer him a bottle.

1.00pm

I Company is marching through the town of Dachau. The soldiers are impressed – it is well kept with neat flower beds, cobbled streets, numerous small shops and a pretty river. Above the houses is an old castle. There had been a short firefight on the outskirts of the town but little else in terms of opposition. White sheets are hanging out of windows – the town has surrendered.

Some soldiers are following a railway line that leads out of the town.

'That's the closest I've been to a free man on our side for more than four months.'

About 1.00pm/6.30pm Burmese time

Royal Australian Air Force Wing Commander Lionel 'Bill' Hudson is lying in the cell he shares with 20 others in Rangoon jail in Burma, listening to a commotion by the main gate. He's half asleep and can't be bothered to investigate what's going on. This morning there had been the regular *tenko* (roll call) at 6.45, followed by a Sunday service, and then Hudson had headed back to his cell to have a nap – it's been a hot week in Rangoon.

It has been a strange few days. There have been explosions and fires to the east of Rangoon. The Japanese guards lit their own fire in the jail compound and started burning papers and what looked to the POWs to be medical records. Four days ago at 9.30 in the evening an Allied aircraft flew low over the jail. 'That's the closest I've been to a free man on our side for more than four months,' Hudson confided to his diary later. Then the following day 200 of the fittest POWs were led away by some of the Japanese guards to an unspecified destination. Hudson asked why he was being left behind (he is the nominal leader of the Allied servicemen in the camp). 'You – trouble-maker,' one guard replied. Hudson fears that the 200 men will be used as hostages in negotiations with the advancing British and Australian forces.

The guards who left have been replaced by raw recruits, with new shoes and uniforms, and they don't mind if the POWs forget to bow to them.

Hudson, an Australian from New South Wales, was captured by the Japanese through what he knows was his own stupidity. On 19th December 1944, he flew his Mosquito from his base in Assam into Burma – he had no specific mission; Hudson just wanted to test out his guns on what's known as a low-level 'rhubarb' – seeking targets of opportunity. Hudson and his navigator Jack Shortis were flying just above the treetops when the Mosquito hit a branch, which badly damaged the port engine. They dropped out of the sky 'like a falling leaf', Hudson wrote later, and were soon captured and taken to Rangoon jail. Rangoon, like the rest of Burma, had been overrun by the Japanese in early 1942; it took the invaders only 127 days to push the British out of the country. The fall of Burma, following the loss of Hong Kong and Malaya, had been a humiliating defeat.

The Japanese are brutal conquerors. When Hong Kong was taken, hospital patients were bayoneted in their beds, and nurses and nuns raped. Prisoners of war are treated with contempt for having surrendered. The Allied prisoners in Rangoon jail have witnessed many examples of sadistic cruelty. The badly burned crew of a USAAF Flying Fortress were left to die a slow death in solitary confinement; those who are too sick to work in the jail's candle factory are given two bottles every morning, and expected to fill them with dead flies. When the able-bodied return in the evening, they help collect flies and put them in the bottles, so the sick can evade punishment.

1.10pm

Operation Merlin is underway. Minutes ago, B Squadron of the 12th Lancers had radioed to say that they had successfully driven over the causeway into Venice. Now Geoffrey Cox and the rest of the 2nd New Zealand Division are heading east out of Padua, and people are on the streets and hanging out of windows cheering them. Italian flags are being thrown at the vehicles as they pass, and the Kiwis are obligingly wrapping them around their canvas canopies and gun barrels. As the Kiwis pass partisans on the road they shout '*Ciao!*' in their best Italian.

Claus Sellier and Fritz are eating a large lunch in a hotel dining room in the German town of Reichenhall. They've walked across the border from Austria this morning. The hotel had been turned into a makeshift army hospital a few months ago, but now all the patients have gone. As they helped themselves to food a doctor came in and told them, 'Eat as much as you want! The kitchen doesn't know how many patients we have in the hotel - nobody told them that there aren't any.'

'Let's get those Nazi dogs! Take no prisoners! Don't take any SS alive!'

1.15pm

In a railway siding outside the town of Dachau, men from Felix Sparks' 45th Infantry Division have found a long line of railway wagons. Lying in and around them waist-deep are hundreds of decomposing corpses – some naked, others in shredded blue and white uniforms. Some have crawled out of the wagons and have then been butchered by the tracks. Many of the dead in the wagons have their eyes open, as if staring at the Americans.

One GI feels it's as if they are saying, 'What took you so long?'

Sparks arrives on foot, looks at the scene and vomits on the ground. Around him, his men are angry; he can hear them shouting.

'Let's get those Nazi dogs!'

'Take no prisoners!'

'Don't take any SS alive!'

They have counted 39 wagons – all of them full of bodies. Sparks orders one group of men to follow him into the camp, and another group to follow I Company Commander Lieutenant Bill Walsh. Walsh realises now that a concentration camp is nothing like a New York POW camp.

The railway wagons had come from Buchenwald concentration

camp as part of the Nazi policy to keep the prisoners away from the invading armies. At the start of the journey three weeks ago there were 4,800 prisoners; by the time the train arrived at Dachau, only 800 had survived. They were left to die in the wagons.

On the other side of the camp's perimeter wall, Sparks finds himself in a rose garden at the back of a large house. The contrast with what he's just seen makes his head reel. Together with two men, Sparks explores the house, keeping an eye out for booby traps. In one room they find children's wooden toys scattered on the floor, and other signs of a hasty departure. Sparks reckons it must have been the home of an SS officer who has long since fled with his family.

By the railway tracks, Bill Walsh and his men have discovered four SS men with their hands on their heads. Walsh pushes them into a wagon and shoots them with his pistol.

1.30pm

At Stalag VII-A at Moosburg, Major Elliott Viney is roaring with laughter as their former SS guards are humiliated. As the guards are led out of the camp, the newly liberated POWs shout to the GIs whether the German was 'good' or not. Those hated by the prisoners are given a heavy kick up the backside by a GI only too happy to oblige.

In Milan, Second Lieutenant Alan Whicker is waiting in the office of the governor of Milan's city jail with one of his British army cameramen. A short time after his appeal for information regarding the whereabouts of the suspected traitor John Amery, he was sent a message giving his location. Amery walks in looking very pale and says straightaway, 'Thank God you're here. I thought they were going to shoot me!'

With Amery is his third wife Michelle, described later by Whicker as 'an appealing brunette in a dark trouser suit'.

Amery is keen to win Whicker's sympathy.

'I've never been anti-British. You can read the scripts of my broadcasts through the years and you'll never find anything against Britain. I've just been very anti-communist, and if at the moment I'm proved wrong, well – one of these days you'll find out that I was right...'

Amery is relieved as Whicker leads him and Michelle from the jail and away from the threat of the partisans. Whicker hands them over to Sergeant John Martin of the Intelligence Corps. John Amery strikes Whicker as 'pleasant and reasonable' – but Amery's troubles are far from over.

Boldt, von Loringhoven and Weiss are setting off on their mission to meet up with General Wenck. They leave the Führerbunker through the underground garage carrying maps, sub-machine guns, camouflage jackets, steel helmets and sandwiches from the dining-room trolley. Von Loringhoven cuts the red staff officer bands off his trousers. If they are caught by the Russians he won't want his captors to know that he is officer rank. The three men emerge from the exit on Hermann-Göringstrasse and are immediately forced to shelter from a mortar attack. Moments later a round of machine gun fire whistles over their heads; the bullets embed in the wall behind them. As they cross Hermann-Göringstrasse heading for the Tiergarten, they pass the first dead bodies, soldiers and civilians lying where they fell. The smell of decomposition is overwhelming.

Back in the upper bunker, Nicolaus von Below, the Luftwaffe adjutant who also hopes to leave, is suggesting to General Burgdorf that he would also be more useful if he were sent on a mission. Burgdorf tells him that that is a decision for Hitler.

Von Below goes down to the Führerbunker and waits in the corridor to speak to the Führer.

Lieutenant Colonel Felix L. Sparks has walked further into the residential part of the Dachau complex. Suddenly he sees Lieutenant Bill Walsh chasing a German soldier. Walsh is shouting, 'You sons of bitches! You sons of bitches!'

Walsh catches the German and starts beating him over the head with the barrel of his rifle, yelling, 'Bastards! Bastards! Bastards!' Sparks shouts at him to stop, but Walsh keeps hitting and hitting. Sparks draws his .45 and cracks Walsh over the head with its butt. Walsh falls to the ground and lies there weeping.

'I'm taking command of the company!' Sparks shouts to the men around him.

It takes seven men to take Walsh away and calm him down.

> **We stood aside and watched while these guards were beaten to death... we watched with less feeling than if a dog were being beaten.**
>
> Dachau inmate Rabbi David Eichorn's
> letter home, 29th April 1945

About 1.40pm

Those Dachau inmates who haven't been held in the prison area of the complex are slowly starting to emerge from their huts and are running as fast as they can towards their liberators. They surround the GIs and kiss and shake their hands. A weak old man holds out a stained cigarette to a GI, who hesitates.

'Take it,' another inmate says, 'That's the only thing the guy owns in the world.'

Albert Guerisse is a Belgian doctor who worked for the British

Secret Operations Executive (SOE) under the pseudonym of Pat O'Leary. He has been a prisoner of the Germans for two years, after the escape line for Allied airmen he was running was infiltrated and betrayed. In Dachau he has been tortured and is under sentence of death. Liberation has come just in time.

Guerisse watches as an immaculately turned-out SS officer, Lieutenant Heinrich Skodzensky, approaches an American officer as if he's on a parade ground.

'*Heil Hitler*! I hereby turn over to you the concentration camp of Dachau, 30,000 residents, 2,340 sick, 27,000 on the outside, 560 garrison troops.'

The American officer hesitates for a moment, then shouts at Skodzensky, '*Du Schweinhund!* Sit down here!' and points to the back of a jeep. The officer then turns to Guerisse and gives him an automatic rifle saying, 'Come with me', offering Guerisse a chance to take his revenge on the SS officer. But Guerisse is too weak to move.

'No, I'll stay here...' he says.

The American drives out of the camp with Skodzensky. Then Guerisse hears gunshots.

A group of about 50 SS prisoners are being lined up in front of an eight foot wall in Dachau's coal yard. The yard is now empty except for a layer of black coal dust on the ground. Felix Sparks has ordered that a light machine gun be trained on them. A private from I Company comes up to him.

'Colonel, you'd better see what we found...'

Sparks sets off and has walked about 50 feet when the machine gun suddenly goes off behind him. Another GI then opens fire. Sparks turns and runs back into the coal yard. He pulls out his .45 and, firing shots into the air, orders his men to stop. Sparks then runs towards the machine gunner who is still firing, kicks him in the back, grabs him by the collar and drags him away from the gun.

'What the hell are you doing?!' Sparks shouts.

'Colonel, they were trying to get away!'

Sparks knows that's a lie. Looking towards the Germans, he can see about 17 have been killed; many others have dived to the ground. Sparks orders that the wounded be taken into the hospital in the camp grounds.

Two of the battalion medics refuse to help the wounded SS men.

The shooting in the coal yard will haunt Felix Sparks for many years to come. Arland Musser, a stills photographer, and Henry Gerzen, a film cameraman, recorded what happened. Their pictures were sent to the head of the Seventh Army, General Arthur A. White, who decided that the shootings needed to be investigated. On 1st May Sparks was told he was being sent back to the United States.

The investigation took place a couple of days later – 23 men gave their testimony. The investigation discovered that I Company Commander Lieutenant Bill Walsh, after becoming 'hysterical in Dachau shortly before the shootings in the coal yard, had given the order to the machine gunner to "let them have it."' The report concluded that the 17 deaths were in effect executions ordered by Walsh.

On his way home, Sparks got as far as Le Havre and was then told he had to return to Seventh Army headquarters, which by now had been successfully set up in Munich. General Patton himself wanted to see him. When the two men met, Sparks was in for a surprise.

'Didn't you serve under me in Africa and Sicily?' Patton asked.

'Yes, sir, I did. I would like to explain what happened in Dachau...'

'There is no point in an explanation. I have already had these charges investigated, and they are a bunch of crap. I'm going to tear up these goddamn papers on you and your men.'

And he did so there and then.

Patton said to Sparks, 'You have been a damn fine soldier. Now go home.'

Despite the investigation, rumours persisted that it was Felix Sparks who had ordered the killing of the SS men. Then, in the early 1990s, four photographs were published for the first time, taken by a GI named Robert Goebel who had witnessed the shootings. They showed Sparks firing his pistol in the air, and with his left hand outstretched, desperately motioning to his men to stop. In the background bodies lie in a heap against the wall.

Remain Firm, Fair, Aloof and Aware.

GI Pocket Guide to Germany

About 2.00pm

Today is Nina Markovna's 17th birthday. Chalked on the wall by her bunk bed are the names of her three American boyfriends. Bob and Mike are both soldiers, and Jack is a pilot. Jack is on his way to see her in a jeep that's piled high with coats, dresses, hats and shoes.

In May 1942 Nina, her mother and her brother Slava were taken from their home in Russia by the Germans to be Ostarbeiter – Eastern workers in Germany. Nina's father is away serving with the Red Army.

After a two-week journey by train in a cattle wagon, the Markovna family were taken to a market square in a Bavarian town with hundreds of others and handed over to factory owners eager for cheap labour. They were all given a cloth badge to wear on their chest with OST written on it. It reminded Nina of the slave markets she'd read about in Uncle Tom's Cabin.

For the next three years they worked in a number of factories; in one they built explosives for V1 flying bombs; in another they turned second-hand clothes into garments such as aprons. Some of the clothes were very expensive dresses, suits and coats; a Polish worker said that they'd come from Oswiecim, a place the Germans called Auschwitz. The name meant nothing to Nina. Sometimes she would find American dollars sewn into seams. The money came in useful to bribe guards for extra food.

At the end of 1944, the Markovna family were moved to what would be their final camp, based in an abandoned theatre on the outskirts of the German town of Triptis. Twelve people are squeezed into the theatre's old dressing room; Nina and her brother have a bunk bed by the window. Lying there on 13th February, she watched the night sky turn orange as the RAF bombed Dresden 90 miles away.

Then on 15th April, their SS guards ran into the woods, shedding their uniforms and changing into civilian clothes.

Soon after, the Americans arrived. Nina was fascinated by how they walked – not rigid like German soldiers or undisciplined like Russians, but in an easy, free, yet self-controlled way. Their tight uniforms were particularly appealing. The Americans were unfriendly at first but when they realised Nina was Russian their mood changed.

'Hey, Russky! Hey, there! War kaput!'

'Don't cry. You're free!'

In the days since then, the Americans have been regular visitors to the abandoned theatre, bringing food and cigarettes for all the ex-prisoners. Nina has been treated to rides on motorbikes and in jeeps. Soon she has her three boyfriends – Bob, Mike and Jack.

Lying on her bunk, Nina hears Jack's jeep pull up outside.

He shouts, 'Ninochka! Come out! Hurry! Happy birthday, young lady!'

He shows her the jeep, piled high with clothes and shoes.

'Select what you like! Whatever fits you. The rest pass on to others.'

Nina asks where he got them all.

'I plundered a few deserted Nazi houses.'

Seeing Nina's concern – a few days ago she would have been shot for looting – Jack says, 'Don't worry, kid, no one will come for these clothes. The Nazis all ran.'

Nina chooses three dresses, a navy-blue coat, a kimono and five hats. Jack tries to persuade her not to take the shoes with heels, as he's not very tall. Nina says she'll wear them only when she's sitting.

Soon Nina's mother and the other women in the camp are modelling hats and dresses for each other, and laughing in a way they haven't done for a long time.

Bob, Mike and Jack will have been warned repeatedly about fraternising with the enemy.

'The Germans must be ostracised,' General Eisenhower said earlier in the year, and ordered that press photographs of his soldiers fraternising with the German population should be stopped by the censors. He issued GIs with a guide to Germany telling them, 'You are in enemy country! These people are not our allies or friends.' There was a $65 fine if they were caught fraternising. The fact that Nina is Russian means that spending time with her and her family is possible.

The British soldiers too were warned about fraternisation. A War Office guidebook said, 'You are about to meet a strange people in a strange, enemy country. Many of them will have suffered from overwork, underfeeding and the effects of the air raids and you may be tempted to feel sorry for them. [But their] hard luck stories will be hypocritical attempts to win sympathy. Germans must be regarded as dangerous enemies.'

'I'm very sorry I can't give you a better farewell present.'

2.00pm

Hitler is lunching with Eva Braun and the secretaries. Until the autumn of 1942, shortly after the start of the Battle of Stalingrad, Hitler used to eat with his adjutants, but he found himself put off his food by conversation about what was turning out to be the bloodiest single battle in history. He began to share meals only with women. The secretaries had a rota to make sure that someone was with him for every meal, including tea in the early hours of the morning. They were instructed not to bring difficult issues into the conversation, but today it is Hitler who raises a difficult subject, which has been preying on his mind.

'I will never fall into the enemy's hands, dead or alive. I am leaving orders for my body to be burned so that no one can ever find it.'

Traudl Junge eats mechanically, without noticing what she is eating, as the conversation turns to the best method of suicide.

Hitler says, matter-of-factly, 'The best way is to shoot yourself in the mouth. Your skull is shattered and you don't notice anything. Death is instantaneous.'

Eva is horrified. 'I want to be a beautiful corpse... I'm going to take poison.'

She shows the secretaries a little brass box that contains a phial of cyanide, which she keeps in the pocket of her dress.

'I wonder if it hurts very much? I'm so frightened of suffering for a long time... I'm ready to die heroically, but at least I want it to be painless.'

Hitler assures her that death by cyanide is painless: 'The nervous and respiratory systems are paralysed within seconds.'

Gerda Christian and Traudl Junge exchange glances, and then turn in unison to the Führer. 'Do you have any phials which we could use?' Neither woman is keen to commit suicide, but they believe that the poison could be preferable to capture by the Russians.

The Führer nods. He will make sure that they each get one. 'I'm very sorry I can't give you a better farewell present.'

Nicolaus von Below, who has been waiting in the corridor to speak to the Führer, gets his opportunity after lunch. He asks permission to attempt a breakout.

Hitler is discouraging. 'It is no longer possible to get through the Russian lines.'

Von Below is determined. '*Mein Führer*, I believe I will be able to reach General Wenck in the south-west.'

'If you get that far you should head for Admiral Dönitz's headquarters in the north. I will give you a written permission. *Alles gute.*'

Dönitz's headquarters is the ideal destination as his wife and children are not far from Plön Castle, along the Baltic coast. Von Below goes to prepare. He decides he will take only the permission, some food and a machine gun.

Thirty-two-year-old British Lieutenant Commander Patrick Dalzel-Job is speeding in his jeep away from the port of Bremen. He is heading towards a vast arsenal of mines belonging to the German navy, which he believes is hidden in woods nearby – it's been completely undetected throughout the war.

Dalzel-Job is a naval intelligence officer with exceptional skills – he can navigate midget submarines, dive, parachute, and in 1940 he helped evacuate 5,000 civilians from the Norwegian city of Narvik (for which King Haakon of Norway awarded him the Ridderkors *or* Knight's Cross*). In 1942 Dalzel-Job was back in occupied Norway leading commando raids to assess the strength of the German forces there.*

Now in Germany, Dalzel-Job is a member of the British 30 Assault Unit whose job it is to secure enemy intelligence material before the Germans have time to destroy it – and also before Allied troops overrun it (Dalzel-Job wrote later that his own side was 'often the bigger risk to their preservation').

30 Assault Unit (named after the number of their underground office in the Admiralty) are the invention of the deputy to the Director of Naval Intelligence, Ian Fleming, a man who Dalzel-Job finds 'kind, but cold with an eye to the main chance'. They are not Fleming's only invention. T-Force is a unit designed to track down all non-naval intelligence, and are currently still working in Bremen. Dalzel-Job has no time for T-Force. As far as he is concerned they always arrive late and are little more than looters. (Dalzel-Job is tough on looters. A few days ago near Bremen he found that a royal marine had taken two watches from a shop. He made the marine go back and return them to the owner. 'It seemed to me that an army which was supposed to be fighting for a principle could not afford the traditional soldiers' perquisites of looting and rape,' he said later.)

30 Assault Unit are in effect Fleming's own private army, and were so successful in North Africa and Italy that they now have a whole Marine commando unit assigned to them. As a result, the scout cars and jeeps that make up Dalzel-Job's team are carrying as many marines as they can as they race through the north German countryside.

Bremen has been a great success for 30 Assault Unit. Last

Thursday, 26th April, Dalzel-Job himself was asked by the Burgomaster to accept the surrender of the city, and he placed the police and all other services at his disposal. But Dalzel-Job was more interested in getting to Bremen's shipyards where he'd heard from German POWs and civilians that there were some of the new and much-feared Type XXI U-boats. Sure enough, in the shipyards he discovered 16 new U-boats and two destroyers. His team worked all through Thursday night sifting through technical data left behind by the naval engineers.

On Friday more British troops arrived, along with the press and army officials. Dalzel-Job recalled, 'When a staff officer arrived from 52nd Division and asked me to sign a receipt for the 16 submarines, it was the last straw. I told the Royal Marines to put up a sign saying the shipyard belonged to 30 Assault Unit.'

They are now getting close to the town of Hesedorf and the naval arsenal. Dalzel-Job and his team have been travelling across Europe since D-Day and are experts in gathering information from both German soldiers and civilians. He finds that the civilians in particular are often willing to talk 'in the first shock of seeing us arrive'. It's through these contacts that he's established the where-abouts of the valuable arsenal.

Although Patrick Dalzel-Job was not especially inspired by Ian Fleming, it seems Fleming was inspired by him. Many years later, Fleming told Dalzel-Job that James Bond was in part modelled on him. As soon as the first books came out in the early 1950s, Peter Jemmett, a former member of 30 Assault Unit, recognised Dalzel-Job as the Bond prototype. 'In contrast to a number of people who have claimed that they were James Bond, Patrick has never made any fuss about it,' Jemmett said. Dalzel-Job wrote that Fleming could write witty minutes on operational intelligence reports, 'but was the last person I would have suspected of writing best-sellers.'

143

About 2.15pm/7.45pm Burmese time/9.15am EWT

Wing Commander Lionel 'Bill' Hudson is wide awake now – from the balcony in his prison block in Rangoon jail he can see a small fire beyond the main gate. The jail is divided into different compounds like spokes in a wheel – one for the British and Australian troops; one for the Indians and Gurkhas; and another for captured Chinese. Hudson looks towards the Japanese guards' compound and it seems to him suspiciously quiet. He wrote later, 'Some intuition, or was it the extraordinary stillness, told me that something strange was in the air.'

Under the light of a full moon, Hudson walks round the balcony until he comes to the front of the prison block. There is no guard. He decides to wait to see if one appears. It is wise to be cautious – even a minor transgression, like failing to bow to a guard, can result in a beating.

Hudson climbs onto the low balcony wall and drops to the ground.

The American military have arrived in Piazzale Loreto in Milan. They're ordering that the bodies of Mussolini and his mistress be taken down from the meat hooks where they've been hanging and delivered to the city morgue so that autopsies can be carried out.

A US army photographer will accompany the bodies to the morgue where he arranges the couple in a macabre embrace for a picture that will be sent around the world.

In Caserta, near Naples, SS-Obergruppenführer Karl Wolff signs the surrender of German forces in Italy – just under one million men – to the Allies. Lieutenant General Morgan signs on behalf of Field Marshal Alexander. American, Russian and British officers look on in silence.

'Ich habe Schmerzen – Schmerzen.'

Geoffrey Cox's Venice-bound convoy has stopped for a moment by a small park. A man who is looking very pale and is being helped to walk by his wife and two daughters approaches the New Zealander's jeep.

'This is my first day out of hiding for a year,' he says in Italian. 'A year in a cellar. A year in a cellar. A year in a cellar...' he says again and again.

The convoy moves on and soon comes across the aftermath of a battle that ended only a short time before. Cox gets out of his jeep and heads towards a ditch near the road. There he sees a group of about 20 German soldiers lying dead or dying. The partisans have taken their guns.

A middle-aged soldier mouths to Cox, *'Ich habe Schmerzen – Schmerzen.'* 'I'm in pain – pain.'

A group of press photographers arrive and start taking pictures; a priest dashes over and starts hearing the German soldiers' mumbled confessions. The photographers ask the priest to shift position so they can get a shot of him where the light is better. He obliges.

Every day Cox sends out an intelligence report for the division. In the report for 23rd April he explained why the Germans continue to fight: 'Even though it is obvious to the vast majority that Germany has lost the war, they are quite prepared to fight on so long as it is the easiest thing to do and so long as there is somebody there to tell them to do it.'

'I hope there is no word or phrase in this outpouring of my heart that unwittingly gives offence.'

President Truman is not having a relaxed Sunday morning. He is reading a cable sent by Churchill to both him and Stalin about the vexed question of Poland. Churchill expresses his 'distress' at the misunderstandings that have arisen about the plans agreed at Yalta for the future of Poland. The British and Americans want a new Polish government to include those politicians who have been in exile in London. Stalin, Churchill suspects, wants the government he's installed in Lublin to be the sole government of Poland. As to Stalin's recent suggestion that Yugoslavia should be the model for Poland, Churchill refuses to accept that, as 'Marshal Tito has become a complete dictator'. Churchill goes on to say that, in 1944, the Allies agreed to the Polish–Russian border (known as the Curzon Line) and now Stalin should meet his side of the bargain, 'namely the sovereignty, independence and freedom of Poland...' Truman reads the final paragraph of Churchill's cable. He remembers its words for a long time to come.

'There is not much comfort in looking into a future where you [Stalin] and the countries you dominate, plus the Communist parties in many other states, are all drawn up on one side, and those who rally to the English-speaking nations and their associates are on the other. It is quite obvious that their quarrel would tear the world to pieces and that all of us leading men on either side who had anything to do with that would be shamed before history... I hope there is no word or phrase in this outpouring of my heart that unwittingly gives offence.'

There is little that Truman can do today. He will wait on developments at the UN Conference in San Francisco when it reconvenes in the afternoon. He begins to get ready to go to church.

This telegram from Churchill was considered by his assistant private secretary Sir Jock Colville to be 'a final appeal to resolve the Polish impasse'. The Prime Minister had written it on 27th April and sent it to the Foreign Office to be approved, with a note saying, 'Pray consider this very carefully with your experts in the Russian section and make me any suggestions you like. But do not try to mar the symmetry and coherence of the message.'

'You son of a bitch, if you touch another of my men, I'll kill you right here.'

2.15pm

Felix Sparks has reached the prison compound within the Dachau complex. It is surrounded by a water-filled moat about 15 feet wide, and a ten-foot-high barbed-wire fence. There is a large wrought-iron gate. Above it is a sign saying '*Arbeit Macht Frei*' ('Work Sets You Free'). On the other side of the fence are thousands of celebrating prisoners shouting, 'America! America!'

Some others are tearing informers limb from limb. Elsewhere prisoners are hunting down their former guards, some of whom have disguised themselves in camp uniforms, and are beating them to death with shovels.

Flags of the Allied nations are hanging on the perimeter wire. The prisoners had been secretly making them over the past few weeks out of bits of cloth.

Sparks orders his men not to throw food as he fears it will start a fight among the starving prisoners. There are over 30,000 people in Dachau – Poles, Russians, Catholic priests and Jews.

Three jeeps pull up by the gate, and in the first Sparks recognises General Henning Linden of the 42nd Infantry Division. He is followed out of the jeep by an attractive woman wearing US army fatigues and a German army jacket. She is Marguerite Higgins of the *New York Herald Tribune*.

'General, I have a lady reporter here who would like to interview some of the prisoners.'

'She can't go in there,' Sparks replies, 'We're not going to open that gate.' He can see that hundreds of people are pressed against it; his orders are not to let anyone out until they have had medical attention.

'I'll take the responsibility for it,' Linden says.

'General, you're not in your area – you're out of your combat zone, and I take my orders from my commanding general.'

As they are talking, Marguerite Higgins jumps out of the jeep and opens the gate. There is chaos as the prisoners surge forward. Sparks orders his men to fire over their heads and to get the gate closed. Shots ring out. Terrified, Higgins runs back to her jeep.

General Linden is furious.

'I'm relieving you of command! I'm taking responsibility,' he yells.

'No, this is not your area, you are not relieving me of my command,' Sparks shouts back. He turns to a soldier and says, 'Private, escort this general and his party out of here.'

The shocked private steps forward towards Linden, who promptly picks up his swagger stick and hits the soldier on the helmet. This is the final straw for Sparks. He recalled later, 'It had already been a long and trying day. I exploded at that point...'

Sparks hauls out his .45 and shouts, 'You son of a bitch, if you touch another of my men, I'll kill you right here!"

Linden sits down in the jeep. Then out of the third vehicle, a battalion commander runs towards Sparks.

'You can't talk to my general like that! I'll see you after the war!'

'You son of a bitch – what's the matter with right now?!'

The battalion commander hesitates, then returns to his jeep. As they pull away General Linden shouts at Sparks, 'I'll see you before a general court martial!'

Sparks recalled, 'That was the last thing that was worrying me at that point...'

It is the evil things that we shall be fighting against – brute force, bad faith, injustice, oppression and persecution – and against them I am certain that the right will prevail.

Prime Minister Neville Chamberlain, 3rd September 1939

Marguerite Higgins got her exclusive, although she never did get inside the prison compound. Her harrowing report of the liberation of Dachau will appear in newspapers around the world in two days' time.

Richard Brown, a submarine designer living in Ipswich referred to it in his diary later that day: 'That sort of thing, and we've heard a lot of it, lots of which I haven't recorded because one just doesn't want to, illustrates to me what we have been fighting. "Evil things" Chamberlain said... though we didn't know what he meant, we know now and we Britons only just escaped similar horrors.'

2.30pm/3.30pm UK time/8.00pm Burmese time

At Bletchley Park, Buckinghamshire, the centre for the British government's Code and Cypher School, the team intercept a message sent by Heinrich Himmler to Ernst Kaltenbrunner – an SS general and the Director of Reich Main Security. The message reads:

'Situation in Berlin very strained. Situation on Eastern Front west of Prenzlau very difficult.

'Reports on the enemy wireless are malicious perversions of a conversation that I had with Bernadotte.

'It is clear that to fight is the only possibility, since the other side is at present absolutely at one against us.

'Equally malicious and untrue is the other assertion that I with [Werner] Naumann, have prepared a detailed declaration concerning the Führer's death. Naumann is in Berlin. I am outside. We have not spoken to each other for a fortnight.'

Himmler is terrified that he could be arrested and executed on Hitler's orders for having had peace talks with the Swedish Ambassador, Count Bernadotte. He is busy denying to everyone the news reports that these talks have taken place.

In Rangoon jail, there is still no sign of the Japanese guards. Bill Hudson is walking cautiously towards the main gate. It looks dark and sinister. There, to his astonishment, he finds two letters attached to it, neatly written in broken English.

Rangoon.
29th April, 1945
Gentlemen, Bravely you have come here to the prison gate. We have gone keeping your prisoner safely with Nipponese knightship. Afterwards we may meet again at the front somewhere. Then let us fight bravely each other. (We had kept the gate's keys in the gate room.)
   Nipponese Army.

Rangoon.
29th April, 1945
To the whole captured persons of Rangoon Jail. According to the Nippon military order, we hereby give you liberty and admit to leave this place at your will. Regarding food and other materials kept in the compound, we give you permission to consume them as far as your necessity is concerned.

We hope that we shall have an opportunity to meet you again at battlefield of somewhere.

We shall continue our war effort eternally in order to get the emancipation of all Asiatic races.

Haruo Ito
Chief Officer of Rangoon Branch Jail

The Japanese were told to defend Rangoon to the last man, but decided to flee the city, as they knew British forces were only days away. It is a bold act of disobedience as today is Emperor Hirohito's birthday.

About 3.00pm/11.00pm Okinawa Time

In the toilets opposite the switchboard, the Führer's beloved Alsatian, Blondi, is trembling as her handler, Sergeant Fritz Tornow, holds her nose and forces her jaw open. One of the Reich Chancellery doctors, Werner Haase, crushes a cyanide capsule inside her mouth with a pair of pliers. Blondi falls sideways, 'as if struck by lightening'.

Tornow can't hide his distress from the Führer who comes, very briefly, to inspect the body. Hitler wants to see for himself that the cyanide which the treacherous Himmler has provided does actually work. The telephonist, Rochus Misch, is overwhelmed by the poison's smell of bitter almonds and rushes out of the switchboard room to the cellar of the new Reich Chancellery to get away from it.

Tornow carries Blondi's body up to the Chancellery gardens, where he buries it. He comes back down for Wulf and the four other puppies. Following orders, he takes them to the garden and shoots them before burying them with their mother.

In one of the network of caves under Shuri Castle on the Japanese island of Okinawa, General Cho has been addressing his fellow commanding officers. He has outlined his plan to smash the American forces that invaded the island on 1st April. If the Americans secure Okinawa, then the invasion of Japan will be next. The generals have been drinking plenty of sake all evening. A vote is taken and Cho's plan is unanimously adopted. They decide that the fightback will begin on 4th May.

Orders are issued to the Japanese soldiers on Okinawa that they must 'display a combined strength. Each soldier will kill at least one American devil'. The Japanese fail to repulse the Americans, and almost all the defenders die, but by the time the island is lost they have inflicted very heavy casualties – over 7,500 GIs killed and over 36,000 wounded. The Americans will conclude that an invasion of Japan would be equally bloody. The atomic option to end the war becomes more appealing for President Truman.

On 22nd June, the day Okinawa surrenders to the Americans, General Cho and General Ushijima (who is in overall command of the Japanese forces on the island) kneel on a white sheet on a ledge overlooking the Pacific Ocean. Wearing their full dress uniform, including medals and swords, they unfasten their tunics; Ushijima then takes a dagger from a waiting staff officer and stabs himself in the stomach. Cho does the same. He leaves a handwritten note: 'I depart without regret, shame, or obligations.'

At Stalag IV-C in the Sudetenland, British POWs Bert Ruffle and Frank Talbot are enjoying a German beer together with their mates Terence 'Lofty' Whitney (Royal Navy), Harry 'Shoe' Smith and Bunny Humphries (both Rifle Brigade). They are amazed that the guard let them hang onto the crate of beer that they found in Brüx, having been sent to pick up building materials. The POWs have noticed a change of attitude in the guards – they know that the war is almost over. Some of them have been spotted with civilian clothing on under their uniforms.

Later that day Ruffle writes in his diary: 'There is not so much shouting and telling us to hurry up all the time, and if we worked or not made no difference to them. Yes, there was a wind of change!'

Lieutenant Claus Sellier is standing by the side of an Autobahn close to the Austrian border in the German Alps. He is shocked by what he sees – nothing but lines of filthy stranded trucks in both directions, and slumped in the fields around are groups of weary-looking soldiers. They have no petrol and nowhere to go. Claus turns to Fritz and says, 'Let's get away from here. Let's find a farm and stay overnight and rest. None of this makes sense to me anymore.'

He recalled later, 'The once formidable German military machine was a dying corpse, struggling, but barely alive.'

3.30pm

A convoy of three cars carrying a group of young aristocratic friends, and laden with rice, flour and tinned goods, is travelling through the Austrian Alps, heading for Moosham Castle, the family home of the Count and Countess Wilczek. The Count and Countess's daughter, Sisi Wilczek, is one of the passengers in the front car, sitting with her handbag and a shoebox on her lap. Until the beginning of April, Sisi had been living in the family palace in Vienna and working as a nurse. On 3rd April she managed to catch the last train to leave Vienna before the arrival of the Russian forces. She gathered all the family's remaining cash – several million marks and several million Czech kronen – and stuffed them into the shoebox which she has clung to for the last three and a half weeks. She is now only hours from her destination. The young people in the convoy were on the edges of the 1944 plot to kill Hitler and have seen many of their friends executed for their involvement.

Shortly after passing through the town of Bad Aussee, Sisi and her companions realise that there is no sign of the third car. They pull over and decide to get out and stretch their legs while they wait for it to catch up. Eventually the third car arrives and the convoy continues slowly up the mountain road. After about four miles Sisi suddenly shrieks. She has left her handbag and the shoebox on the roadside where they stopped.

The front car turns back, while the others wait. They reach the spot and to Sisi's huge relief, she immediately spots the shoebox on the side of the road, but there is no sign of her handbag. They decide to drive a bit further to see if they can find the person who has taken it and soon catch up with two women riding bicycles. Sisi's handbag is dangling from one of the handlebars. There's an unpleasant altercation as the women insist the handbag is theirs and threaten to call the police. But Sisi is not going to leave without it. When the car turns around and heads back to join the others, Sisi has her family fortune and her handbag safely on her lap.

Geoffrey Cox is driving through the streets of Mestre, a suburb of mainland Venice. There are thousands on the streets to welcome the Allied troops – but it's the girls that Cox notices most: they are sunburned and, as he wrote later, had 'greeting and invitation in their eyes... The Italian men greeted us warmly enough, with relief and with thanks, but in the eyes of the girls there was something akin to ecstasy'.

What Geoffrey Cox witnessed was seen across western Europe by the liberating forces. A Dutch woman wrote about seeing a Canadian tank for the first time on the streets of the Hague: 'All the blood drained from my body, and I thought: there comes our liberation. And as the tank came nearer, I lost my breath and the soldier stood up – he was like a saint.'

4.00pm/11.00am EWT/9.30pm Burmese time

President Truman is with his wife and daughter at the Foundry Methodist Church in Washington. Their pew is draped in black and surmounted with a black cross in memory of President Roosevelt. Truman is feeling uncomfortable about all the attention he is getting in the church. He feels as if he is distracting the congregation from their worship.

In Swarthmore, Pennsylvania, the poet W.H. Auden is in the throes of packing. He is about to leave America and travel on a US military passport to Germany. He has been recruited by the US Strategic Bombing Survey to a team tasked with surveying the effects of Allied bombing on German morale. Auden is originally from Birmingham, England, but controversially moved to the United States in January 1939, timing that many of his friends and readers saw as a betrayal of Britain. He is a fluent German speaker, having lived in Berlin from 1928 to 1929. Although he is gay he is in fact married to a German woman, Erika Mann, the daughter of the German writer

Thomas Mann. The couple married in 1935 to enable Erika to gain British citizenship and escape the Nazis. The person Auden really considers himself married to is the American poet Chester Kallman, who is currently watching him attempting to pack. Kallman tells friends that the scene looked 'as though a mythical beast had gotten drunk and wandered through shitting books and soiled shirts'.

In Rangoon jail, the prisoners are celebrating by drinking tea, with sugar they've found in the Japanese stores. But the concern now is how to stop the Allies bombing the jail – they may not realise that there are POWs in Rangoon.

In the green room in the Reich Chancellery, Joseph Goebbels and his family are at a farewell party for some of the Hitler Youth who have worked for him. About 40 people have gathered, including some staff and patients from the emergency hospital. Everyone is served pea soup and the Goebbels children are passed from lap to lap. After the meal the Hitler Youth sing some of their songs. Goebbels asks for some of the old Nazi fighting songs. He listens with tears running down his cheeks. Then his children gather around the table and start singing to the accompaniment of a young soldier playing an accordion:

> *The Blue Dragoons, they are riding*
> *With drum and fife through the gate,*
> *Fanfares accompany them,*
> *Ringing to the hills above.*

The children, who are very practised singers, go through their repertoire of German folk songs and lullabies. Staff Lieutenant Franz Kuhlmann, who had been brought along by another officer, is very struck by the ghostly, unreal atmosphere. He later recalled that it felt as if everyone in the room knew that 'this was a farewell for ever, the end of a world for which millions had fought and shed their blood, and that all the sacrifices had been in vain'.

> *Kids are kids all over the world – except in Hitler's Germany. Sure they're lovable, but ten years ago the Jerry that got your buddy was lovable too. It's tough to do, but make the kids realise now that war doesn't pay; they may remember when they start thinking about the next war!*
>
> *US Armed Forces Radio*

About 4.30pm

In the hills above the chaos of the Bavarian Autobahn, the young German lieutenants Claus Sellier and his friend Fritz are standing outside a barn beside a picturesque farmhouse. They know there are people inside the barn as the door was shut as they approached.

'Don't be afraid,' Claus calls, 'we're passing through and we would like to sleep in your barn.'

Silence.

'We'll help you with repairs around the house.'

The barn door opens slowly and the two soldiers see the frightened face of a young girl. She then slams the door shut. Claus gives their names and their ranks. After a while the door opens and the girl appears with three younger girls holding onto her skirt. She tells them that her name is Barbara and that she's 15, and she introduces her two sisters and a cousin. Their fathers are away fighting in the war, and her mother died four months ago.

'Come into the house. I've just finished baking bread,' Barbara says.

'And I helped make cookies!' adds the cousin.

5.00pm

The light is beginning to fade when Johannmeier, Lorenz and Zander, the Hitler testament couriers, reach Pichelsdorf Bridge over the River Havel. A battalion of Hitler Youth volunteers are holding up the bridge in the hope that General Wenck's 12th Army will soon cross it and relieve the centre of Berlin. The three men are exhausted by a traumatic journey through the ruins of Berlin, passing huddled women and children, and exhausted soldiers hiding in burned-out houses. They have succeeded in getting through three lines of Russian soldiers: one at the Victory Column in the Tiergarten, the second at the Berlin Zoo station and the third just before Pichelsdorf. They squeeze into the battalion commander's small concrete bunker and sleep.

5.15pm/6.15pm UK time

Bletchley Park intercepts a message from Karl Hermann Frank, the notoriously violent head of the police in Prague and Reich Minister for Bohemia and Moravia. It is addressed to Heinrich Himmler. Frank wants to know what to do if 'something happens to the Führer'. He demands to be informed immediately of any developments. Prague is one of the last major European cities still under Nazi control. Frank is trying to retain power, but at the same time anxious to evacuate key German personnel before the Russians arrive. He shares Himmler's hope that it may be possible to negotiate a peace with the Allies and join forces to defeat the Russians.

About 5.30pm

At the labour camp in the abandoned theatre in the German town of Triptis, Nina Markovna's 17th birthday celebrations continue. She is sitting on her bunk trying out chewing gum for the first time. Nina has seen the Americans chewing constantly and so wants to try it herself. All her American admirers are here. Bob, who'd brought a leather suitcase full of sweets, cognac and food, is sitting next to Mike on the next bunk.

'What's next?' Jack asks.

Nina spits out the chewing gum and points to a can with a picture of a pineapple on its label. Bob opens the can.

'It's not the whole fruit. It's just the juice squeezed out of it. Try it!'

Nina has her first fruit juice.

She then moves on to peanut butter. With a spoon she devours a whole jar. The three Americans and her brother Slava are watching wide-eyed and with some concern. Bob gives the remaining two jars to Slava.

'Take it. Hide it from her!'

About 6.00pm/7.00pm UK time

The officers who have escaped from the Führerbunker, Boldt, Weiss and von Loringhoven, reach the underground shelter at Berlin Zoo Station, having made their way past two lines of Russian soldiers, dodging gunfire and leaping over shell craters and decaying bodies. When they get to the Zeiss-Planetarium they decide to go inside to rest. It has taken the three men four hours to scramble along a distance that would normally be a 30-minute walk. They lie down, exhausted and gaze up at the artificial sky of the domed planetarium roof. Beyond it, visible through a shell hole, they can see the real, darkening sky.

In Bletchley Park a message to Hitler is intercepted. It is another telegram from Karl Hermann Frank in Prague. Heinrich Himmler is copied in. The message reads:

'My Führer,

'In view of the latest Reich situation, I request immediate reply giving freedom of action in domestic and foreign policy for Bohemia and Moravia in order still to exploit all possible opportunities for the rescue of Germans here from Bolshevism.'

6.15pm

In Berlin, Yelena Rzhevskaya of the Russian SMERSH intelligence unit is interviewing a German nurse. The woman has been caught trying to break through the Russian lines to get home to her mother. She has discarded her uniform cap but is otherwise still dressed as a nurse. She admits she has been working in an emergency hospital in the Reich Chancellery cellars. She tells Rzhevskaya that people there said that Hitler was 'in the basement'.

Yelena Rzhevskaya and her colleagues waste no time. They follow the route of the Soviet tanks towards the Reich Chancellery, passing through broken barricades and driving over rubble-filled ditches in an American jeep. As they approach the centre of the city the air thickens with acrid fumes, smoke and dust. Rzhevskaya feels the grit on her teeth.

6.30pm

In northern Italy under the shadow of the Alps, the 2nd New Zealand Division has ground to a halt on the banks of the River Piave. As the troops get comfortable for the night, engineers are building a bridge so that the advance to Trieste can continue. (They are calculating the width of the river based on the information supplied by Geoffrey Cox's aerial intelligence team who have always proved themselves to be accurate.)

A short while ago, Cox saw a milestone saying that Trieste is only 125 kilometres away. Their orders are to get to the city before Marshal Tito's Yugoslav forces. Tito, who has fought with the Allies, is desperate to seize the port and make it part of a new Yugoslavia.

7.00pm/2.00pm EWT

At the Brooklyn Navy Yard, in the shadow of a brand-new 45,000-ton aircraft carrier, Mrs Eleanor Roosevelt, dressed in black, is addressing the thousands of shipyard workers who built the vessel. The carrier was to be called USS *Coral Sea*, but with the death of her husband three weeks ago, the navy decided that she should be named the USS *Franklin D. Roosevelt*.

'My husband would watch this ship with great pride. So today I hope this ship will always do its duty in winning the war. I pray God to bless this ship and its personnel and to keep them safe, and bring them home victorious.'

Mrs Roosevelt pulls a lever and a bottle of champagne smashes onto the bow. Slowly the USS *Franklin D. Roosevelt* rumbles down the slipway and into the East River. British and American vessels nearby sound their whistles in tribute.

By the time the fully fitted-out USS Franklin D. Roosevelt *sails from New York in October, the war will be over. During her 30 years' service, the carrier will acquire a number of nicknames (necessary for a ship with such a long name), including 'Swanky Franky' and 'Rosie', and in the 1970s towards the end of her career, 'Rusty Rosie.'*

In the dark waters beyond the Kola Inlet on the Norwegian coast, close to the Russian port of Murmansk, the 14 German U-boats that make up the wolfpack codenamed *Faust* are waiting for the very last Arctic convoy to set sail. The convoy of 24 merchant ships plus a Royal Navy escort are about to make their final return to Britain, having delivered munitions, tanks, food and raw materials to the Soviets. The Arctic convoys have been travelling from Britain, Iceland and North America to Russia since 1941.

In Berlin, the Russian SMERSH reconnaissance unit has had to abandon their jeep because the streets of the city centre are blocked by the rubble of ruined buildings. Their street maps are useless as street signs have been destroyed by shelling. Yelena Rzhevskaya asks Berlin citizens for directions to the Reich Chancellery. Most people are helpful; many have white sheets and pillowcases hanging from their windows as signs of surrender, ignoring SS threats of execution for anyone who displays a white flag. Some people are wearing white armbands. Rzhevskaya notices an elderly woman taking two young children across a road. All three are wearing white armbands. The children are neatly dressed, hair combed, but the woman is distressed and, Rzhevskaya notes, hatless. She is crying out to no one in particular, 'They are orphans! Our house has been bombed! They are orphans!'

7.15pm

Just off the Norwegian coast, in the *Faust* wolfpack, U-boat Captain Willi Dietrich and his crew on board *U-286* have been at sea for the last 12 days. Dietrich has commanded U-boats in the German Navy since 1943 but has never successfully torpedoed an enemy vessel.

U-286's sonar detects the merchantmen and Royal Navy ships of the Arctic convoy sailing away from the Kola Inlet. Dietrich sees his opportunity.

Lookouts on the escort frigate HMS *Goodall* spot the wake of a torpedo on the surface of the water heading straight towards them. Her skipper James Fulton orders evasive action. The torpedo shoots past.

In northern Germany, the German speakers in Lieutenant Commander Patrick Dalzel-Job's 30 Assault Unit (the intelligence-gathering team created by Ian Fleming) have spent the afternoon getting information from the Burgomaster of Hesedorf and other civilians about the location of the German naval arsenal hidden in woods nearby. 30 Assault Unit are now poised at the arsenal's entrance, ready to go in. With them is an M3 Stuart tank (nicknamed a 'Honey' after a US tank driver remarked 'she's a honey') that Dalzel-Job asked the Irish Guards to provide as extra backup; his unit consists of just 30 men and they have no idea what they will find. He gets a colleague to take his photo at the entrance to the arsenal.

7.27pm

In the Arctic seas off Norway, a second torpedo is racing towards HMS *Goodall*. This time it is too late for the frigate to take evasive action. Captain Willi Dietrich in *U-286* has his first hit. The torpedo explodes against the bow of the *Goodall*. Captain James Fulton and 94 crew are killed. Almost all are under the age of 25. The rest of the crew abandon ship. There are 44 survivors. HMS *Goodall* is the 2,779th and last Allied warship lost in the fight against Germany.

> **I have suffered terrible anxieties, and experienced terrible things myself. My parents couldn't protect me.**
>
> **Jutta, a German schoolgirl**

About 7.45pm

In a cellar beneath an apartment block in the town of Thüringen on the outskirts of Berlin, 17-year-old Lieselotte G. (the 'G' is for anonymity) is writing her diary. Two weeks ago she returned from boarding school to be with her mother. Lieselotte's father is a soldier fighting in Riesa, 120 miles to the south. Her brother Bertel is with the *Volkssturm* – the German territorial army – defending east Berlin. Lieselotte is glad she's home but frequent air raids mean that they have to constantly run to the cellar, and there are power cuts that last up to four hours. A white flag flies outside their apartment.

Last Sunday the Russians arrived. Thüringen had been ready for them for weeks. The woods nearby were cut down and tank traps dug in the streets (although the locals called them 'laughter traps' as they believed the Russians would find them so small and funny).

Lieselotte wrote in her diary that although Nazi propaganda had depicted the Russians as murderers and rapists 'they all behaved pretty decently and did nothing to us, even though we were shaking with fear'. But shortly after she finished writing that entry, everything changed. Later that night, Lieselotte's apartment was damaged by a bomb and she and her mother had to move in with their neighbours. Some Russian soldiers then came into their housing block and helped themselves to the food in the empty apartment. Terrified, Lieselotte and her mother hid in the cellar until they'd gone. For the past week, whenever they see a Russian soldier coming, they hide.

Now, a week after the Russians started breaking in, Lieselotte has her first opportunity to update her diary.

'Hundreds of people killed themselves in our district last Sunday. Our pastor has shot himself, his wife and his daughter, because the Russians broke into their cellar and started doing it with his girl. Our teacher Miss K. hanged herself because she is a Nazi. It's lucky the gas is off, otherwise even more people would have killed themselves; we might have too... I thought a Russian would take me... I would have had an abortion, I don't want to bring a Russian child into the world.'

Lieselotte's family all survive the war, and Thüringen becomes part of East Germany.

'See Them – Lest You Forget'

8.00pm/9.00pm UK time

The German naval arsenal is bigger than Lieutenant Commander Patrick Dalzel-Job ever imagined. It has 200 stores filled with mines and is linked by over 20 kilometres of roads – all hidden by trees. The Allies had no idea that it was here. Some of the mines are of a revolutionary type Dalzel-Job has never seen before.

30 Assault Unit have based themselves in the arsenal's large naval officers' mess. Bizarrely it has a huge white porcelain vomitorium, with chromium handles and, as a joke, a sign in large black letters saying, '*Für die seekranke*' (For the seasick).

Suddenly there are mortar explosions outside – the Germans are in the woods around them.

Michael Hargrave is still in England. Together with two other medical students, he's huddled round a fire in their hut back at their transit camp near Cirencester. By now they should have been in Germany and on their way to Bergen-Belsen to help the sick and dying.

At midday the students were told that storms over the continent meant it was too dangerous for their Dakota to fly – two had been lost in the past week, and the RAF weren't taking any unnecessary risks. Hargrave is flattered by their concern for the students' safety but depressed they won't be flying today. They hope to go in the morning.

In Bergen-Belsen the work of saving lives continues. In the past week, the sick have been moved from the camp to a nearby Panzer training school that's been turned into a makeshift hospital. Even its parade grounds are full of beds and straw mattresses. Soon it will be the largest hospital in Europe, with 13,000 patients.

Twenty-five-year-old Private Manny Fisher has been helping transfer the sick. He's written in his diary: 'I simply could not look at these human wrecks for more than a few seconds. I found my eyes filling with tears, and had to turn away from my soldier-comrades. Some are beyond human aid and will soon die. But they are happy and look forward to living again even though they might know it is only for a short while.'

The wards are often in a state of chaos. The patients sometimes fight for what little food there is, and basic equipment is lacking. Bedpans sometimes double up as feeding tins. Five hundred new patients arrive every day, and the British doctors and nurses and the 48 Red Cross volunteers who arrived a few days ago are struggling to cope. Lieutenant Colonel James Johnston, the senior medical officer at Bergen-Belsen, requested medical personnel from England, and was shocked when a few days ago 60 German doctors freed from POW camps arrived.

A Red Cross nurse wrote home, 'They strut about the place in a most alarming fashion terrifying all the inhabitants. However the British Tommy is marvellous in taking them down a peg or two.'

On their second day, the German doctors ignored an order to parade at 7am, so Lieutenant Colonel Johnston threatened to hang their senior officer. After that they were more obedient.

German nurses drafted in from nearby towns and cities have added to the tension in the camp. When a group from Hamburg arrived on a ward for the first time, they were set upon by patients (some of whom were dying) armed with knives and forks. Troops were called to rescue the nurses who were by then covered in blood, their uniforms torn to shreds. This is the atmosphere that Michael Hargrave and the other volunteers face in the coming weeks.

Michael will finally arrive in Bergen-Belsen on 3rd May, and be put in charge of Hut 210. Over the next few weeks he treats patients suffering from typhus, diarrhoea and severe malnutrition, and makes careful notes and drawings in his diary about the various conditions he encounters. One day in the camp he comes across a huge pile of boots about 20 yards long and 12 feet high that had belonged to those who'd perished before the British arrived.

'...the shoes at the bottom were squashed as flat as paper so you can imagine how many thousands of pairs of shoes were there, and each pair had once had an owner, and though the Germans may have destroyed all records of the camp, this pile of shoes and boots bore mute and absolutely damning evidence of the number of people who had died...'

In May and June a strange sort of normality will appear in the makeshift hospital in the Panzer training school. Dances are organised, attended by British soldiers and patients, with music provided by an RAF band.

One doctor wrote later of the survivors: 'Some could hardly walk, others looked as if they'd break in two.'

A library will be established; Yehudi Menuhin and Benjamin Britten come to give performances, and in June, Laurence Olivier's 65-strong Old Vic Company perform Bernard Shaw's Arms and the Man *for the soldiers and medical staff.*

Just before Michael Hargrave leaves England, a consignment of lipstick will arrive at Bergen-Belsen (no one knows who'd ordered it) and it has a remarkable effect on the female survivors. Lieutenant Colonel Mervin Gonin wrote, 'At last someone had done something to make them individuals again; they were someone, no longer merely the number tattooed on the arm. That lipstick started to give them back their humanity.'

Only yesterday, on 28th April, the British finally buried in mass graves the last of the corpses that they'd discovered when they first entered Bergen-Belsen. Most of the soldiers and medical staff smoke all the time as a way of hiding the atrocious smell.

Cameramen from British Movietone News and from the British Army Film Unit are filming footage in and around the huts. For stills photographer George Rodger, on an assignment for *Life* magazine, the scenes at the camp are all too much. After realising he is trying to find the most photographically pleasing composition of bodies, Rodger is so ashamed he stops taking pictures. For the rest of his life he avoids war zones and concentrates instead on the people and wildlife of Africa.

The Ministry of Information is keen to collect images to prove to the German people that reported atrocities are real. The famous film director Alfred Hitchcock has been recruited to help compile the footage into a documentary for cinema release.

When he is shown the harrowing footage from Belsen, Hitchcock is so shocked he stays away from Pinewood Studios for a week. One of Hitchcock's aims will be to show how close the camps are to German towns, and that local people must therefore have known about them. But by the time the film is finished, British politicians are keener to reconstruct Germany than humble its people. The film won't be shown until 1984.

However, cinema newsreels in May 1945 will show footage from Belsen. Outside a cinema in Kilburn, north London, a sign is put up: 'See Them – Lest You Forget.'

Bletchley Park pick up a message from Heinrich Himmler replying to Karl Hermann Frank in Prague:

'Ref. yours of 1900 hours.

'What do you mean by freedom of action in domestic and in particular in foreign policy?'

Having been accused of treason by Hitler, Himmler is not going to be seen to give any encouragement to any independent foreign policy initiatives.

Bletchley don't pick up any reply from the Führerbunker, but they intercept a message to Frank from the Plön headquarters of Admiral Dönitz. Frank is curtly reminded that he has already had instructions for the removal of the German population from the Protectorate of Bohemia and Moravia.

In London the white stone of BBC Broadcasting House has turned a dark-grey colour during the war years, and it has bomb damage on its west side. The BBC's civil engineering department has decided that these battle scars should remain as a memento of the war years. In one of the building's news studios, newsreader Stuart Hibberd is reading the nine o'clock bulletin, and it's full of details of the death of Mussolini.

Later that evening Hibberd updates his diary: 'He had been

shot like a dog, together with members of his Cabinet and others, and his body afterwards publicly displayed in Milan, hung up like a turkey in a Christmas market.'

This was one of the last broadcasts in which he would say, 'Here is the news – and this is Stuart Hibberd reading it.' In a few days the BBC will request that their newsreaders return to pre-war anonymity. There had been so many fake radio stations broadcasting propaganda out of Germany that in 1939 the BBC decided their newsreaders should be identified by name. They became some of the most well-loved personalities of the war years, both in Britain and in occupied Europe.

On 3rd May, a Norwegian named H. Bloemraad wrote to Hibberd and the other BBC newsreaders from his home in Larwik. He'd been in hiding since December when the Germans conscripted all men between 17 and 40.

'It was a welcome quarter of an hour at nine o'clock in the evening, when your well-known voices told us of the day. In spite of the Germans and their prohibitions and the betrayers they made use of, we have been able to listen to your news regularly. And our relationship, although we are unknown to each other, became ever closer.

'And now, at the bottom of our misery and hunger, we are hearing your voices telling us of rumours about peace... As soon as our Germans are in their cages I'll bring this letter to the post office.'

In his diary the politician Harold Nicolson notes the response of Mrs Grove, his London housekeeper, to the news of the deaths of Mussolini and Clara Petacci. Mrs Groves thinks the Italian dictator thoroughly deserved what he got, 'a married man like that driving about in a car with his mistress...'

8.15pm

The Royal Marines attached to Dalzel-Job's 30 Assault Unit are finding it hard to fight the German troops in the woods surrounding the naval arsenal. They've sent out patrols, but the Germans are either small in number or unwilling to take them on. They keep disappearing into the trees. Fortunately, the aim of the German mortars is erratic, so there are no British casualties so far – but a German self-propelled gun is being more precise.

30 Assault Unit will be forced to defend the arsenal for another two days. On 1st May the Irish Guards send a platoon to help them deal with the remaining German resistance. Remarkably Dalzel-Job never has a man killed or wounded under his command. 'From the first I held a firm and quite irrational faith that unlike my father [who died on the Somme when Dalzel-Job was three years old] I should survive and that no man of mine should be killed.'

The [Allied] soldiers were mentally packing their bags for home while they were still shooting their last shots.

Photographer Robert Capa

About 8.45pm

Nina Markovna's 17th birthday is ending with a dance. They are making good use of the old theatre that is her family's temporary home. Nina has looked forward to dancing with the soldiers and pilots who visit the camp. In ballet school before the war she had learned to tango and waltz, and she wants to impress the young Americans with the 'Western Salon' dances she knows.

But the Americans don't want a formal dance; instead they are showing Nina their newest craze, which they call 'the

Jitterbug'. To Nina they do resemble large jittering bugs as they move furiously across the dance floor. She tries to copy them, but just feels stiff and ridiculous, while they dance as if they were born to do it.

In Rome, 41-year-old Military Policeman Benedict Alper is writing one of his regular letters to his wife Ethel at home in the US. Since he was posted overseas in September 1943, he has written to her almost every day. (He missed two days after they had a spat when Ethel accused him of having fallen in love with a young army nurse.)

Alper tried to enlist only hours after the Japanese attacked Pearl Harbor, but was turned down because he was over the draft age and he didn't have 20/20 vision. Still keen to do his bit, he went on to try and join Marine Intelligence, the Coast Guard, the Harbor Antisubmarine Patrol – even the Red Cross. After a year of trying, he was accepted by the Military Police.

Alper writes to Ethel, 'Here all we think of is when do we go home, now it's in its final hours… we have lost time together, my sweet, chances to make love, but not love itself, that is, if anything stronger than it was. Surely we will never take each other for granted again, and I promise not to be inconsiderate ever again, or angry, or any of the silly things I have kicked myself for so many times since.'

'It takes a proper chap to run straight down the course.'

9.30pm

General Sir Bernard Montgomery is retiring for the night, as he always does at this time. His TAC HQ (Tactical Headquarters) is based in an isolated group of farm buildings outside Soltau, south of Hamburg. It is his 26th TAC location since the D-Day landings the previous June. Monty is not staying in the farm itself; he has his own caravan, which was captured in the North African desert two years ago from an Italian officer. In it Monty keeps photographs of enemy generals to help him decide what sort of men they are, and how they might react to any moves he may make against them.

Monty is a skilled military commander, much loved by the British people. He is a complex man. Major Peter Earle sat next to him at an evening meal on 12th April and summed up Monty in his diary that night as 'a bounder: a complete egoist, a very kind man, very thoughtful to his subordinates, a lucid tactician, a great commander'.

Monty frustrates General Eisenhower with both his caution in battle and his tendency to mislead him with his 'successes'. Monty always tries to keep 'Winston's podgy finger' out of his campaigns, much to the Prime Minister's frustration (Churchill came close to sacking Monty on a visit to TAC HQ in July 1944).

Monty knows that the end of the war is in sight and his staff can see that he is more relaxed. He has more time to write to his 15-year-old son David, a pupil at Winchester College. On 10th April, using paper captured from the commander of the German VI Army Corps, he wrote to David about his school report: 'I do not think that this report is very good; except for the Chemistry. I should say that you have been playing the fool a good deal... You must give up trying to dodge the rules, and fooling the masters. Anyone can do that, but it takes a proper chap to run straight down the course.'

Last week there was better news for David. His father sent two parcels – one contained captured pictures of the German field marshals Rommel and Kesselring, the other containing a cake, a box of chocolates and a tin of sweets.

On 3rd May, a German peace delegation led by Admiral von Friedeburg will arrive unexpectedly at Monty's headquarters, offering the surrender of all the forces in the north of Europe. Monty emerges from his caravan looking deliberately casual in old corduroy trousers and a grey turtle-necked sweater and trademark black beret.

Monty greets von Friedeburg by bellowing, 'Who are you and what do you want? I've never heard of you!'

One of Montgomery's staff whispers to a colleague, 'The chief is putting on a pretty good act.'

To which the colleague replies, 'Shut up, you son of a bitch, he has been rehearsing this for six years!'

Monty will then lecture von Friedeburg about the bombing of Coventry and the mass murder of Jews at Belsen. Later he sends a message to Field Marshal Sir Alan Brooke in London, 'I was persuaded to drink some champagne at dinner tonight.'

In the Sudetenland, Corporal Bert Ruffle is standing up to his knees in a mud-filled railway truck with three other POWs. They had been promised some light night work by the Stalag IV-C guards – all they had to do was empty the trucks of rubble, then claim extra rations when they finished the job. But Ruffle can see that the Germans were lying – the truck is filled with mud, bricks and large boulders. The men open the side gate of the truck and the mud pours out in a torrent. They start shifting the bricks and boulders.

'Hanging upside down.'

About 10.00pm/11.00pm UK time

The Allied POWs of Stalag VII-A have been celebrating their

174

liberation by cooking the produce the GIs brought with them, and a lucky few have been smoking cigars. Now they are being told by the Americans that the news of the liberation of their camp was read out on the BBC an hour ago.

Major Elliott Viney writes in his diary of the joy of a better diet at last, 'A bash [celebration] lunch and a potato-less dinner. So ends four years, eleven months and one day.'

Hitler is sitting at the table in the Führerbunker conference room, reading a transcript of a radio broadcast which announces the death of Mussolini. The announcement of Il Duce's death was accidentally picked up by an orderly who was trying to tune a shortwave radio. Hitler's valet, Heinz Linge, is standing behind him. One of Linge's responsibilities is to ensure that the Führer has access to pencils, spectacles, magnifying glasses, atlases and compasses at all times. On this occasion Hitler needs neither spectacles nor a magnifying glass as the transcript has been typed on a special typewriter in extralarge Führer font. He does, however, require a pencil, which he uses to underline three words: 'hanging upside down'.

Hitler's mind turns immediately to the question of the timing of his suicide. He has not completely given up hope that Berlin can be relieved. Oblivious to military realities, he envisages a multiple assault: General Wenck's 12th Army, with the support of General Busse's 9th Army, attacking in the south, and General Rudolf Holste's Panzer Corps in the north. As the telephone no longer works, he orders Rochus Misch to send a radio message to General Alfred Jodl to try to establish the military position:

'Inform me immediately:

1. Where are Wenck's spearheads?
2. When will they attack?
3. Where is the 9th Army?

175

4. Where is the 9th Army going to break through?
5. Where are Holste's spearheads?'

Hitler's questions reflect his complete disconnection from the military realities. None of his commanders believe in the possibility of saving Berlin any more. Wenck's 12th Army is desperately trying to create an escape route to enable the remnants of Busse's 9th Army to retreat to the River Elbe; 25,000 soldiers and many civilians who have fled the city are trapped without supplies in the Spree forest to the south-east of Berlin, and are now collapsing with hunger and exhaustion. Meanwhile General Holste in the north is making plans to abandon his troops and escape with his wife and his two best horses.

Boldt, Weiss and von Loringhoven, the three young officers who are trying to escape to Wenck's 12th Army, have become trapped in a shelter in the south-west corner of the Tiergarten. Berlin's great park resembles no-man's-land from the last war. It is full of muddy craters, and the trees are shredded to ribbons. The shelter is so tightly packed with people that it is difficult to breathe and impossible to sit. The three men have no idea how they are going to find the River Havel in the darkness of this moonless night. A colonel from the Home Guard, very impressed by the fact that these men have come from the Führerbunker, offers them use of an armoured vehicle and a guide.

'You know you must never be frightened of me when I snap.'

In the long gallery at Chequers, Churchill is watching a movie with some of his staff. One of his secretaries leaves the room to take a call. It is a message from the staff of Field Marshal Sir Harold Alexander saying that the German Army in Italy has surrendered. Delighted at the news, Churchill dictates a telegram for Stalin: 'It looks therefore as if the entire German forces south of the Alps will almost immediately surrender.'

Churchill is an avid fan of films; screenings are a regular occurrence at Chequers. 'Let it roll!' Churchill shouts when he is ready for the film to start. The night before it had been a 1939 film of Gilbert and Sullivan's, The Mikado; *'Yet again, with the PM accompaniment singing all the songs,' his secretary Marian Holmes noted in her diary. Favourites include the wartime Noël Coward film* In Which We Serve, *Walt Disney's* Bambi *and Laurence Olivier and Vivien Leigh's epic* Lady Hamilton *(which the Chequer's projectionist's notebook records he watched 17 times. Nelson's line about Napoleon – 'You cannot make peace with dictators. You have to destroy them – wipe them out!' – must have been especially popular with the Prime Minister). Such was his dedication to his films that on 10th May 1941, when he was told that Hitler's deputy Rudolf Hess had been captured in Scotland, he declared, 'Hess or no Hess, I'm going to watch the Marx Brothers.'*

Hitler is also a great film lover and before going into the bunker he liked to watch a film a night. Mrs Miniver, *the story of a British family struggling heroically at the start of the Second World War, is one of his surprise favourites. He loves* The Hound of the Baskervilles *and* Mutiny on the Bounty *and he is a massive fan of Mickey Mouse. For Christmas 1938 Joseph Goebbels gave Hitler 12 Mickey Mouse film reels.*

Churchill is loved and revered by most of his staff, but he can have a nasty temper. When Marian Holmes first met him in 1943, he shouted at her, 'Dammit, don't go!' as she headed for the door when she thought the dictation was over. When he had finished all his papers, Churchill looked at her over his spectacles and said with a smile, 'You know you must never be frightened of me when I snap. I'm not snapping at you but thinking of the work.'

This apology may have had something to do with a letter that Churchill's wife Clementine had written to him in 1940, in which she told him that his 'rough sarcastic & overbearing manner' meant that he was in danger of being 'generally disliked by [his] colleagues & subordinates'. Clementine went on, 'It is for you to give the Orders & if they are bungled – except for the King, the Archbishop of Canterbury & the Speaker you can sack anyone & everyone – therefore with this terrific power you must combine urbanity, kindness and if possible Olympic calm... You won't get the best results by irascibility & rudeness...'

The letter would have had particular impact as it is believed to be the only letter Clementine wrote to her husband that year.

10.15pm

Johannmeier, Lorenz and Zander, the three couriers who are carrying Hitler's testaments, have climbed down underneath Pichelsdorf Bridge. They manage to find two small rowing boats. Johannmeier takes one, Zander and Lorenz the other. They set off, under cover of darkness, south down the River Havel. They plan to row for about ten kilometres to the Wannsee bridgehead where they hope to find Wenck's 12th Army. Behind them the smouldering capital glows red, ahead the darkness of the river on a moonless night.

10.30pm

Lieutenant Claus Sellier is lying awake in the straw of Barbara's alpine barn, pondering what to do next. Fritz is asleep close by. In Claus's jacket is the second of the two packages that they've been asked to deliver by their camp commander. This one has to go to the army provision headquarters at Traunstein about 20 kilometres to the north.

After arriving at the barn, they spent the rest of the afternoon splitting wood and helping prepare the evening meal. They talked about the war and reassured the girls that, despite rumours in the village, when black GIs arrive, they won't eat them alive. Claus told them about 23-year-old Jesse Owens, the black American athlete who won four gold medals at the Berlin Olympics in 1936 and had become friends with his German competitors.

Protecting Barbara and the girls seems more important than their army mission right now. He and Fritz could use Barbara's father's clothes and pretend to be farmers until he comes home. Yet he has a duty to finish their task. Undecided, Claus can't get to sleep.

Off the Arctic Coast U-boat captain Willi Dietrich and his crew on the *U-286* are still celebrating the success of their attack on HMS *Goodall*. But the convoy escorts are hunting for them – and the frigate HMS *Loch Insh* has detected a strong signal. As the ship passes above *U-286*, Captain Edward Dempster orders depth charges to be released. All 51 men on board *U-286* are killed.

'One gradually assumes the attitude of a lion-tamer... To show fear is to fare worst of all with them, it provokes them visibly to attack.'

11.00pm

In a camp run by the Soviet law enforcement agency the NKVD (a forerunner of the KGB) in Rothenstein on the outskirts of the East Prussian city of Königsberg, 35-year-old Dr Hans Graf von Lehndorff is helping carry the last of 400 patients up to the second floor of his makeshift hospital. Yesterday the number of patients dying increased dramatically as dysentery and typhoid spread through the camp, and the Russians want the diseases contained. The camp is being used to detain and interrogate prisoners (including Jews who had looked forward to being liberated by the Russians). Many are kept in a large cellar that is so crowded the inmates are forced to stand.

Von Lehndorff has been a prisoner here since Königsberg surren-dered in early April. Before that he worked as a surgeon in the city, where he witnessed the apocalyptic scenes as the Russians fought for the town. The Red Army has behaved with particular brutality in East Prussia. Drunk after raiding a brewery, the soldiers stormed through Von Lehndorff's hospital raping nurses and even patients in their beds – many wanting to avenge what the German troops had done in their homeland. Even the official Soviet history of the war will conclude 'not all Soviet troops correctly understood how they had to behave in Germany... In the first days of fighting in East Prussia, there were isolated violations of the correct norms of behaviour'.

Von Lehndorff could have fled Königsberg, but his Christian faith compels him to stay and help the sick. He comes from an aristocratic family (Graf means Count) and he is a member of the Confessing Church – the Protestant movement opposed to Nazism (whose leaders include Pastor Martin Niemoller, who is currently a prisoner with Payne-Best). Von Lehndorff's mother, also a member of the Confessing Church, has been arrested by the Gestapo, and his cousin was executed for being part of the July 1944 plot to kill Hitler.

Von Lehndorff looks with dismay at the second floor of the hospital. A group of Polish prisoners have been forcibly removed to make way for the 400 patients, and have left the rooms in a disgusting state. Von Lehndorff and the other medics lack mops and water to clean the floor, but they do what they can. Some of the sick are in bed, others are lying on the floor or on the wooden boards on which they were carried up. Von Lehndorff had hoped to put them in rooms according to their illness, but there's only been time to separate the men from the women.

The move hasn't helped the patients – if anything they are in a worse state than before, as the rooms are draughty with most of the window panes having been broken or stolen. The Russian officers who have been supervising the move have now gone back to their barracks for the night.

Von Lehndorff has learned over the weeks how to deal with the Red Army. He wrote in his diary a few days ago, 'One gradually assumes the attitude of a lion-tamer... To show fear is to fare worst of all with them, it provokes them visibly to attack. Audacity, on the other hand, can get one a surprisingly long way...'

The driver of the armoured car which has been put at the disposal of the three officers escaping the bunker, Boldt, Weiss and von Loringhoven, decides he can't go any further through the rubble-strewn streets. The three officers get out at the Olympic Stadium where a Hitler Youth unit is based. This is the vast, circular amphitheatre where, nine years earlier, Hitler hoped to display to the world the supremacy of the Aryan race, but was in fact confronted by the brilliance of the black American athletes who won 14 medals between them. The building is one of the very few in the city which remains almost completely unscathed by the war. It is empty except for a small number of teenage soldiers. The three men find some shelter and try to get some sleep.

In the Arctic seas the skipper of HMS *Loch Insh*, Edward Dempster, is still on the hunt for the rest of U-boat wolf-pack *Faust*. *Loch Insh*'s sonar picks up another strong signal. Dempster again orders depth charges. This time *U-307* is hit. Badly damaged, the submarine surfaces, and the crew of the *Loch Insh* are able to pick up 14 survivors out of the 51 German submariners.

U-307 is the last U-boat of the war to be destroyed. There are no further attacks from the remaining 12 U-boats that make up *Faust*. The final Arctic convoy is able to continue its journey and arrives in the Clyde docks in Scotland on VE Day, 8th May.

During the war, 27,491 German submariners were killed. Of the German navy's 863 U-boats, 754 had been sunk or damaged beyond repair. They had sunk 148 Allied warships and 2,800 merchant ships.

In the Führerbunker switchboard room, Rochus Misch falls asleep with his head on the telephone junction box.

11.30pm/12.30am UK time

At Chequers, although the film is over, Churchill is up late dictating telegrams. One sent to Field Marshal Sir Harold Alexander in Italy congratulates him on the German surrender there: 'The British, Americans, New Zealanders, South Africans, British-Indians, Poles, Jews, Brazilians, and strong forces of liberated Italians have all marched together in that high comradeship and unity of men fighting for freedom and for the deliverance of mankind. This great final battle in Italy will stand out in history as one of the most famous episodes in the Second World War.'

Churchill has been staying up very late in the last few months and spending much of the day in bed working. The Prime Minister talked with his aides until nearly 5am last Friday, and then on Saturday until 3am watching newsreels. His staff have noticed that his work is suffering. Sir Jock Colville, Churchill's assistant private secretary noted in his diary, 'The PM's box is in a ghastly state. He does little work and talks far too long...'

Churchill was also feeling exhausted. In his memoirs he wrote: 'At this time I was very tired and physically so feeble that I had to be carried upstairs in a chair by the Marines from the Cabinet meetings under the Annexe.'

German civilians flee over a demolished bridge acros
the River Elbe, 1st May 194

Monday 30th April 1945

Midnight/5.30am Burmese time

Nicolaus von Below, the Luftwaffe adjutant who is making his way home to his wife and children on the Baltic coast, steps out of the Chancellery garages on to Hermann-Göringstrasse. The street is an inferno. There are fires on all sides and the night air is thick with smoke. The surface of the street has been devastated. He has to make his way in the darkness over a confusion of cables, torn-down tram wires, building rubble and bomb craters. As he picks his way towards the Brandenburg Gate and the River Havel, on the same route travelled by the two groups of officers yesterday, von Below feels an enormous flood of relief. As he writes many years later, 'With every step it became clearer to me that I had left nothing left to do. It was all the same to me whatever happened now. I was free at last of all the responsibility and depressing burden of the Hitler years.'

Further along the route, the three testament couriers are rowing as silently as they can down the River.

Wing Commander 'Bill' Hudson is in the Commandant's office at Rangoon jail. The Commandant and the Japanese guards have gone, leaving letters of explanation on the main gate. Hudson is the highest-ranking officer among the 668 Allied prisoners and so has taken charge. He knows he's free, but doesn't feel much emotion. He is writing his diary by the light of five candles that are slowly spreading wax across the table. A Japanese doll sits in the middle of the table; next to her is half a bottle of sake. Birds are singing noisily outside as Hudson writes.

'This day is a frightening one. Anything may be in store for us.' As a precaution he has padlocked the prison gate from the inside. The POWs may be at risk from the Burmese population, many of whom had welcomed the Japanese as liberators. Before he shut the gate, Hudson peeped out for a quick look at freedom. Rangoon means 'end of strife' but he can't believe that's quite true yet.

About 00.15am

In the camp in Rothenstein on the outskirts of Königsberg, Dr Hans von Lehndorff is eating a meal that consists only of sugar. Holter, the camp's translator, found it – von Lehndorff didn't ask where he got it from, but guessed he stole it from the Red Army kitchens. Von Lehndorff is sitting on a bed by the door of their makeshift ward with three other medics. They don't trust the water supply, so there is nothing to wash the sugar down with, but they all enjoy the sensation as it hits their stomachs.

In a neighbouring room are the doctors' assistants, including 20-year-old Erika Frölich. She came to see von Lehndorff a few weeks ago after she injured a finger. Having been treated, Erika started clearing up the chaos in the medical centre, without being asked. She has only had some basic medical training but von Lehndorff is hugely impressed by how good she is at diagnosing illnesses and instantly winning the trust of the patients. Erika even has a good rapport with the Russian soldiers – which has probably saved her life. She's looking after a woman who earlier today gave birth to a stillborn child.

00.30am

At a railway siding in the Sudetenland, POW Bert Ruffle and his gang of three have finished emptying their truck of mud, bricks and boulders. It's taken them three hours and they are exhausted. Their German guard tells them that, as they know the way back to Stalag IV-C, they can walk there by themselves. The POWs stagger through the dark, covered in mud. Ruffle vows that he will never do hard labour again.

In the switchboard room of the bunker Rochus Misch is woken from his doze by a message from Hitler. The Führer wants to know whether there has been any reply to the questions radioed to General Jodl a few hours ago. Is there any news of the progress of the German combined attack forces which are supposed to be relieving Berlin? There isn't.

1.30am

A group of about 25 guards and servants are summoned from the Reich Chancellery building to the Führerbunker. Hitler tells them of Himmler's treachery and his intention to take his own life rather than be captured by the Russians.

'I do not want to be put on show like an exhibition in a museum.' He shuffles along the line of people and shakes hands with each of them, thanking them for their service. He tells them they are released from their oath of loyalty. They must try to make their way to an area controlled by the British or Americans rather than fall into Russian hands.

On the second floor of the camp outside Königsberg, Dr von Lehndorff is wide awake. It's quiet and the only sound is the creaking of floorboards as people make their way to the corridor to use the buckets placed out there to act as a latrine. Von Lehndorff heads for the corridor too. He's glad it's dark so he can't see the others and they can't see him. He finds it a humiliating experience.

'Eyes... filmy like the skin of a soft ripe grape...'

2.00am/3.00am UK time

In London and the south-east of England snow is settling on the blossom of the trees. After a mild month, the cold weather this weekend has come as a surprise, as there have been no weather forecasts available to the public since the outbreak of war. Weather predictions are something only the military have access to, as they can determine the success – or otherwise – of their ground operations or bombing raids.

In the Führerbunker, SS doctor Professor Ernst Schenck is looking Hitler in the eye, and although the Führer appears to be staring back at him, his eyes say nothing. There is no expression. They are 'like wet pale blue porcelain, glazed actually more grey than blue... filmy like the skin of a soft ripe grape'. The whites of his eyes are bloodshot and there are dark black bags beneath. Schenck is not clear why he has been woken from a deep sleep and summoned to meet the Führer, but he is one of four medics who have been called to this meeting. He is exhausted. He has been working in the emergency hospital in the Reich Chancellery all week, carrying out operations on the endless stream of wounded who are brought in. Schenck is by training a research doctor, not a surgeon. His more experienced colleague, Dr Werner Haase, guides him through the more complex operations. Haase is suffering from tuberculosis and has difficulty breathing. He lies on a hospital bed beside the operating table and talks Schenck through the necessary incisions.

Schenck has spent most of the war working in Dachau concentration camp, developing nutritious sausages for soldiers, experimenting on the prisoners. He has never been so close to the Führer. The diminished, hunched man with his shaking limbs is nothing like the inspiring leader he has admired from afar. Schenck is a man whose mind always turns to diagnosis. This, he thinks, is a clear case of Parkinson's disease.

Noticing the food stains on the front of Hitler's military jacket, Schenck suddenly becomes aware of the state of his own uniform. It is spattered with encrusted brown blood – not his own. He has worked and slept in it for as long as he can remember.

Hitler takes Schenck's hand and gives it a jerky shake, a 'cold fish, flapping gesture'. He moves along the line of medics, shaking their hands in turn with mumbling thanks for their work. The others summoned for this unexpected meeting are Dr Haase, who killed Hitler's German Shepherd Blondi a few hours earlier, and two nurses.

One of the nurses, Erna Flegel, has been helping to look after the Goebbels children during the last week. Flegel is a stolid woman who does not flinch as she dresses the hideous injuries of the wounded who are brought into the emergency hospital – but now, when Hitler takes her hand, she breaks down, sobbing, 'My Führer! Have faith in the final victory. Lead us and we will follow you!'

Hitler doesn't respond. He starts speaking, but his words,

Schenck notices, seem 'not aimed at anyone in particular'. He is 'just summing things up; speaking, as it were, for the ages'. At last Hitler turns slowly away. Schenck and the two nurses leave, but Dr Haase is asked to stay.

2.15am

The magnificent 270-foot long, three-masted barque *Gorch Fock* is slowly sinking into the Baltic Sea. She is a training ship for the German navy, moored just off the island of Dänholm. There is no one on board; her crew were deployed elsewhere as the Russians advanced. At midnight the harbour master Hans-Heinrich Beerbohm received an order that the *Gorch Fock* shouldn't fall into Russian hands (they've already tried to sink her using tank shells), and so he dispatched two of his men to open the ship's seacocks. The men are watching from their motor launch as the *Gorch Fock* slowly settles on the seabed, her masts protruding above the waves.

> After the war, the Gorch Fock *will be salvaged and taken as war reparations by the Russians, to be renamed* Tovarishch *and used as a training vessel until the 1990s. She is now once more in German hands under her old name, and is a museum ship moored close to where she sank in 1945.*

2.30am

The testament couriers from the bunker have become separated on the River Havel. Only Johannmeier has managed to row as far as their agreed destination at the Wannsee bridgehead. In the darkness Lorenz and Zander have landed on the Schwanenwerder not far from the lakeside house where the Goebbels children were living until a week ago.

'Like a Rhineland carnival queen.'

Dr Schenck is sitting drinking schnapps in the corridor in the upper bunker. As the doctors and nurses walked back to the Reich Chancellery after their meeting with Hitler, they came upon a big party of drinkers and were invited to join them. Two secretaries now appear with a third woman. Someone whispers to Schenck that this is Frau Hitler. She sits at one end of the table 'like a Rhineland carnival queen', knocking back the drink, dominating the conversation with chirpy stories. Schenck has never heard of her before, and certainly never met her. He can't tell whether the tremor in her voice is caused by a lisp or by alcohol.

3.00am

In the Führerbunker switchboard room, Rochus Misch is woken again as General Jodl's replies to Hitler's questions about a combined attack come through on the radio:
  '1. Wenck's spearhead is stuck south of Schwielow Lake.
  2. Consequently, the 12th Army cannot continue its attack on Berlin.
  3. The 9th Army is fully encircled.
  4. Holste's corps has been forced into a defensive position. Attacks on Berlin have not advanced anywhere.'
There is no good news.

In frustration, Hitler orders Martin Bormann to send a message to Admiral Dönitz: 'Immediate ruthless action must be taken against all traitors.' It is Heinrich Himmler he has in mind.

191

About 4.00am/6.00am Cairo time

Twenty-year-old Pilot Officer Anthony Wedgwood Benn is cleaning five pairs of shoes. He is on leave, and together with other young RAF officers, is heading by train from their base near Cairo to Jerusalem. Wedgwood Benn has got up early to clean both his and his friends' shoes as he feels that it's good for him to do something he hates, plus he knows deep down he likes being thanked by others for small gestures such as this.

The papers say that the end of the war is in sight, and Wedgwood Benn hopes that the news will come when they are in Jerusalem. At this stage in his life he is a devout Christian, and for him the trip is a spiritual pilgrimage, and he has with him H.V. Morton's book *In the Steps of the Master*. He is keen on politics too (his father William Wedgwood Benn, 1st Viscount Stansgate, had been an MP and Secretary of State for India) so he is also reading *Palestine – A Land of Promise* by a Dr Lowdermilk of the US Soil Conservation Commission.

Wedgwood Benn has only recently got his wings after finishing his pilot's training. Like many RAF cadets, he was sent by ship to the relative safety of Rhodesia to be taught to fly in old Tiger Moths. A few days ago, in his diary – which he started in 1940 when still a pupil at Westminster School, and which he will continue for the rest of his life – Wedgwood Benn confessed to being afraid of 'ditching, crashing, being taken prisoner, torture by Japs, these things are working on my imagination...' Last June his brother Michael was killed in a flying accident, and his death has affected him deeply. Wedgwood Benn has sown his brother's wings on his own battledress, and when he flies he always wears Michael's gloves. The day after he heard the news, he flew his plane to a height of 6,000 feet and decided to do a spin, inspired by Michael's courage as a pilot.

He wrote in his diary that night, 'My voice is rather like his when it is muffled and so I picked up my speaking tube and said 'Hello James [as Anthony is called by his family], this is old Mikie speaking' – but it made me cry so I stopped.'

Wedgwood Benn finishes cleaning the shoes, and the Palestine Railways locomotive carries on heading east through the desert for Lydda, where tomorrow the pilots will change trains for Jerusalem.

At the end of his leave Anthony Wedgwood Benn will be told he is being posted home, and in June he sails on the troopship Carthage. *The general election campaign has started, and so he organises hustings on board ship and makes a speech entitled 'Why I Will Vote Labour'. After finishing his studies at Oxford, he will work as a magazine salesman and a BBC producer. Then in 1950 he will win the Bristol South East by-election, and so at 25 enter Parliament as the 'Baby' of the House, where he will remain until 2001.*

At Stalag IV-C, the German guards come into Bert Ruffle's hut to get the men up and out to start work. Ruffle worked last night clearing out railway trucks, so he can stay in bed all day.

'How are we going to get past this grey building?'
'Neustroev! That grey building is the Reichstag!'

Dr Schenck is desperate for a pee. He gets up from the table of drinkers and realises that his need is too urgent for him to go all the way back to the Reich Chancellery. He hurries down the staircase to the lower bunker. It is normally guarded by two armed guards but they seem to have disappeared. The Führerbunker is ghostly quiet except for the drone of the diesel generator and the more distant sounds of a boisterous party, somewhere in the Reich Chancellery. He creeps along the corridor, looking for the latrines. Through an open doorway he sees the Führer standing by a table, leaning his weight on one hand, in deep conversation with Dr Haase.

Hitler is anxious that he and Eva die at exactly the same moment. He wants to use a foolproof method of cyanide and shooting. They agree that he will have two pistols, in case one jams, and two cyanide capsules, in case one is a dud. Eva Braun will also have two capsules. Hitler will put one capsule in his mouth and hold the pistol at eyebrow level at a right angle, the muzzle on his temple. He will fire and bite simultaneously.

Haase then goes through to Eva Braun. She is worried that she will lose her resolve if Hitler dies first. Haase tells her to bite the moment she hears a shot. She has a pistol in reserve, but she doesn't want to use it.

In the Ministry of the Interior, about 600 yards from the Reich Chancellery, a Soviet kitchen has been set up in the basement. A vat of porridge is being hurriedly cooked as an early breakfast for the troops who are about to take part in a dawn assault on the Reichstag. Stalin has identified this government building as the one that symbolises control of Berlin. He has ordered that the red flag should be flying from the Reichstag rooftop in time for Russia's national May Day holiday tomorrow.

On the top floors of the ministry, the battle for Berlin is still being fought. As Russian soldiers make their way up the stairs,

German defenders are attacking them with grenades and sub-machine guns.

On the first floor, a centre of military operations has been set up. Captain Neustroev, the battalion commander who is about to lead the assault on the Reichstag, is studying a map with his regimental commander. Neustroev is struggling to get his bearings.

'How are we going to get past this grey building?'

'Neustroev!' the senior commander exclaims, 'that grey building is the Reichstag!'

Neustroev is stunned. He had not realised how close they were to their ultimate target.

General Shatilov, who is in overall command of the 150th Rifle Division, is bursting with excitement. He can't resist informing the Front headquarters that the Reichstag is as good as won. He knows Stalin wants the news in time for tomorrow's May Day parade.

4.30am

As the first light of dawn begins to brighten the smoky Berlin sky, the escaping officers Boldt, Weiss and von Loringhoven can just make out three Russian tanks – their guns pointing in the direction of Pichelsdorf Bridge. The Hitler Youth have lost control of it, but remain in position on the far side. As the three officers approach there is no reaction from the Russian tanks, the Russian soldiers are sleeping. The officers are able to crawl unnoticed across the bridge, and slip down to the far bank. It is the start of a cold, wet day.

In the Führerbunker Hitler retires to bed. The party of drinkers in the upper bunker disperses and Eva Hitler goes down to her room. Schenck and the nurses make their way back to the Reich

Chancellery. Upstairs, in the new Reich Chancellery building, a raucous party is still in full swing, despite the risk of shelling. Behind the door of the Chancellery dental surgery a woman is being strapped into the dentist's chair. By day this room is used for tooth extractions, by night it is the most popular place to have sex.

In the Ministry of the Interior breakfast is dished up; the Russian soldiers who are going to lead the attack on the Reichstag queue for dollops of undercooked porridge.

German snipers are in position in the Reichstag itself and in the nearby Kroll Opera House. There are about 5,000 German troops defending the Reichstag; they are made up of SS, regular army, Home Guard, Hitler Youth and 250 sailors who have been airlifted into Berlin in the past week. The Germans have dug a network of defensive channels around the Reichstag. The centrepiece is a moat, which was created when shelling smashed an underground tunnel, allowing water to seep through from the River Spree.

5.00am

Sisi Wilczek finally arrives at her family home of Moosham Castle, near Salzberg. It has been snowing during the night and Sisi and her friend Missie Vassiltchikov, both wearing their restrictive nurses uniforms, had to dig the car out of a drift about an hour ago. Missie has worked with Sisi in Vienna but has never visited Moosham Castle before. She is amazed at the size of it – a medieval battlement surrounding an entire village. The Wilczeks are one of the richest families in the Hapsburg Empire. Sisi hands her parents the fortune contained in the shoebox that she has managed to smuggle out of Vienna, and she and Missie collapse with exhaustion into a four-poster bed.

In Berlin heavy shelling shakes the Reich Chancellery bunkers.

In the basement of the Ministry of the interior, the company of Russian soldiers of the 150th Rifle Division, who are going to lead the attack on the Reichstag, have finished their breakfast and are checking their weapons.

6.00am/midnight Central War Time (CWT)

On the second floor of the makeshift hospital in the camp outside Königsberg, Dr von Lehndorff has discovered that a number of his patients died in the night. Some have died in their beds; others have died in the corridor on their way to the latrine buckets. One died while squatting on a bucket. Von Lehndorff starts to help carry the dead bodies into a bathroom.

Soon there are 36 bodies stacked several metres high; most are almost naked as other patients have taken their clothes to keep warm. Von Lehndorff notices that they are all men; women seem to be able to survive better. Although some of the dead have their papers, von Lehndorff knows that the Russians won't bother to record their deaths; there will be no official account of where or how they died. Those that have survived have lost the will to live.

General Mohnke, commander of the Zitadelle, the government district in central Berlin which includes the Reich Chancelleries, is summoned to Hitler's rooms in the Führerbunker. Hitler is sitting in a chair beside his bed wearing a black satin dressing gown on top of his nightshirt and soft leather slippers. He wants to know the latest on the Russian position.

'They have reached the Tiergarten, somewhere between 170

and 250 feet from the Reich Chancellery. On all sides they are within a few hundred yards of the Reich Chancellery, but for now their progress has been halted.'

'How long can we hold out?'

'Twenty or 24 hours at most, *Mein Führer.*'

'In the end these decadent Western democracies will fail.'

'*Jawohl, Mein Führer.*'

Hitler stands up and shakes Mohnke's hand. 'Good luck and thank you. It wasn't only for Germany!'

The first company of Russian soldiers from the 150th Rifle Division battalions charge out of the Ministry of the Interior, heading for the Reichstag across Königsplatz. The wide leafy square at the heart of Berlin's government district is now a cratered wasteland. The soldiers run for about 50 metres before they are thrown to the ground by a hurricane of German fire from the Reichstag building on one side and from the Kroll Opera House on the other. Meanwhile, a premature message of triumph is radioed to Moscow from General Shatilov, commander of the 150th Rifles. Stalin is informed that the Reichstag has been taken.

The presses of the *Chicago Herald-American* are printing their first editions. They carry the latest dispatch from their young correspondent, John F. Kennedy, at the international conference in San Francisco that's deciding the shape of the United Nations.

'There is a heritage of 25 years of distrust between Russia and the rest of the world that cannot be overcome completely for a good many years... This week in San Francisco will be a decisive one in Russian–American affairs. It will be a real test of whether the Russians and Americans can get along.'

This will be a major theme of Kennedy's presidency. In fact, he will recruit for his administration many veterans of the San Francisco conference.

The conference marks a turning point in JFK's life. In a few days' time he will say to close friend Charles Spalding, 'Charlie, I've made up my mind – I'm going into politics.'

'Geez, Jack, that's terrific! You can go all the way!'

'Really?'

'All the way!'

Although his time in San Francisco was when the young JFK began to take life more seriously, he still enjoyed a busy social life. One evening, during the six weeks of the conference, lying on his hotel bed dressed for a black-tie dinner, holding a cocktail in one hand and a telephone in the other, he left a message for the editor of the Chicago Herald-American.

'Will you see that the boss gets the message as soon as you can reach him? Thank you. Here's the message: "Kennedy will not be filing tonight..."'

6.30am

For the second day in a row Hitler's valet, Heinz Linge, finds that the Führer is already dressed and is lying on his bed, fully clothed in his uniform jacket and black trousers. Hitler gets up and comes to the door. He puts his finger to his lips and shuffles quietly down the corridor. The three drinkers, Bormann and generals Krebs and Burgdorf, are asleep on the benches outside his room. Beside them are bottles of schnapps and loaded pistols, safety catches off. Both secretaries, Traudl Junge and Gerda Christian, can be seen through the open doorway of the conference room where they are sleeping on camp beds.

Linge accompanies the Führer down the corridor to the switchboard room. Hitler radios a message to General Weidling, the new Commandant of Berlin, asking for an update on the military situation. The reply comes quickly: the Russians are in immediate proximity to the government district.

The Russian company leading the attack on the Reichstag remains on the ground, trapped by the crossfire in Königsplatz.

Another division of Russian soldiers is sent to empty the embankment buildings behind the Kroll Opera House in order to surprise the German snipers from behind.

'His private life was notorious for its irregularities.'

7.00am/8.00am UK time/3.00pm Okinawa time

This morning's *Times* newspaper has a story on page two about the students heading to Belsen, 'Medical Students for Belsen Camp. Treating the Starved.'

There is also a story that the Dean and Chapter of St Paul's are preparing a report on the cost of repairing the damage to the cathedral. It was hit three times in the Blitz, resulting in considerable damage to the high altar and the organ. A sum not less than £100,000 is suggested.

'When the report is made public it is likely that there will be not only a nation-wide but an Empire-wide response, for St Paul's has stood as a symbol of all that free men have fought for during nearly six years of war.'

The Times also has a half-page looking back on Mussolini's life.

'The man who first organized modern dictatorship in Europe and furnished a pattern by which German Nazism was quick to profit; who had successfully defied the League of Nations and seemed to rank in the tripartite agreement with Germany and Japan, among the directing forces of the world, lies dead by the hands of his own countrymen among the ruins of the country he has brought low.' The piece ends disapprovingly, 'His private life was notorious for its irregularities.'

Eva Hitler hurries up the concrete steps from the Führerbunker to the Reich Chancellery garden. She has a sudden urge 'to see the sun once more'. The garden has been wrecked by shelling and the sky is darkened by smoke from the battle of the Reichstag. She hesitates briefly before returning to her bedroom. She has barely slept.

On the island of Okinawa, where it's the 30th day of the American campaign to capture the island in the face of fierce Japanese opposition, the commander of the US forces on the island, General Simon Bolivar Buckner, is attending an unusual wedding. On the lawn outside his headquarters, a captured Japanese captain is about to marry an Okinawan woman. The ceremony was delayed because the bride needed to fix the sash on her kimono. Everything is being captured by an army press photographer.

'Bring 'um in!' a sergeant shouts.

For the past few months, the Japanese have been telling the native Okinawans that if they are captured by the Americans they will be tortured and executed, and that they should kill their women before the GIs get them. On 5th April General Buckner wrote in his diary that two Okinawan men 'who killed their wives because the Japs told them they would be raped to death, became very hostile to the Japs when they surrendered themselves [to the Americans] and found this not to be true. One attacked a Jap prisoner'.

The wedding is therefore a useful propaganda exercise to show that the Americans treat their POWs fairly and that Okinawans have nothing to fear.

Buckner and about 50 US soldiers watch as the army chaplain reads a civil service that is then translated for the couple. The ceremony is soon over; an accordion plays and the groom makes a speech which is duly translated. Then the sergeant on duty shouts, 'Take 'um home!'

The following day at a two-hour press conference, Buckner will face critical questions about what the reporters call the 'Hollywood wedding'. At the end of the conference, Buckner, who has no love of the press even though his father was a newspaper editor, will reckon he's persuaded some of the reporters that the wedding was a useful exercise, but that other reporters will 'want to raise controversial bad feeling for sensational purposes'.

On the day of the press conference, Buckner travels to two frontline observation posts – he is fond of seeing for himself how the battle is progressing. These are not popular visits as it often provokes Japanese fire when the enemy spots a general. On 18th June, Buckner visits the 1st Marine Division wearing his three silver stars prominently on his helmet. The marines ask him to remove the helmet and change it for one less conspicuous. Buckner replies that he isn't afraid of the Japanese and refuses to take it off. Moments later a US battalion command post radios that they can clearly see the general's stars. Buckner agrees to take off his helmet, places it on a rock nearby and puts on a regular one instead. But he's been spotted. A Japanese shell explodes on the rock next to him. General Buckner dies at a battalion aid station shortly after, as a young marine private repeats, 'You are going home, General; you are homeward bound...'

7.15am

White frost covers the bodies of the dead in and around the railway wagons outside Dachau concentration camp. To medical officer Lieutenant Marcus J. Smith of the US army, the frost looks like nature's shroud. Smith has only just arrived, and was summoned yesterday to do what he can for the survivors. Smith notices mutilated bodies of SS guards on the ground.

Nearby there is an ornate signpost that says *SS KonzentrationsLager* (Concentration Camp). The road to the administrative area is shown by three figures – a bugler leading two soldiers. On the sign indicating the road to the prison there are two figures dressed as peasants – one holding an umbrella and the other an accordion. A third figure, a soldier, is playing a cello.

> **The 30th April found us in the position of some passengers in an old-time sailing ship crossing the ocean – we had mutinied and removed officers and crew, but did not yet know how our further course was to be set nor who would navigate.**
>
> **Captain Sigismund Payne-Best**

7.30am

Adolf Hitler follows his wife's example and heads up the steps to the Reich Chancellery garden. He climbs slowly, and as he reaches the top the sounds of shelling intensifies. He doesn't open the door, but turns around and makes his way back down.

7.45am

Lieutenant Claus Sellier and his friend Fritz are packing their few belongings. They've decided that, although it is tempting to help Barbara and the girls on the farm, they should finish their mission and go to Traunstein to deliver the final package. Once that's done, Claus is determined to go home.

8.00am

In a hotel in the Italian Alps five miles away from the village of Niederdorf, 26-year-old Fey von Hassell is getting used to being free. She is one of the 120 prisoners who, thanks to British secret agent Sigismund Payne-Best, has been led by partisans to safety. Yesterday, their SS guards fled, leaving their weapons behind.

The Lago di Braies is a huge hotel with over 200 rooms. Fey has one to herself, with a view over an emerald lake that's so beautiful she keeps staring out at it.

In his room, Payne-Best is also captivated by the view. Despite the cold, he's been out on the balcony many times to take it all in. He recalled later, 'For five and a half years I had been starved of the beauties of the world...'

Over the past weeks Payne-Best has reassured his fellow prisoners with his calm authority and the way be dealt with their SS captors. Yesterday afternoon they had been impressed further with how he had helped transform a cold hotel closed for the winter, without food or drink, into a haven. Local people had willingly provided food, wine and tobacco. The local German army commander had even sent 60 bottles of Italian brandy – but as yet no soldiers to protect the former prisoners as he'd promised. It seemed there was more than enough food for everyone, but they were soon running out, so the hotel kitchen had to produce more. Payne-Best reckons that old prison habits die hard, and that food is being smuggled up to bedrooms just in case things take a turn for the worse.

Up in her room, Fey von Hassell is in torment. Her father Ulrich von Hassell was the former German Ambassador to Italy who had been dismissed by Hitler in 1938 because of his criticism of Nazi policies. After the failed bomb plot of 20th July 1944, Ulrich von Hassell was arrested and under interrogation admitted to involvement in plots against Hitler. He was hanged soon after.

Even though Fey had no involvement, in September she was also arrested along with her two young sons Corrado and Roberto (her husband Detalmo was safely in Rome). The boys were taken away, and for eight months Fey was a prisoner in a succession of concentration camps. She has no idea where Corrado and Roberto are.

Although Fey is enjoying the comfort of the hotel, now that she has time to think she feels the separation all the more. As she went to sleep last night, she could hear Corrado's desperate cries, exactly as she'd heard them as she was led away by the Gestapo.

Fey contemplates leaving Lago di Braies to start looking for them, but feels too weak to make the journey.

American soldiers come to the camp to look at us. A group of them were led to a block. In a washroom lay 50 corpses that had died – starved, exhausted. One of the officers started crying when he saw that. Strange to think of a man coming from battle, who sees corpses all the time... crying at the sight of our dead. But I

> **know what our dead look like, so shocking that even
> the tears of a warrior are understandable.**
>
> **Edgar Kupfer-Koberwitz, Dachau inmate**

In Dachau US medical officer Lieutenant Marcus J. Smith has walked through the main gate under the metal sign *Arbeit Macht Frei*. The few inmates who have braved the cold crowd around him and his small team of orderlies. There is the sound of gunfire in the distance.

'Is it safe?' one of the inmates asks Smith.

'Yes. The Nazis are all gone; they will never come back; we have driven them away; soon the war will be over.'

The men try to smile. Smith wishes he had been here yesterday when they were liberated to have seen their faces then.

The inmates volunteer to be guides.The Americans walk to the first barrack block, but they have to wait as the inmates can't walk as fast as them. There are bodies all around the barracks. Smith goes in.

In Berlin, in the upper bunker corridor, one of the kitchen orderlies is clearing the table of the debris – glasses, bottles of schnapps and cigarette ends left by the overnight drinkers – so that the Goebbels children can have breakfast there.

In the small room which the six children are sharing, Helga and Hilde, the two oldest girls are helping the younger ones get dressed. They have now been in the bunker for a week and their clothes are getting rather grubby. They brought pyjamas but no spare clothes, as their parents didn't expect them to be staying very long.

To the Editor of the Daily Telegraph
May I suggest that, after his death, Hitler should be

**buried in an unmarked grave at Buchenwald, amongst
his victims? By this means his name would be indissolu-
bly linked, for all time, with the horrors he loosed upon
the world, and even Germans would find it difficult to
make a national hero out of him.
Yours faithfully**

F.W. Perfect, London NW11.

About 8.30am/9.30am UK time

In her house in a village on the outskirts of Coventry, Clara
Milburn is reading the letters page of the *Daily Telegraph*.
Clara's son Alan has been a POW in Germany since Dunkirk
in 1940, and she always scans the papers for news of his prison
camp Stalag VII-B. There is news of the men liberated from
Stalag VII-A at Moosburg, but not of Alan's camp.

Clara is fascinated by the idea suggested in a letter that
when Hitler dies his body should be buried at the Buchenwald
concentration camp with his victims, to prevent him becoming
a hero and his grave a place of pilgrimage.

*Later today Clara will write in her diary about today's events as she
has done for the last five years. ('Things go well in Burma... but we
seem so preoccupied with events in Europe that our minds cannot
take in all the happenings there too.') Clara ends her diary for the
30th April by writing: 'May tomorrow – the month of Alan!'*

*Clara's hunch is right. On 9th May, she receives a telegram from
him saying he'll be home soon. The next day, Alan is back at their
kitchen table eating boiled eggs and bread and butter, and then
later walking with his mother to the grocer's for double rations,
shaking hands with the people they meet along the way. That night
she writes her final ever entry, 'Here the "Burleigh in wartime"
diary ends with victory bells... Alan John is home!'*

The Goebbels children are sitting around the upper bunker table, eating a breakfast of jam and butter and bread. One thing that they all appreciate is that here in the bunker they are allowed as much food as they like. Their parents have been very strict about keeping to the rations that ordinary Germans are allowed, and in the fridge at home each child has had their own tiny labelled ration of butter, milk and eggs to last them the week.

Magda Goebbels is lying on her bed. She can hear the chat and clatter of the children from her room, but she can't face seeing them and has no appetite for breakfast.

'You know how it is. You have to suppress your feelings a bit in wartime.'

In a hotel called Haus Ingeborg, in the centre of Oberjoch, close to the border with Austria, a 33-year-old scientist named Wernher von Braun is having breakfast. In 15 years' time, von Braun will be receiving almost as much fan mail as Elvis Presley, be able to count Walt Disney as one of his friends and be known to millions of American children as 'Dr Space'. Breakfast is a painful process as von Braun broke his left arm in a car accident a month ago, and it's in a heavy cast. He is waiting for the US army to arrive in the town – he has information he knows they want.

For the past few years, Wernher von Braun has been the leading rocket scientist in the world, helping devise, develop and build the V2 (*Vergeltungswaffe-2*, Retaliation Weapon-2). With him in the hotel are other leading German rocket scientists, together with trunks, briefcases and boxes containing the crucial data they need to continue their work in the west.

At the end of 1943 von Braun had shown Hitler colour footage of the V2 and explained what it was capable of. The rocket is 46 feet long, can travel at 3,600mph and can carry a ton of explosives. Its range is 225 miles, so if launched from Holland, much of the south-east of England is within its reach. Hitler declared that it would be 'the decisive weapon of the war' and ordered its mass production. The burden of producing both the V2 rocket and the V1 flying bomb was given to slaves working under appalling conditions in secret factories in Germany. The first V2s didn't roll off the production line until January 1944, because von Braun and his team had made over 63,000 modifications to its design.

The first V2s fell on England that September, and soon began to inflict tremendous casualties. On 25th November a V2 landed on a Woolworth's store in New Cross in London killing 160 people and injuring 108. By the end of April 1945, V2s had killed 2,754 people and injured 6,523.

George Orwell wrote in December 1944, 'People are complaining of the sudden wallop with which these things go off. "It wouldn't be so bad if you got a bit of warning" is the usual formula. There is even a tendency to talk nostalgically of the days of the V1. The good old doodlebug did at least give you time to get under the table.'

In June 1945, when von Braun will be in Bavaria in the middle of negotiations with the Americans about coming to the US, he will give an interview to Gordon Young of the Daily Express. *He speaks about a visit he'd made to London in 1934, 'I did all the regular things you know – the British Museum and the Houses of Parliament, and lunched at the Savoy.'*

'But didn't you feel a bit odd about trying to smash it up after-wards?' Young asks.

Von Braun laughs. 'Well, you know how it is. You have to suppress your feelings a bit in wartime.'

Von Braun always maintained that his reason for developing the V2 was for space exploration.

> *A few days later, von Braun would be on his way to the United States; several V2 rockets were shipped out soon after. His work for NASA in the 1950s and 1960s (in particular his development of the Saturn V booster rocket) would be decisive in putting man on the moon. In 1960 a Hollywood film was made about his life called I Aim at the Stars. Some suggested at the time the full title should be I Aim at the Stars, But Sometimes I Hit London.*

In Dachau, medical officer Lieutenant Marcus J. Smith is staring at a German diary for 1940 that he'd picked up a few days before. He is reeling from the squalor he has just seen in the barracks. Smith looks for a blank page and comes across a list of important German dates.

'May 1st. Public Holiday.'

'I wonder if it will be celebrated here?' he thinks.

'May 22nd 1813 Richard Wagner's birthday.'

'May 29th 1921 Hitler becomes leader of the Nazi Party.'

Smith finds a blank page and starts a list, thinking, 'What do these people need? Everything.'

'George Thomann from Akron, Ohio.'

9.00am

The Russian army reaches Ravensbrück camp, 56 miles north of Berlin. They find about 3,500 sick and dying women and several hundred men. It is estimated that about 50,000 women died at the camp in the six years since 1939.

Thirty-four-year-old Leo Goldner is one of the prisoners at the Allach sub-camp at Dachau where prisoners are employed in the production of porcelain. He is close to the gate when the first American soldier of the 42nd 'Rainbow' Division arrives.

The soldier shouts, 'You are free!'

'What's your name? And where are you from?' Goldner shouts back.

He never forgets the answer: his liberator is George Thomann from Akron, Ohio.

Another Allach prisoner, a Hungarian woman called Sarah Friedmann, is collapsing with hunger when the Americans enter the camp. She only arrived a couple of weeks earlier, having survived a death march from Birkenau. The soldiers start handing out cans of food and oil. Friedman eats a little but, as she later recalled, 'Many of us perished that day as a result of overeating, because they were not used to such fat and nourishing food in their stomachs.' Those who died are known as 'canned-goods victims' – people who survived concentration camps and death marches but who now die of overeating the rich food.

Across Germany hundreds of camp inmates and starving civilians are dying every day from eating food that their intestines can't cope with. Canadian troops hand out cookies, which cause acute thirst, and then the water taken to assuage the thirst causes the un-digested biscuits to swell – resulting in burst stomachs and death.

In the Bavarian Alps 15-year-old Barbara has taken the two young German lieutenants Claus and Fritz to an elderly neighbour so they can listen to her radio and get news of the war.

'I don't listen to it any more,' the old lady says. 'All day long they play military music, and there are bits of news in between, but it's always the same: "We're winning the war..." Yet in town they are saying there are American tanks on the Autobahn. I don't know who to believe.'

They all sit and drink milk and listen to a station broadcasting from Rosenheim near Munich. The woman is right – the news-reader says emphatically that the Germans are winning and Hitler is in control.

A neighbour arrives – a tall, skinny farmer aged about 80. He has heard from the girls that the young officers need a lift into Traunstein. He's happy to take them to the door of the army provision headquarters.

'Maybe they'll trade their stores for my apples,' he jokes. 'They won't need what they've got for much longer.'

The farmer also knows that it will be far safer for him to travel if he has two army officers in his truck.

I think they have forgotten us entirely in England. I don't think there'll be many left to ring Victory bells. The BBC has forgotten us too.

Letter from a Channel Islander, late 1944

9.30am/10.30 UK time

In Britain the BBC bulletins and newspapers are full of the news about the death of Mussolini and the battle for Berlin. As usual there is no news of the only part of the British Isles occupied by the Germans – the Channel Islands. The islands are an embarrassment to the government, and they have decided that any reference to the occupation in the press or by the BBC would be bad for the public's morale. There was no mention of the islands in the King's Speech last Christmas, and as recently as March Churchill refused a request from the Home Secretary to mention the suffering of the islanders in a speech. 'I doubt if it will be possible for me to introduce the subject into my broadcasts. These have to be conceived as a whole, and not as a catalogue of favourable notices.' The Channel Islands are a reminder to him of the humiliating invasion of June 1940 and Britain's inability to recapture territory only 12 hours away by boat.

The government knows a little of what has been happening on the islands thanks to escapees who have sailed over to liberated France. They've told how a group calling themselves the 'Guernsey Underground Barbers' has got together to punish women who have 'misconducted themselves with Germans'. They've also reported that the German troops are reduced to eating horsemeat and their uniforms are falling apart, and that the islanders are starving too. The British government was initially reluctant to help, fearing that providing supplies for the island would only prolong the occupation. However, on 27th December 1944, after a long delay, a ship named the *Vega* docked at St Peter Port with 100,000 food parcels.

The painting of V-signs is a particular issue for the Germans. One man chalked a 'V' on a German soldier's bike saddle so it would leave the mark on his trousers – for which he got 12 months in prison. 'V' badges made of British coins are pinned inside many lapels.

But there is by no means a united front against the German occupiers. For the past four years radios have been illegal – to be caught in possession of one means many months in prison, and at one point in 1943, the police were getting 40 anonymous letters a day denouncing neighbours for owning a radio (it's believed they were paid £105 each for the information). The islanders have been constructing their own radios – every public telephone box on Jersey and Guernsey is out of action as the handsets have been stolen to make headphones.

By the end of April, the occupying forces have more important matters to worry about. Food is so scarce that German troops have been eating limpets from the seashore, and stealing crops from fields. One farmer has been murdered protecting his property. But the majority of German soldiers are showing discipline, even when the islanders deliberately eat their Red Cross parcels in front of them to provoke them.

It's said that there are no pets left on the Channel Islands as they've all been eaten.

In the public library on Berlin's Ravennee-Strasse, 53-year-old teacher Willi Damaschke is hiding among the bookshelves. He had to flee his house a few days ago, and since then has been moving from place to place – last night he broke in through the library's front door.

Outside the battle is raging. Damaschke looks at the spines of the books – August Winning's *The Book of Science*; Felix Timmerman's *The Hernat Family*; books by Wilhelm Scholz and Regina Holderbusch. Damaschke reflects on how he used to spend time among these shelves in peacetime.

Damaschke gets out a pocket diary from his coat. In it he writes, 'A wretched life! I'd like to get back to the house, but the courtyard's under heavy fire...'

10.00am/11.00am UK time

On the other side of the city, Russian tanks and self-propelled guns are rolling over Moltke Bridge to support the infantry assualting the Reichstag. The first company has suffered many casualties. The survivors are trapped. The sky above them is as black as night.

Martin Bormann rises from the corridor bench in the Führerbunker, nursing a hangover. He makes his way to the upper bunker to grab some sandwiches from the trolley in the corridor. He takes a couple to eat and stuffs some extras into his pockets.

In Prague, the Nazi leader of Bohemia and Moravia and head of the police Karl Hermann Frank makes the first of a series of broadcasts on Czech radio announcing that any uprising against German rule will be 'drowned in a sea of blood'.

The population know what Frank is capable of. Following the assassination of Reinhard Heydrich in 1942, Frank orchestrated massacres in the Czech villages of Lidice and Ležáky in order to punish the local population. These villages were burned to the ground. All the men were shot. The women and children were separated and initially sent to concentration camps. All pregnant women were forced to have abortions. Eventually most of the children were gassed, though a few were considered suitable for 'aryanisation' and were sent to live with German families. Of the 94 children living in these two villages only 19 survived.

In the Danish border town of Padborg, a freight train made up of 56 carriages has arrived at the station. Inside are 4,000 women from Ravensbrück concentration camp 440 kilometres away in Germany. None of the women are Danish.

Hans Henrick Koch from the Danish Ministry of Social Welfare is watching the massive train pull in. Koch has spent the past two years trying to get aid to the Danes (mostly Jews and communists) who have been sent to concentration camps and prisons in Germany.

Koch watches as railway staff open the doors of the carriages, and women surge out – they refuse to be held back. The women then search for wood and kindling, and make fires all along the railway track. They've brought with them small pans in which they start to cook potatoes. Koch wrote later that it was a 'strange and sad sight'.

This is not the last trainload of women to arrive at Padborg. Two days later Hans Henrick Koch witnesses the arrival of 2,800 women who are in an even worse state. When they leap out of the carriages, half-naked and crying, they start eating grass and potato peelings left over from the trackside cooking of the 30th April. Some Danes throw them bread, and the women fight over it 'like wild animals', Koch observes.

The majority of the people crossing the border from Germany into Denmark in the final days of the war were Danes and Norwegians. Between April 1940 (when Germany invaded Norway and Denmark) and May 1945, 9,000 Norwegians were imprisoned in Germany. The majority survived, although 736 of the 760 Norwegian Jews arrested died. From a total of almost 6,000 Danes, 562 died, including 58 Jews. Food parcels sent by their governments helped keep the non-Jewish death rate low, but so did the attitude of the Nazis to Scandinavians, whom they regarded as racially similar. The Reverend Conrad Vogt-Svendsen, a Norwegian minister, asked a Nazi official why Germany was letting these Scandinavian prisoners go free.

'It is now time to save the best of the remaining people of western Europe,' he replied.

Most of the Scandinavian prisoners were collected in an initiative organised by the neutral Swedish government, known as 'White Buses', after the Red Cross vehicles used to transport the prisoners. Lisa Borsum, who as a member of the Norwegian resistance had smuggled Jews into Sweden, remembered dancing with joy in the aisle of the bus that had rescued her from Ravensbrück. It looked, she said later like 'a garland of white hope' when she first saw it.

Part of the White Buses deal was that every other vehicle should carry a Gestapo officer. Many joined in the celebrations of the liberated prisoners – laughing and sharing their food.

With the encouragement of his Swedish masseur, Felix Kersten, Himmler himself authorised the Scandinavian prisoners' removal as a goodwill gesture, as part of his plan to negotiate a peace treaty with the Allies. Such was Kersten's influence that on 21st April 1945, Himmler hurried back from Hitler's birthday celebrations in Berlin to Kersten's estate at Hartzwalde – a few miles from Ravensbrück concentration camp – to meet the Swede Norbert Masur of the World Jewish Congress and agree to spare the lives of the remaining 60,000 Jews in camps in Germany.

At Euston Station in London, 17 German army generals are being escorted by Military Police to a train that will take them to POW camps in the north of England.

10.30am

Traunstein has recently been wrecked by Allied bombs and is deserted. A farmer is driving Claus Sellier and Fritz through town. They tell him to pull up outside the headquarters of the town's military commander. Suddenly they hear a female voice inside yell, 'American tanks are in the town!'

Then there is a single shot. The two men run inside and find the military commander slumped dead on the floor, the muzzle of his rifle still in his mouth.

Forty kilometres away, in the village of Prutting, Annmarie Cramer is settling into a lakeside holiday hut with her six children. It is a place she knows from pre-war family holidays. She and the children left their home near Breslau in January. Her husband, an academic turned ordinary soldier, Ernst Cramer, managed to get them onto one of the last planes to leave Breslau before the Russians arrived. It took them to Berlin, where they caught a train, which took two weeks to reach Bavaria. She feels very lucky that she has managed to get here with all the children. The train was absolutely packed and one of her sons had to be heaved in through a window after it had started moving. They had only just passed through Traunstein Station before it was destroyed by bombs. At least they didn't leave on foot, like many others she knows, or on a ship like the *Wilhelm Gustloff* where so many thousands lost their lives.

Annmarie doesn't yet know that her husband has just been killed in a gun battle with Americans near Leipzig. He was a very reluctant soldier. As a teenager he had fought in the First World War and been held in France as a prisoner of war.

In January, when he said goodbye to his family at the airport in Breslau, he asked his oldest daughter to help her mother with the little ones. He didn't think he'd survive. He felt he'd used up all his luck in the last war.

On 30th January, the Wilhelm Gustloff *had set off from Gotenhafen on the Baltic coast. It was taking part in Operation Hannibal, the evacuation of German civilians and military personnel from East Prussia before the Russian army swept in. There were believed to be 10,582 people on board, including the crew and about 5,000 children. At 10pm Hitler's final broadcast to the nation was played on the ship's loudspeaker system. Shortly after it finished the ship was hit by a torpedo from the Russian submarine S-13. The* Wilhelm Gustloff *was travelling with a motor torpedo boat escort but the submarine sensors had frozen. Only 1,252 people were rescued. It remains the most catastrophic loss of life in a single sinking.*

The streets are deserted. There are no more streets. Just torn-up ditches filled with rubble between rows of ruins. What kind of people used to live here? The war had blown them away.

Ruth Andreas-Friedrich, diary entry, 30th April 1945

About 11.00am

In Traunstein, Claus and Fritz are digging a grave for the town's military commander in his housekeeper's back garden. She is in tears, as she feels responsible for his death. She'd told him she'd heard that American tanks had arrived. As a proud officer who'd never recovered from defeat in the First World War, he could not bear the shame of losing another war.

A white ox is walking through the rubble of the streets of Berlin. Through the bars of her basement window, 34-year-old Ruth Andreas-Friedrich watches it, transfixed by its large gentle eyes and heavy horns. Also watching the ox are other members of the small anti-Nazi resistance group she helped found. For the past few days they have had little water and hardly any food.

They slip out of the basement as quickly as they can, grab the ox by its horns and pull it into a courtyard. They have brought knives with them.

> **Going to war was the only unselfish thing I have ever done for humanity.**
>
> **David Niven**

Infantry platoon leader John Eisenhower is walking through a forest by the Mulde River near Leipzig. He is part of the 3323rd SIAM (Signals Information and Monitoring) company; a unit of officers who have been trained as observers, operating between headquarters and the frontline. For the past few weeks he has spent time with Patton's Third Army, moving at speed throughout Germany, in what a journalist has described as 'the greatest armoured joy ride in history'.

John has with him a camera that his father the Allied Forces

Supreme Commander General Dwight D. Eisenhower sent him a few months ago. In it are pictures he took at Buchenwald concentration camp on 14th April. John had tried to conceal the camera for fear of being intrusive, but the inmates repeatedly urged him to take pictures of the emaciated prisoners and hundreds of corpses.

John Eisenhower's unit is collecting weapons and equipment from German soldiers who have surrendered. As he walks through the forest a German officer suddenly appears. Eisenhower points his pistol at the man's chest. The officer clicks his heels and gives a Nazi salute, saying, 'I surrender.'

John Eisenhower is unimpressed. What he's seen at Buchenwald has made him angry at the way the German army expects to be treated in a civilised manner. Eisenhower thinks that the arrogant Nazi salute is not worthy of a soldier who is, in effect, now a prisoner of war.

'*Sie saluten comme ça*, do you get it?' Eisenhower says.

The German bows slightly and follows Eisenhower meekly to his jeep.

John Eisenhower's mother Mamie has been concerned for her son's safety ever since he arrived in Europe in November 1944, and hopes that her husband can get John a safer posting.

The General wrote to Mamie, 'Don't forget that I take a beating every day... I constantly receive letters from bereaved mothers, sisters, wives, and from others that are begging me to send their men home, or at least outside the battle zone, to a place of comparative safety... As far as John is concerned, we can do nothing but pray. If I interfered even slightly or indirectly he would be so resentful for the remainder of his life...'

In fact, Eisenhower's staff have ensured that John is kept away from the battlefield. In the autumn of 1944, General 'Sandy' Patch's son had been killed in action, and Patch was so shattered by the loss that he was unfit for duty for some time, plus they don't want John Eisenhower captured by the Germans.

Encounters like John Eisenhower's were common in the final days of the war. Many soldiers had to make snap decisions about the German soldiers they encountered. Lieutenant Colonel David Niven of the Rifle Brigade (and Hollywood) was driving his jeep through the countryside near Brunswick when he passed a farm wagon with two men sitting behind the horse with sacks on their backs as protection from the rain. Niven slammed on his brakes. One of them was wearing army boots. Niven pulled out his revolver, walked up to the cart and told the men to put their hands up and get their papers out. The man with the boots didn't have any papers.

'Who are you?' Niven asked.

The man gave a name and said he was a general. Instinctively, Niven saluted and told them they could put their hands down.

'Where are you coming from, sir?'

'Berlin,' the General replied wearily.

'Where are you going, sir?'

'Home, it's not far now... only one more kilometre.'

After a long pause Niven said, 'Go ahead, sir, but please cover up your bloody boots.'

The General closed his eyes, sobbed, and the wagon moved on. Years later, David Niven told friends that he wondered if it had been Martin Bormann.

In the makeshift hospital in Königsberg camp, medical orderly Erika Frölich has won the friendship of the Polish lady who distributes the food in the hospital. As a result people are receiving generous portions. Dr Hans Graf von Lehndorff reckons Erika probably diagnosed the woman's medical condition – she's certainly managed to find some pills for her from somewhere – and has earned her gratitude.

Von Lehndorff watches as Erika hands out soup in metal army bowls to her patients and the medical staff. More sick people are arriving all the time – including some Russian soldiers.

Von Lehndorff tries to remain calm, despite the constant demands and the impatience of the Russians who are never happy with anything. In a small room nearby is a woman Erika has been looking after, who is about to give birth to twins.

On the lawn in front of the camp's main building, about 50 prisoners are marking out two large Soviet stars in the grass for the May Day celebrations tomorrow. One star is being made out of red pansies planted in the soil, the other made with brick dust.

Two hundred miles to the south in the town of Garmisch, the world-famous composer Richard Strauss is arguing with an American major named Kramers. The US army arrived in the Bavarian town this morning and immediately started looking for places where their troops could be billeted. Strauss's large house would be perfect for their officers. Kramers' men have already started moving furniture out and even Strauss's ill wife has had to move from her room.

Strauss is 81 and his grandson, also called Richard, begs him not to get himself worked up, but he is persisting.

'I am Richard Strauss, the composer of *Rosenkavalier* and *Salome*,' he says to Kramers. This has the desired effect – the Major stops what he's doing and shakes the composer's hand. He assures Strauss that he and his family will be left alone.

The war has been a difficult time for Richard Strauss. In 1924 his son Franz married Alice von Grab, who is Jewish. Franz and Alice had two sons, Richard and Christian. Strauss tried unsuccessfully to rescue Alice's mother from Theresienstadt concentration camp, and then in 1944 Franz and Alice were arrested by the Gestapo. Strauss intervened to save them, agreeing to keep them at his home under house arrest. In his diary at the end of the war he wrote, 'The most terrible period of human history is at an end, the 12-year reign of bestiality, ignorance and anti-culture under the greatest criminals...'

We have already given away whatever we had in our pockets that was edible or smokable. We can do nothing for these half-dead people except find out what is going on, let them know we care, and then look for help.'

Lieutenant Marcus J. Smith

11.15am

In Berlin, the ox is lying in a pool of blood. It's surrounded by men, women and children shouting and screaming as they fight for the meat. Some have brought buckets to take away their spoils. No sooner had the beast been slaughtered than people began to emerge out of the rubble. Ruth Andreas-Friedrich wonders if they could smell the blood. She stands back, watching.

'The liver belongs to me!' someone growls.

'The tongue is mine! The tongue is mine!' someone else shouts as five people try to pull it out of the ox's throat.

Ruth walks away feeling utterly miserable. She writes later today in her diary, 'So that is what the hour of liberation amounts to. Is this the moment we have awaited for 12 years? That we might fight over an ox's liver?'

In the prison hospital at Dachau, medical officer Lieutenant

223

Marcus J. Smith has met some of the inmates who volunteered as doctors, and are doing what they can with primitive and inadequate supplies. They are weak and confused. One is a Spanish doctor who has been in Dachau since the Spanish Civil War. Another, a French doctor who served in the trenches in the First World War, showed Smith how to recognise typhus fever – something he has never seen before.

Smith is thinking about lines from John Milton's *Paradise Lost*:

> *With shuddering horror pale, and eyes aghast*
> *View'd first their lamentable lot, and found*
> *No rest... shades of death...*
> *Where all life dies, death lives...*
> *Abominable, inutterable, and worse...*

With the support of the tank fire and the heavy artillery that has arrived over Moltke Bridge into the heart of the capital, the 150th Rifle Division have reached the moat surrounding the Reichstag.

'You're on fire, sir. May I put you out?'

About 11.30am/12.30pm UK time

At Chequers, Churchill is still in bed working, surrounded by papers and smoking a cigar. He's dictating to Marian Holmes – one of his secretaries. Marian suddenly smells burning – and it's not the cigar. John Peck, another of the duty secretaries, comes in and starts pointing frantically at the Prime Minister. Cigar ash has set light to the lapel of his bedjacket, and Churchill is so absorbed in his work he hasn't noticed.

John Peck says, 'You're on fire, sir. May I put you out?'
'Yes, do,' Churchill replies unconcerned.

Churchill's habit of working in bed could be off-putting for his staff. Lieutenant Commander Baird-Murray, who worked in Churchill's Map Room, recalled, 'It was sometimes disconcerting when reporting to him at 8am as he lay in bed, as Nelson, his big black cat, was usually jumping about on the bed playing with his toes moving about under the blanket, but nevertheless no detail however small escaped him.'

Composer Richard Strauss is at the piano of his house in Garmisch playing a waltz from *Rosenkavalier.* His audience consists of American soldiers, who shortly before were clearing out the house to make it into an army billet, but are now holding signed photographs of Strauss and enjoying the delightful music.

In the Führerbunker Eva Hitler is dressed, made up, ready, at a loose end. She asks Traudl Junge to come into her room. 'I can't bear to be alone with my thoughts.'

It's hard to know what to talk about. They try to remember happier times. The spring in their home town of Munich. Eva Hitler suddenly leaps up and opens her wardrobe. She pulls out a silver fox fur which has been one of her favourite coats. She holds it towards Traudl Junge. 'Frau Junge, I'd like to give you this coat as a goodbye present.' She fondles the soft fur. 'I always love seeing well-dressed women. I like the thought of you wearing it – I want you to have it now and enjoy it.' She holds the coat open and Junge slips her arms into the sleeves and pulls it around her. 'Thank you,' she says. She feels very moved, though she can't imagine where and when she might wear it.

The Commander-in-Chief of the Dutch armed forces, Prince Bernhard of the Netherlands, is being driven through the streets of a small town named Achterveld, just a few miles inside Allied lines. The Prince is married to Juliana, the heir to the Dutch throne; many of the streets have Dutch flags flying as today is her birthday. Some people are leaning out of their windows shouting greetings to him.

'How's the Princess?'

'It's good to see you again!'

The Prince is heading for St Josef's School, where a meeting will take place that will decide the fate of the Dutch people.

Two days ago a meeting at St Josef's between the Allied delegation led by Major-General Sir Francis de Guingand, and the German delegation led by Ernst Schwebel, reached an agreement that the Germans would not fire on Allied planes dropping food to the starving Dutch. Since yesterday morning, Operation Manna has been progressing well, with about a thousand tons of food dropped on four designated zones marked by white crosses and red lights.

Also making his way to St Josef's is the man who today will lead the German delegation to hammer out the terms of the truce: the hated Reich Commissioner in the Netherlands, Arthur Seyss-Inquart. In 1939 Hitler appointed him Deputy Governor of Poland, where he enthusiastically persecuted the country's Jewish population. In Holland he oversaw the deportation of thousands of Dutch Jews to concentration camps, and 400,000 people to Germany as labourers. In the past few weeks the killing has continued, with the SS carrying out mass public executions, while Seyss-Inquart has been trying to save his own skin by negotiating a separate peace with the Allies.

Earlier in April, to Seyss-Inquart's fury, the Dutch resistance stole his car, with its distinctive number plate *RK1*

(*Reichskommissar 1*). What he doesn't yet know is that Prince Bernhard, who spotted it last night in a nearby town, is currently being driven in it.

> **Tomorrow is 1st May, and I shall sign off this letter to you, and meanwhile the guns are thundering here, they're making things good and hot for the Fritzes... there's no time to sleep, we're hammering and hammering away at them, luckily we have no shortage of shells.**
>
> **Pyotor Zevelyov, a Russian soldier**

11.45am

Hitler shuffles along the corridor to the telephone switchboard. He pauses in the doorway. Misch stands up, awaiting orders, but there are none. Without saying anything, the Führer turns away and shuffles back to his room.

Midday

Seyss-Inquart is arriving at St Josef's School. The Reich Commissioner can't believe his eyes. Prince Bernhard is taking photographs leaning against his own precious, stolen *RK1* car.

Hitler summons the military staff for the daily situation conference. General Weidling, Commandant of Berlin, leads the briefing. He is very pessimistic.

'Munition is running out. Air supplies have become impossible. Morale is very low. Fighting only continues in the city centre. The battle of Berlin will be over by evening.'

A week ago Hitler sent out an order for Weidling, then commanding a Panzer division, to be captured and executed by firing squad for retreating in the face of the enemy. Weidling learned of this when he telephoned the bunker to report, after two days without telephone communication. General Krebs, sitting in the report office, informed him 'with conspicuous coldness' that he had been condemned to death for treason and cowardice. Weidling's reaction was to make his way straight to the Führerbunker to protest his innocence to Hitler in person. Hitler was so impressed by Weidling's bravery in coming to see him that he not only cancelled the execution order, but also made Weidling Commandant of Berlin.

Hitler is silent for a long time. Then he turns to General Mohnke, who, at six that morning, had suggested there might be 24 hours left. In a weary voice Hitler asks Mohnke his view. Mohnke nods heavily. He agrees with Weidling. Hitler pushes himself slowly out of his chair.

Weidling asks permission to ask a final question. If they run out of ammunition, will the Führer give permission for the remaining soldiers to attempt a breakout from the city? Hitler turns to General Krebs. Krebs agrees that permission to break out should be given. Hitler then orders it to be confirmed in writing, that small numbers can attempt to break out so long as it is clear that Berlin will never surrender.

In Prague rumours that the Allies are approaching the city take hold and the people start crowding in the streets to welcome them. Karl Hermann Frank, Nazi head of police, gives orders for the streets to be cleared. Anyone who refuses to leave the streets is to be shot.

It is the beginning of a week of tension before the Prague Uprising in which 1,694 civilians and almost 1,000 German soldiers will die in three days. The Germans will regain the city on 8th May, only to surrender to the Soviet Army a day later.

Yelena Rzhevskaya of the SMERSH Russian intelligence unit is waiting in the centre of Berlin for the Reich Chancellery to be captured. She talks to a young woman with a thin little boy. The woman's husband was sent to the front two years ago. She hasn't seen him since. She can't stop talking about him and Rzhevskaya can see how this upsets the boy, who is making 'painful grimaces'. The woman is at a loss. For a long time she coped with her husband's absence by making a list of jobs for him to do when he got home – replacing a door handle, a window catch in their apartment. Now her entire apartment block has been destroyed by shelling.

It was fun being in Germany proper. After five negative years we were at last bringing the war into the country of the people who had started it. If you shelled a house because there was a machine-gunner in it, it was a German house and no longer did some wretched French or Dutch family go homeless.

John Stirling, 4th/7th Royal Dragoon Guards

Many of the British troops fighting in Holland and Germany are veterans of several bloody campaigns. Twenty-six-year-old gunnery officer Jack Swaab of the 51st Highland Division has seen action in Tunisia, Sicily and Normandy. He's in a tent on the outskirts of Bremen, which surrendered to the British four days ago, updating a diary he's kept since 1942. He can't be too overt about it as diaries are a breach of regulations. Over the last few months Swaab has recorded his impressions of the German population ('there seem to be so many children... it makes me nervous to see them – seeing in them the seeds of another war…'); the morale boost of seeing a British newspaper ('you don't realise how well you're doing until the *Daily Mail* tells you!'); and the hidden dangers ('the budding of the trees holds a menace here… the forests are still sheltering deserters, saboteurs…')

Swaab is feeling low – he's ill and therefore 'LOB' (left out of battle), and yesterday Jerry Sheil, one of the division's finest commanding officers, was killed. Brigadier Sheil was returning from a military conference in a village near Bremen and had swapped places with his driver, who was feeling tired. Their jeep went over a mine – the driver survived, but Sheil was killed.

Swaab is writing, 'What utterly bloody luck on a man who'd come all the way from Alamein without a scratch. What good people we are losing in these final stages. Milan and Venice taken, the Russians and ourselves converging on Lübeck, Hitler reportedly dying of a stroke…'

Swaab has had some news – he should be home on leave by 8th May.

'Leaving the battery on the 5th… sent C. no.68 last night telling her.' (His letters to his girlfriend Clare are all numbered in case they are delivered out of sequence.)

Jack Swaab does indeed get home on 8th May – VE Day. After sailing in the morning from Calais, by the afternoon he is celebrating on the streets of London. Exactly three years to the day he would get married – but not to Clare.

Independently working among the British troops already in Bremen are members of an elite team known as T-Force (T standing for Target; the unit disapproved of by 30 Assault Unit's Patrick Dalzel-Job). Their mission is to capture the non-naval technological secrets of Nazi Germany before the Russians do, and to ascertain what secret weapons may have been passed on to the Japanese.

The last five years of warfare have shown just how technologically advanced the Germans are – not just in producing V2 rockets and V1 flying bombs, but also jet fighters, infra-red gun sights and chemical weapons.

Like 30 Assault Unit, T-Force is the brainchild of Ian Fleming of Naval Intelligence. He sits on the committees that decide T-Force's targets and the order in which they should be captured, listing them in the so-called 'Black Books' issued to the unit's officers. Fleming will later use elements of the exploits of T-Force in his Bond novels, particularly in Moonraker, *published in 1955.*

In the past few weeks T-Force have uncovered a uranium research laboratory hidden within a silk factory, and the German army's Anti-Gas Defence School close to Bergen-Belsen, where chemical shells were tested. They found hastily vacated laboratories with notebooks still open on desks, and photographs that showed that the chemists had been testing out their inventions on the inmates of Bergen-Belsen. One T-Force member wrote, 'It certainly seemed that we were winning the war not a moment too soon.'

Since Bremen surrendered on the 26th, the men of T-Force have been scouring the ruins of the city. Over the past three days, T-Force have blown open 95 safes in their search for documents and caches of money. Often when the safes blow, billions of marks are sent fluttering into the air and down onto the soldiers, who are under strict instructions not to keep any. This order is not always obeyed.

About 12.30pm

Eva Hitler is in her bathroom with Liesl, choosing her final outfit.

The Goebbels children are playing in their bedroom. Magda Goebbels is lying on her bed.

Hitler sends for Martin Bormann, his private secretary, to come to his study. Bormann, who has already started the day's drinking, stands before the Führer in the crumpled suit he slept in.

Hitler begins, 'The time has come. Fräulein Braun and I will end our lives this afternoon.' He never called her Frau Hitler. 'I am giving Günsche instructions to cremate our bodies.'

It is the conclusion Bormann has dreaded. He has made every effort to persuade the Führer to escape to Obersalzberg, but now he can only accept the inevitable end.

Claus Sellier and Fritz have at last arrived at their final destination. For six days the two young Mountain Artillery officers have been on a mission to deliver vital documents. 'Guard them with your lives!' the commanding officer of their training school had told them. The army provision headquarters in Traunstein is deserted. At the gate there is an elderly cigarette-smoking guard who tells them that the base closed last week, and that today is his last day on duty. There is no one to receive Claus's documents.

Claus walks through the complex with its neat rows of tents, blankets, shoes and uniforms. In one room he disturbs a group of civilians helping themselves to equipment, who then flee through a hole in the fence.

The farmer who drove them to Traunstein can't believe there is so much in the stores. 'Is all this unprotected? There's enough stuff for an army... I'm glad that I brought you!'

Claus tells him to load up his truck and to take supplies for Barbara and the girls. The farmer starts helping himself.

'I'll come back tomorrow, and I'll bring a few friends.'

In St Josef's School, the meeting between the Germans and the Allies to settle the terms of the truce to allow planes to drop food supplies to the Dutch has yet to begin. Prince Bernhard, the Dutch representatives, Eisenhower's chief of staff Major-General Walter Bedell Smith, Major-General Sir Francis de Guingand and the other Allied officers are enjoying an excellent lunch. Seyss-Inquart and his delegation are locked in a classroom.

'It is time to get the petrol… I don't want to end up in some Moscow waxwork display.'

Twenty-two-year-old Ernst Michel is working on a farm in Saxony, making sure that his jacket sleeve covers the tattooed number he was given at Auschwitz. Around his waist is a leather belt with many holes – he has lost so much weight in captivity that he has had to cut more and more notches.

A week ago Michel and his two friends, Felix and Honzo, were part of a group of prisoners being marched from the Berga concentration camp. They escaped as darkness fell by pretending they needed to go to the toilet, and fled into the woods.

After days wandering around the countryside they approached a deserted farm and knocked on the door, pretending to be forced labourers separated from their truck after an air attack. They said they would work for food and lodging. The farmer's wife gave them food, but Honzo warned they had to eat it slowly as their stomachs weren't used to it.

So the three men have spent the past few days working in the fields and slowly feeling their strength coming back. The farmer and his wife don't ask the men any questions; they are just grateful for the help.

Michel survived Auschwitz because of his skill in calligraphy. In the summer of 1943, while in the camp hospital, an administrator came in asking for someone with very good handwriting. He needed someone to write the death certificates of those being shipped to Birkenau and the gas chamber. 'No matter how they had died, I was to write "heart attack" or "weak of body" for the cause of death,' Michel recalled. 'You could not say "gas chamber". I had to say only one of those two things.'

At the end of the war, Michel will work for the Displaced Persons Section of the US-controlled German zone, and then as a reporter for German newspapers at the Nuremberg trials, insisting that his by-line be 'Special Correspondent Ernst Michel. Auschwitz number 104995.'

During the trials Michel will be feet away from Nazis such as Hermann Göring, Rudolf Hess and Joachim von Ribbentrop as they are tried by the Allied Military Tribunal.

'The scum who were responsible for the greatest crimes against humanity sat less than 25 feet away from me...' Michel said later. 'There were times when I wanted nothing more than to jump up and grab them all by the throat. I kept asking myself: How could you do this to me? What did my father, my mother... ever do to you?'

One day Göring's lawyer says that his client wants to meet Michel – Göring has read his reports of the trial. Michel is taken to his cell. But when Göring puts his hand out in greeting, Michel looks at it, then his face – and freezes. 'What the hell am I doing here? How can I possibly be in the same room with this monster and carry on a conversation? Should I blame him for my lost childhood? For the death of my parents?' Michel thinks. He bolts for the door, over-whelmed with emotion.

Michel's sister Lotte had gone missing during the war, but in 1946 she sees one of her brother's reports in a newspaper, and they are reunited shortly after.

12.45pm

Hitler summons his adjutant Otto Günsche. Like Rochus Misch, Günsche is seen by others in the bunker as a gentle giant. They find his physical presence reassuring. He is six foot six and broad-shouldered, a quiet, obedient man, with a long serious face.

Hitler tells him, 'It is time to get the petrol. Tell Kempka we need it now, urgently. I don't want to end up in some Moscow waxwork display.'

Hitler's voice is calm but his driver, Erich Kempka, can hear the panic in Günsche's voice when he calls the underground garages.

In the kitchen in the upper bunker, Constanze Manziarly is supervising the cooking of Hitler's last meal. There's a big pan of water coming to the boil for spaghetti and one of the orderlies is making a vinaigrette dressing for a salad. Like Hitler, Manziarly is an Austrian. She started working for Hitler in Obersalzberg in 1943. She quickly became his favourite cook as she has been trained in the Viennese/Bavarian cuisine that Hitler loves. She is a plump, kind, self-effacing woman who takes great trouble to prepare gentle vegetarian dishes which suit his delicate stomach and to bake the sweet, moist cakes he loves.

Across Berlin people are destroying evidence of any link to the Nazis. Posters or photographs of the Führer are smashed and thrown in with the rubble on the streets. Women are throwing out their photographs of the men they love because they are wearing German army uniform.

'The immediate post-war world will not have a good word to say about me – but later histories will treat me justly. You will all experience things that you cannot even imagine.'

1.00pm/8.00am EWT

Intelligence officer Geoffrey Cox has decided to head into Venice. The engineers of the 2nd New Zealand Division are in the process of building a bridge over the River Piave, and until it's completed they can't continue their advance to Trieste. A trip to Venice would be useful, as Cox knows that the partisans there have telephone contact with groups behind German lines. He is also desperate to see one of the most beautiful cities in the world.

The Germans, who seized power in Venice in September 1944 after the overthrow of Mussolini, fled yesterday, and the partisans took control. The Germans had threatened to blow up the city, but were dissuaded from doing so by the Patriarch of Venice.

Venice has had a good war – the greatest number of casualties are the 200 who fell into the canals during the blackout. There is rationing, and the city has had to cope with 200,000 refugees, but otherwise life has continued as normal. The Allies recognised that Venice was a city whose precious architecture and art treasures meant it should be bombed only after securing the highest authorisation. Nevertheless, in 1940 Venetians were instructed to build air raid shelters – a task made difficult in such a water-logged city.

America is waking up to sensational headlines, such as 'MUSSOLINI AND PARAMOUR EXECUTED BY ITALIAN PATRIOTS'. 'REDS STABBING BERLIN'S VITALS'. But there are small domestic war stories too – many papers cover the tale of a Baltimore woman who lost her wallet a week ago and has had it returned, minus $5 but with an IOU saying, 'I borrowed the $5 I found. My husband is being shipped out so we had gone to Baltimore to see the sights and naturally money comes in handy. Please don't be angry.'

Hitler sits down for lunch with Constanze Manziarly and the two secretaries, Gerda Christian and Traudl Junge. Eva Hitler has no appetite and has stayed in her room with her maid Liesl Ostertag.

Everyone around the table maintains an artificial composure, as they twirl the plain spaghetti around their forks and prod the cabbage and raisin salad. Hitler gives a monologue on the future of Germany and the difficulties that lie ahead.

'The immediate post-war world will not have a good word to say about me – but later histories will treat me justly. You will all experience things that you cannot even imagine.'

As he drones on the secretaries feel a mounting tension. They are desperate to get away. After the meal, as soon as they politely can, they slip off to find somewhere 'to smoke a cigarette in peace'.

Hitler's monologues are dreaded by his entourage. The Führer has always had a desperate need to be listened to. In the early years of his political career this need was satisfied by addressing crowds, which he undertook with huge enthusiasm, flying from town to town, speaking to several hundred thousand people in three of four stadiums each day. Since the beginning of the war he has withdrawn from public speaking and his generals turn to drink to cope with the tedium of the all-night tirades about modern art, philosophy, race, technology. In the bunker his favoured topics have narrowed further: dog training, diet and the stupidity of the world.

Eva Hitler has chosen a black dress with white roses around the neck, one of her husband's favourites. Liesl has pressed it and is now coiffing Eva's hair.

About 1.15pm/9.15am Bahamas time

Major-General Sir Francis de Guingand is explaining to the Reich Commissioner in the Netherlands, Arthur Seyss-Inquart, the details of the Allied plan to feed the Dutch, and the medical arrangements in place for those suffering from malnutrition.

In Königsplatz, in central Berlin, the Russian 150th Rifle Division are diving for cover. They have not yet succeeded in crossing the moat in front of the Reichstag. They have come under heavy fire from the rear as the anti-aircraft guns from the Zoo tower, two kilometres away, have been turned upon them. Hundreds of Russian soldiers have been killed. The survivors are forced to wait until nightfall.

However, beyond Königsplatz, the German defence fighters have been utterly unable to stop the flow of tanks and heavy artillery over Moltke Bridge into the city centre. Supported by these big guns, the Russians are systematically emptying the buildings around the square to isolate the German fighters in the Kroll Opera House and the Reichstag itself.

Antonina Romanova is an 18-year-old Russian forced labourer planting potatoes on a farm near Greifswald in north-east Germany. She and her fellow labourers work in all weathers, but today at least it is warm and sunny. Antonina notices that the three-storey farmhouse has white sheets hanging out of the windows. She is bemused as the beds were aired only two days ago. What can this mean?

Suddenly she sees some horsemen riding across the field. As they get close they shout in Russian, 'Where are the Germans?' Overjoyed, Antonina and the others kiss the soldiers' boots and pull them from their horses and hug them. 'We were drunk with joy,' Antonina wrote later.

In Nassau, in the Bahamas, the Duke and Duchess of Windsor are having breakfast (the Duke is the former King Edward VIII who abdicated in December 1936). Today is the day that his resignation as Governor takes effect. They have already started packing and will leave the island in three days' time for New York, and eventually France. Edward and Wallace have not been happy in what he calls 'a third-class British colony'. He has asked Churchill to intercede and persuade his brother, the King, to invite him to tea on his return to Europe. It is a courtesy normally extended to former governors, but George VI absolutely refuses. Churchill assures the Duke, 'I have not concealed my regret that this should be so.' Following a visit to Obersalzberg in 1937 when the Duke of Windsor publicly gave Hitler a Nazi salute, he has been widely criticised in Britain for having apparent Nazi sympathies. After the war he will insist, 'The Führer struck me as a rather ridiculous figure with his theatrical posturings and bombastic pretensions.'

We may be destroyed, but if we are, we shall drag a world with us – a world in flames.

Adolf Hitler, November 1939

1.30pm

Twenty-seven-year-old American GI Lieutenant Wolfgang F. Robinow is steering his way through the wrecked streets of Munich in a jeep. There is a machine gun mounted at the back of the vehicle, and sandbags on the floor as protection from mines. With Robinow is his reconnaissance unit of 21 men, whose mission is, as usual, 'To go forward until you meet resistance.'

There are few civilians to be seen in the city, and most of the SS battalions who have defended Munich so fiercely in the past few days have left. (The SS have also faced a three-day insurgence from some citizens of Munich hoping to be spared further destruction.)

Allied bombardment from the air and from field artillery has damaged many of Munich's finest buildings, including the 12th-century Peterskirche and the Wittelsbacher Palais, used until recently as a Gestapo jail and satellite camp for Dachau. The capture of Munich for the Allies will be a symbolic prize – the Nazis call it 'the Capital of the Movement'; General Eisenhower called it 'the cradle of the Nazi beast'.

Hitler had first come to Munich in 1913 with a plan (never achieved) of enrolling at the Art Academy. 'Almost from the first moment... I came to love that city more than any other place. "A German city!" I said to myself...' Hitler wrote in *Mein Kampf.* Now, in Odeonsplatz, Munich's central square, where Hitler joined the crowds celebrating Germany's declaration of war on Russia and Serbia in August 1914, large white letters are painted across a monument: 'I am ashamed to be German.'

Lieutenant Robinow has, in one sense, come home. Until the age of 14 he lived in Berlin, but then in January 1933 his life changed.

Robinow went to his Boy Scout troop and was told it was now called the Hitler Youth, and that he must find evidence of his Aryan ancestry. He wrote the word 'Aryan' down carefully on a piece of paper as he had never heard it before, and went home. There he discovered for the first time that, despite the fact that he had been raised as a Protestant, all his grandparents were Jewish. He left the Hitler Youth the next day.

Soon after, the Robinow family fled to Denmark and then sailed to the United States. Robinow joined the US army in 1941 and arrived in Germany in early 1945 to act as an interrogator of POWs and Nazi officials.

Making his way through the centre of Munich is nerve-wracking work. He recalled later, 'We never knew what was hiding around the next corner. We didn't have any dogs or tanks or anything like that. Just the jeeps. My soldiers had rifles. I had a pistol. That was it.'

About 1.30pm

Russian soldiers are rampaging through 77-year-old Elisabeth Ditzen's house in the town of Carwitz in north-east Germany. They arrived with swords, rifles and horsewhips. Elisabeth offered them two clocks, but they wanted more. They are now in every room in the house going through every drawer, every suitcase. A soldier heads out of the door, and Elisabeth can see that he is holding her late husband's watch. He stares at her, then shakes her hand and leaves.

In the Führerbunker, the switchboard operator Rochus Misch is sick with panic. In order to stretch his legs he has just been over to the new Reich Chancellery where he saw three men in the corridor. Two he recognised as high-ranking SS officers,

241

but it was the sight of the man they were flanking that terrified Misch. The thin, pale man with close-set eyes is Heinrich Müller, aka Gestapo Müller, chief of the Gestapo. Misch can only think of two possible reasons for his arrival – either he has come to shoot the eyewitnesses to Hitler's death or he has come to blow up the bunker with a time bomb.

About 2.00pm/9.00am EWT

At Blair House on Pennsylvania Avenue, President Truman is saying goodbye to Judge Samuel I. Rosenman, the White House Special Counsel. They have just had a brief meeting to discuss the question of what to do with Nazi war criminals. Stalin is in favour of the execution, without a trial, of high-ranking Nazis – indeed, he half-joked at the Tehran Conference about the need for between 50,000 and 100,000 staff officers to be killed. But Truman wants public trials, and has just asked Rosenman if he would act as his official representative in talks with the Allies.

The letter of instruction that Judge Rosenman has with him concludes, 'Those guilty of the atrocities that have shocked the world since 1933 down to date must be brought to speedy justice and swift punishment – but their guilt must be found judicially...'

One of the British soldiers hunting for war criminals is Lieutenant Colonel Geoffrey Gordon-Creed. In 1944, aged only 24, he was given a jeep and a driver and a Movement Order, signed by Eisenhower, to give him freedom to drive around liberated Europe to assess the threat from 'last ditch Nazi fanatics' – the so-called Werewolves. Gordon-Creed did that job so well that, in early 1945, he was given the task of tracking down war criminals. He was handed a list of 4,000 the Allies were especially interested in.

Gordon-Creed split them into four categories of arrest priority:

Class 1: Supernasties	*24*
Class 2: Nasties	*about 320*
Class 3: Shits	*about 1500*
Class 4: Bastards	*the balance*

2.00pm

Lieutenant Wolfgang F. Robinow's reconnaissance unit is making its way onto Munich's historic 12th-century square the Marienplatz. They are soon surrounded by a group of old people waving and cheering. Robinow can only feel anger at their pleasure. This was the city that supported Hitler and his National Socialists from the start, and where the *Volkischer Beobachter*, the Nazi propaganda newspaper, still has its headquarters.

'And now these people are happy to be "liberated"?' Robinow thinks in disgust.

The young lieutenant spots a police station, and heads across the square with his men.

About 2.15pm

In Dachau, medical officer Lieutenant Marcus J. Smith is being shown the full horror of the camp by the former inmates. He is at the rear of the four furnaces of the crematorium. On a wall is a sign showing a man riding a monstrous pig. The caption reads, 'Wash your hands. It is your duty to remain clean.'

2.30pm

In the main police station in central Munich, Lieutenant Robinow is looking at row upon row of pistols – all boxed and with two tags attached, one showing the number of the pistol and the other the number of the officer who had been issued the pistol. Robinow can only smile at the German efficiency he knows so well. He had expected trouble at the police station and had marched boldly in with his men, but was greeted only by salutes from unarmed officers.

A policeman with Robinow says that, if the Americans are taking the weapons away, he wants a receipt for them. Robinow writes, 'Received this day the 30th of April, 1945, 102 pistols. Signed John Doe. First Lieutenant Infantry US Army.'

Admiral Dönitz has arrived at another police station 500 miles to the north, where Heinrich Himmler has set up his headquarters. Hanna Reitsch has made it clear that Hitler wants Himmler arrested, but Dönitz does not have the forces to overpower Himmler's SS guard. Himmler has kept Dönitz waiting, and finally appears with what Dönitz reckons must be every available SS officer. The room in Lübeck police station is packed. Himmler assures the Admiral that he has had no contact with Bernadotte, and has made no overtures to the Allies. He emphasises that in these difficult times it is vital to avoid internal disputes. It suits Dönitz to take these assurances at face value.

'You have lost the war and you know it.'

In the classroom at St Josef's in the north of Holland, the German and Allied delegations have divided up into different groups to examine in detail the issues to be solved before a humanitarian truce can be agreed. Operation Manna is underway but with no formal agreement saying that the

Allied planes won't be shot down as they carry out their food drops.

'Watching this scene,' Major-General Sir Francis de Guingand recalled later, 'I found it hard to believe I wasn't dreaming, for all intents and purposes it reminded me of a staff college exercise with the best syndicates arguing amongst themselves as to the best way of solving a particular problem.'

While the groups are talking, General Eisenhower's Chief of Staff Major-General Walter Bedell Smith takes the opportunity to talk to Reich Commissioner Seyss-Inquart about the capitulation of the remaining 200,000 German soldiers in Holland. Around a table with sandwiches on it, Bedell Smith pours Seyss-Inquart a large glass of gin and explains to him that he would be held responsible if any disaster befell the Dutch people, and that he expects the war will be over in a matter of weeks.

'I agree,' Seyss-Inquart replies.

Surprised by the answer, Bedell Smith pushes further. He says as the German army is cut off in Holland they should surrender to avoid further bloodshed. Seyss-Inquart replies that he has no orders or authority to carry out such a surrender. Bedell Smith says, 'But surely it is the politician who dictates the policy to the soldier, and in any case our information points to the fact that no real supreme headquarters exists any longer in Germany today.'

'But what would future generations of Germans say about me if I complied with your suggestion? What would history say about my conduct?' Seyss-Inquart replies.

'Now look here,' Bedell Smith says impatiently, 'General Eisenhower has instructed me to say that he will hold you directly responsible for any further useless bloodshed. You have lost the war and you know it. And if, through pigheadedness, you cause more loss of life to Allied troops or Dutch civilians, you will have to pay the penalty. In any case you are going to be shot.'

Seyss-Inquart looks at Bedell Smith and says quietly and slowly, 'That leaves me cold.'

'It will,' Bedell Smith replies.

In Heemstede, a suburb of Haarlem in the Netherlands, Audrey Hepburn's cousin, eight-year-old John Schwartz, is at his grandparents' farm watching the planes of Operation Manna dropping food bags in the large open fields. It is a sight he will never forget. 'It really looked as if there was no end to the planes coming in from the sea, dropping all these bags (instead of bombs).'

A few days later, John Schwartz will personally harvest a can from the Allied food drop. He had just got off the tram from his school in Haarlem and was walking along a small path when he saw a huge pile of discarded cans. He rummaged through and discovered one which hadn't been opened… 'I took it home. My mother opened it and it was full of sausages! A huge feast for the family.'

For a while his journey to school became almost impossible as the roads filled with soldiers retreating and arriving. He remembers standing on the edge of 'Heemsteedse Dreef', the highway leading from Heemstede to Haarlem: 'We could not cross the Dreef because of the endless slow stream of horses and wagons (no petrol for trucks) carrying broken German soldiers in shabby uniforms, pale faces, just looking defeated and humiliated, leaving their camps on their way back to Germany.

'Around the same time. They were American trucks… on the highways in Heemstede. You could not see the drivers behind the trucks' windows if they had black drivers. Very unfamiliar to us. One truck drove into a biker pulling a flat loaded with potatoes. The truck fell over trying to avoid him, the biker lay dead on the

side of the street and the potatoes flew all over, and people were reaping them from the street.'

In Amsterdam, Jacqueline van Maarsen is at school. Like everyone in the city she is longing desperately for the end of the war. Throughout the city, people are dying of starvation. At home Jacqueline's family have no gas or electricity or food. She is constantly hungry, and missing her many friends who have gone abroad, including her best friend, Anne Frank, whose family (Jacqueline thinks) have moved to Switzerland. As her class sit at their desks they suddenly hear the sound of planes. They look out of the window and see the sky is full of Allied aircraft heading towards them. Everybody in the school rushes up the stairs and onto the roof. The children wave everything that can be waved: scarves, books, handkerchiefs. From the rooftop they can see the planes flying over fields on the edge of the city, and drifting black dots falling from the sky. They have no idea that these are bags full of food.

One day in June 1945 Jacqueline van Maarsen will learn that the Frank family had not escaped to Switzerland. Otto Frank, Anne's father, appears on the van Maarsen doorstep; 'sad eyes, thin face, threadbare suit,' as Jacqueline later recorded. He explains how they had been in hiding with the van Pels family for two years. After they were betrayed to the Germans, the men and women were separated. He knows that his wife has died but he doesn't know what has happened to his daughters Margot and Anne. Miep Gies, the woman whose house they hid in, has just given him the diary that Anne left behind. It contains two letters for Jacqueline. The second letter is a reply to an imagined response to the first letter, which she had never been allowed to send. Months later Otto Frank will learn that both girls died of typhus in March in Bergen-Belsen.

'Do your best to get out... and give Bavaria my love.'

About 2.45pm

The Goebbels children are playing quietly in their bedroom in the upper bunker. In the corridor outside, Hitler's secretary Traudl Junge is sitting in an armchair smoking a cigarette. Otto Günsche comes up the stairs from the Führerbunker to call her. 'Come on, the Führer wants to say goodbye.' She quickly stubs out her cigarette and tries to waft away the smell. Hitler disapproves of smoking, and hates the smell of cigarettes. He is always warning his staff that smoking causes cancer, a view many of them regard as eccentric.

Junge follows Günsche down to the Führerbunker corridor where Constanze Manziarly, Gerda Christian and other staff members have gathered together with Martin Bormann and Magda and Joseph Goebbels. They wait for a few moments and then Adolf and Eva Hitler emerge from his study.

Hitler walks very slowly. Junge thinks he is stooping more than ever. He shuffles from person to person, proffering a quivering hand. When it comes to Junge's turn, she feels the warmth of his right hand, but she realises that he is looking through her. He mutters something, but she can't take it in. She is numb, frozen. It's the moment that they have all been waiting for but now it has come she feels completely detached.

Eva Hitler approaches Hitler's valet, Heinz Linge, and says, 'Thank you so much for everything you have done for the Führer.' She leans in and lowers her voice, 'Should you meet my sister Gretl, please do not tell her how her husband met his death.' She doesn't want her to know that Hermann Fegelein was executed on Hitler's orders.

Then Eva goes over to Traudl Junge and jolts her out of her daze by hugging her. 'Do your best to get out,' Eva says. 'It may still be possible. And give Bavaria my love.' She is smiling, but her voice catches.

Joseph Goebbels stands before Adolf Hitler. He is suddenly desperate. He has sworn his loyalty unto death to the Führer. He has demonstrated it by bringing his wife and children into the bunker to die alongside their leader, but the prospect now seems unbearable. '*Mein Führer*, it is still possible to escape. You can oversee the war from Obersalzberg. Artur Axmann can arrange for the Hitler Youth to escort you safely from Berlin. *Mein Führer*, I beg you to consider...'

'Doctor, you know my decision. I am not going to change it. You and your family can of course leave Berlin.'

Joseph Goebbels raises his head and looks the Führer in the eyes.

'We will stand by you and follow your example, *Mien Führer*.'

The two men shake hands. Then Hitler leans on Heinz Linge, and retreats slowly to his study.

At the study doorway Hitler stops and turns to look at Linge. In the last six years, he has been at his master's side at all times. He has had a total of about three weeks' leave. He has always travelled in the same vehicle as Hitler. He has always worn clothes which match Hitler's – a uniform if Hitler was in uniform, civilian clothes if Hitler was in civilian clothes. Linge fixes his eyes on 'the hank of hair, as always, across the pale forehead'.

'I'm going to go now.' The Führer's voice is quiet and calm. 'You know what you have to do. Ensure my body is burned and my remaining possessions destroyed.'

'*Jawohl, Mein Führer.*'

'Linge, I have given the order for the breakout. You must

attach yourself to one of the groups and try to get through to the west.'

Linge swallows. 'What is the point? What are we fighting for now?'

'For the Coming Man.'

It is not clear what he means, but Linge salutes. Hitler offers his hand. He looks exhausted, grey. Then the Führer raises his right arm in his final salute. He turns to go into his study.

Traudl Junge is suddenly seized by a wild urge to get as far away as possible. She rushes out of the Führerbunker and towards the stairs to the upper bunker. There, sitting silently, halfway up, are the six Goebbels children. No one has remembered to give them lunch. They want to find their parents and Auntie Eva and Uncle Hitler.

'Come along,' says Junge, trying to keep her voice calm and light. 'I'll get you something to eat.'

She tells them to sit down at the table in the *Vorbunker* corridor and goes to the kitchen where she finds bread, butter and a jar of cherries.

The children's parents are still down in the Führerbunker. Magda Goebbels is embracing Eva Hitler. The relationship between Germany's first lady and the Führer's consort has always been awkward. Magda, 11 years older, has always been more dominant, more socially confident, but now, as they say goodbye, it is Magda who stands weeping and Eva, calm and controlled, who tries to comfort her. Eva then turns and joins her husband in his study.

Outside the main gate at Dachau, Lieutenant Marcus J. Smith and his medical team are talking with the GI guards. One of the orderlies asks a war-weary sergeant, 'What was it like yesterday? Was it rough getting in?'

'Not bad. We were mad. We got those bastards...'

'Bullseye!'

About 3.15pm

Heinz Linge closes the door behind Adolf and Eva Hitler and for a moment the corridor is quiet. Then suddenly there's a commotion. Magda Goebbels bursts out crying, begging to be allowed to see the Führer for a final time. Linge hesitates. Magda Goebbels is insisting that she has to have 'a personal conversation'. Linge goes through to ask Hitler if he will see her, and he agrees.

It is a very brief conversation. Like her husband, Magda is panicking as the reality of killing their children comes closer. She begs the Führer to leave the capital. If Hitler goes then her husband will agree to go, and she will feel that she and the children can leave too. His refusal is brusque. She emerges from the room crying and Heinz Linge closes the heavy iron security door of the study behind Adolf and Eva Hitler for the final time. People start to drift away from the corridor. Linge goes up the stairs to the bunker exit for a quick breath of fresh air, but he doesn't hang about. He knows it won't be long.

In the Reich Chancellery canteen someone puts on a record and a group of soldiers and nurses start dancing. There is no longer a sense of day or night in this underground world. As their music drifts down, the dancers have no idea what is happening in the Führerbunker.

3.30pm

Hitler's adjutant, the gentle giant Otto Günsche, is standing guard outside the study. Goebbels, Bormann and several members of staff are hovering nearby, waiting for the sound of a gunshot. There is a lull in the shelling. The only sound is the loud drone of the diesel generator.

At the table in the upper bunker corridor the Goebbels children are wolfing down their late lunch, watched by Traudl Junge. Helmut is particularly cheery. He loves hearing all the explosions knowing that they are safe: 'The bangs can't hurt us in the bunker.'

There is the sound of a gunshot.

For a moment they all fall silent. Then Helmut shouts, 'Bullseye!'

Traudl Junge says nothing. She presumes it's the sound of the Führer's gun.

She butters another slice of bread, and asks the children brightly what games they are planning to play after lunch.

3.40pm

Heinz Linge decides that they have waited long enough. He opens the door and enters the study. Bormann is close behind him. They find Hitler and his wife sitting side by side on the sofa. There are two pistols by Hitler's feet, the one he fired and the one he kept as a reserve. He has shot himself through the right temple. His head is leaning towards the wall. There is blood on the carpet, blood on the blue and white sofa. Eva is sitting on Hitler's right. Her legs are drawn up on the sofa; her shoes are on the floor. On the low table in front of them is the little brass box in which she kept her cyanide phial. The poison has contorted her face.

Bormann goes to fetch help and Linge lays out two blankets. As Linge lifts the Führer's body and lays it on one of the blankets he avoids looking at his face – an issue which the Russians will return to again and again during the valet's ten years of interrogations as they seek to establish the details of the fatal gunshot.

3.45pm

The children go back to their bedroom to read and play.

Traudl Junge helps herself to a glass of Steinhäger gin from a bottle that has been left on the table. She knows it's all over.

3.50pm

With the help of three SS guards, Linge carries Hitler's body up the steps to the Reich Chancellery garden. The Führer's head is covered by the blanket but his legs are sticking out. Martin Bormann lifts the wrapped body of Eva Hitler and carries her out into the corridor. Erich Kempka, who has just come up from the underground garages to deliver the petrol, takes the body. He doesn't like to see her being held 'like a sack of potatoes' by a man she so despised, he tells interviewers after the war. Kempka carries her to the stairs where Günsche, who is much bigger and stronger, takes over. He carries her out into the garden and lays her body beside Hitler's in a spot about three metres from the bunker door.

Soviet shells are falling all around as Günsche and Linge pour the petrol over the bodies. Goebbels has brought matches, which Linge uses to light some paper, creating a torch. He hurls the burning paper towards the bodies and then races back to the bunker entrance. A fireball engulfs the bodies as he pulls the door behind him. The funeral party raise their arms and shout '*Heil Hitler*' from the safety of the staircase.

> **Venice absorbed the Eighth Army as it had absorbed so many other conquerors, with a quietness which indicated that all this fighting was a pretty vulgar business anyway.**
>
> Geoffrey Cox

About 4.00pm/11.00am EWT

Two Allied tanks are speeding along the causeway that links Venice with the mainland. They pull up in front of the Santa Lucia railway station at the end of the causeway, and thousands of Venetians arrive to greet them.

Sitting by a deserted Bavarian Autobahn, Claus Sellier is writing in his pocket diary.

'30th April 1945. We completed our mission!'

Earlier at the army provisions store in Traunstein, he and his companion Fritz loaded up two knapsacks each with supplies, including pots and pans to exchange for food. Claus yells as loud as he can towards the Alps, 'I am free at last! This is a great day!'

The young men pick up their knapsacks and head for home.

Four days later on 4th May, Claus and Fritz see an American road-block in the distance. They keep their uniforms on, but bury their pistols in a gas mask box, and mark the spot by placing their belts in the shape of cross in case they need to retrieve them.

At the roadblock the GIs take great interest in Claus's medals, especially a swastika made of gold. Claus doesn't understand exactly what's being said, but he knows an auction when he sees one. A young GI gives the soldier on duty a wad of notes for the gold swastika. Claus notices that all of the Americans have watches from their wrists to their elbows. They try and take Fritz's gold watch, but he fights too hard, shouting in broken English that he demands to see the officer in charge.

Then the GIs motion to Claus and Fritz to roll up their sleeves. All SS soldiers have their blood type tattooed under their armpit. Satisfied that they are ordinary soldiers, the Americans take them to a nearby cemetery where they join other German soldiers sitting on cold, wet gravestones.

Claus and Fritz watch as a civilian is stopped. He protests in good English that as he isn't a soldier he shouldn't be searched. But in his belongings the American soldiers find a photograph of him dressed in an SS uniform – he shouts indignantly that it's a picture of his twin brother. They rip off his white shirt and find a blood group tattoo – further evidence that he's in the military. At gunpoint the man joins Claus and Fritz in the cemetery. It starts to snow.

Two weeks later, the men make it home to their families, looking tired and scruffy.

Around the same time, a farmer outside Munich discovers that two of his scarecrows are wearing the uniforms of the German Mountain Artillery Regiment.

High in the Italian Alps, a mystery has been solved. The 120 *Prominente*, former prisoners of the SS, including Lëon Blum, former Prime Minister of France, Kurt von Schuschnigg, the former Chancellor of Austria, and the British secret agent Sigismund Payne-Best, are recovering from their ordeal in the Lago di Braies Hotel's luxurious rooms. Payne-Best suspects that his fellow guests are hoarding more than just food. Throughout the day, those with rooms on the third floor have been coming one by one to tell Payne-Best that their eiderdowns and pillows have gone missing (he's felt like a combination of host and hotel porter since they arrived). Payne-Best asks one of the ex-prisoners, Commander Franz Liedig (who's come to be seen as a sort of hotel manager), to look into the disappearances. Liedig searches all the floors and finds all the missing eiderdowns and pillows piled up in one room. He never revealed whose room it was.

Payne-Best's belief that former prisoners have a tendency to steal food and bedding without thinking will be confirmed when he comes to pack his things to return home a few days later. He discovers that he has butter, tobacco, tins of spam and milk in his room, and no memory of taking them.

The guests of the Lago di Braies Hotel will be liberated by the Americans early on 4th May. The GIs disarm and arrest the German troops who had been guarding them, in case the SS return. Before they are taken away, Payne-Best addresses the German soldiers, telling them how he respects their bravery in the face of overwhelming odds, and that although difficult times lay ahead for them, there is a brighter future too. He asks the American commanding officer if the German troops could be treated with consideration. The Americans then join Payne-Best and the others for breakfast at the hotel.

As he recalls later, 'they seemed to have expected to find us in extremis, and were certainly surprised when, within an hour of their arrival, they found themselves sitting down to a magnificent breakfast, and being waited upon by a number of pretty and very charming girls.'

President Truman is meeting with Joseph E. Davies, the former Ambassador to Moscow. He wants Davies to go to London and meet Churchill and have one-to-one talks with him, to assess whether the death of Roosevelt has brought about any change in attitude to the United States. Truman has already asked Harry

Hopkins, who was one of Roosevelt's closest advisors, to fly to Russia to meet Stalin on a similar mission. Truman feels there is only so much he can learn from telegrams. Roosevelt's widow Eleanor advised Truman that Churchill 'was a gentleman to whom the personal touch means a great deal... If you talk to him about books and let him quote to you from his marvellous memory everything on earth from Barbara Frietchie to the Nonsense Rhymes and Greek tragedy, you will find him easier to deal with on political subjects'.

Truman can see that Davies doesn't look well and he suggests that maybe a trip to England is not such a good idea. Davies dismisses the suggestion.

In 1941 Joseph E. Davies had published a book called Mission to Moscow *about his time as Ambassador in the 1930s. Two years later it was turned into a film starring Walter Huston as Davies. It was the first pro-Soviet film made by Hollywood, and by the end of the war it was ridiculed for its bias towards Stalin and its naivety about his show trials. America had fallen swiftly out of love with Stalin.*

By the spring of 1945, the American people are prospering – they are enjoying 40% higher disposable income than at the start of the conflict. As a reminder that the war isn't over, the government is encouraging its citizens to take holidays on the West Coast where they are likely to see the burned-out and damaged merchant and navy ships that are taking such a hammering in the Pacific from the Japanese.

George L. Harrison, advisor to the US Secretary of War Henry Stimson, is completing a paper to be put to the Chief of Staff General George Marshall in the morning. It recommends 'the setting up of a committee of particular qualifications' with responsibility for advising the government on the use of the atomic bomb 'when secrecy is no longer fully required'. Harrison warns, 'If misused it may lead to the complete destruction of civilisation.'

President Truman knew nothing about the development of the atomic bomb until two weeks into his presidency. On the day of his swearing in, Secretary of War Stimson had whispered a few cryptic words in his ear about 'the development of a new explosive of almost unbelievable destructive power' – but that was it. In 1944 Truman, then a senator, had made Stimson's life a misery while chairing a committee investigating wasteful military spending. The committee wanted to investigate rumours of costly scientific experiments. On 25th April Stimson found himself in the Oval Office explaining the details and power of the so-called Manhattan Project to someone he had once described as 'a nuisance and a pretty untrustworthy man'.

4.15pm

Hitler's adjutant Otto Günsche goes up the stairs to the upper bunker and drops onto the bench beside Traudl Junge. He takes the bottle of schnapps from her and lifts it to his lips. His large hands are shaking. He is as white as a ghost and stinking of petrol. 'I have carried out the Führer's last order,' he says softly. 'His body has been burned.' Traudl Junge doesn't reply.

Downstairs, Heinz Linge is sorting out Hitler's study: disposing of the bloodstained carpet, medicines, documents and clothes. Günsche leaves Traudl Junge to give orders to two SS officers, Ewald Lindloff and Hans Reisser, to bury the bodies.

Rochus Misch remains at the switchboard; he has been joined by one of the mechanics from the underground garages who helped bring the petrol to the Führerbunker. They sit in silence.

Misch is hyper-alert. He keeps thinking he can hear 'the tread of the death squad's boots sent below by Gestapo Müller to shoot us'. He takes the safety catch off his pistol.

No one can look like a liberator in a gondola.

Geoffrey Cox

About 5.00pm

New Zealand intelligence officer Geoffrey Cox is having a surreal experience. He and other officers are being rowed in a gondola up Venice's Grand Canal. Occasionally people wave from a house or from a bridge as they pass by, but Cox feels like a tourist and is rather embarrassed by the whole experience. Their little flotilla arrives at St Mark's Square and Cox is relieved to get ashore.

In the square, the Italian and Venetian flags hang in front of the cathedral, and below Kiwi troops are being sold food to feed the pigeons. By the lift that takes people up the bell tower, the price list in German is being replaced by one in English. Cox watches as a terrified-looking fascist is led by partisans over a bridge to prison; a noisy crowd follows on behind.

Cox heads to the Royal Danieli Hotel – the best in Venice – where the British and New Zealanders have set up their headquarters (they have done this at speed to prevent the Americans from getting it first).

Cox climbs the stairs to the first floor, where, in a large suite overlooking the Grand Canal, a unit of Italian partisans have made their base. Cox is impressed – they are a group of well-organised and well-dressed students and lawyers who have planned for this day in secret for many months – with the assistance of the US intelligence agency the Office of Strategic Services. Their leader, a pre-war racing driver, had been dropped in by parachute the year before, wearing a business suit and carrying a rolled umbrella. For the next few hours, Cox, his team and the partisans telephone villages on the route to Trieste to find out which bridges are still standing.

5.00pm/6.00pm UK time

As dusk begins to fall, Berlin darkens quickly under the pall of smoke and the Russian assault on the Reichstag restarts. General Shatilov has learned that his overly optimistic claims of having taken the Reichstag have reached Stalin. He is now desperate to get the red flag flying on the roof of the building on the far side of the square.

Captain Neustroev, who is leading the assault unit, is exasperated by the focus on the flag. All his platoon sergeants are vying to be the ones to plant it on the roof.

Half a mile away in the Führerbunker, Goebbels, Bormann and generals Krebs, Mohnke and Burgdorf are sitting in the conference room trying to agree the best course of action. They quickly decide against joint suicide. Bormann suggests a mass breakout, but Mohnke argues that it would be impossible. They decide to try and set up negotiations with the Russians. Meanwhile the Führer's death must be kept secret. Only two people need to know: General Weidling, who is leading the defence of Berlin, and Joseph Stalin. Weidling is summoned from his command post in the Tiergarten.

Churchill's car is arriving back at Downing Street after his long weekend at Chequers. His staff are shocked by the mess of paperwork in his red box. Churchill is determined that, even though the war is almost over, he keeps abreast of events as much as he can. Today he received a letter from Sir

Stewart Menzies (known as 'C'), the head of Britain's Secret Intelligence Service, suggesting that he reduce the paperwork being sent his way.

'Prime Minister, in order to save time in reading I am preparing, until such time as you direct me to the contrary, Boniface Reports as headlines, in the same form as Naval headlines as submitted to you daily.' (Boniface Reports are the information gleaned by spies). Churchill had written in large red letters, 'No' and then 'Certainly not' underlined.

The Prime Minister now puts through a cable to Truman, urging the liberation of Prague and 'as much as possible of the territory of western Czechoslovakia'. He argues that there can be little doubt that this 'might make the whole difference to the post-war situation in Czechoslovakia and might well influence that in nearby countries'. For this reason he wants Truman's Chief of Staff, General Marshall, 'to agree to the dispatch of a message to Eisenhower in order that he should take advantage of any suitable opportunity that may arise to advance into Czechoslovakia'. He adds, 'I hope this will have your approval.'

Truman then consults General Marshall, who sets out his view in a communiqué to Eisenhower: 'Personally... I would be loath to hazard American lives for purely political purposes.'

Radio is the most modern and the most important instrument of mass influence that exists anywhere.

Josef Goebbels

About 5.15pm/6.15pm UK time

Twenty-nine-year-old William Joyce, known to millions of Britons as Lord Haw-Haw, is recording his final broadcast from the Hamburg radio studio of the *Reichs-Rundfunk-Gesellschaft* (Reich Broadcasting Company). Outside in the street, members of staff are standing around a bonfire made up of files, scripts, paperwork and tapes. Joyce is drunk.

'This evening, I am talking to you about... Germany. That is a concept that many of you may have failed to understand. Let me tell you that in Germany there still remains the spirit of unity and the spirit and strength...'

Joyce was born in America and grew up in the west of Ireland. He attended Birkbeck College in London where he got a First. In 1933 he joined Oswald Mosley's British Union of Fascists and became their Director of Propaganda. He eventually left, believing that Mosley wasn't anti-Semitic enough. In August 1939, Joyce headed to Germany with his wife Margaret to start a new life. It was an ill-thought plan and when they realised that if war broke out they would be interned, they tried to return to London. That proved impossible. Looking for employment, Joyce had a radio audition and made his first broadcast on 6th September, three days before the war began.

The radio critic of the Daily Express, *Jonah Barrington, began to make fun of German propaganda and German radio announcers, giving them comic names like 'Winnie the Whopper' and 'Uncle Smarmy'. Having listened to William Joyce, Barrington wrote of his fake aristocratic drawl, 'He speaks English of the haw-haw damn-it-get-out-of-my-way variety...' William Joyce soon became known as Lord Haw-Haw.*

Tonight his speech is slurred and his Irish accent occasionally comes through.

'...I had always hoped and believed that in the last resort there would be an alliance, a compact, an understanding between Germany and Britain. Well, at the moment, that seems impossible. Good. If it cannot be, then I can only say the whole of my work has been – in vain...'

At the peak of Joyce's popularity in January 1940, it's estimated that seven million people listened to him on Radio Hamburg, having retuned after the BBC's nine o'clock bulletin finished. The Times *even started listing his broadcasts in their radio column, and the BBC became so concerned at Joyce's popularity that they moved their most successful show, Arthur Askey's* Band Waggon, *to be at the same time at his broadcasts.*

But as Lord Haw-Haw became an increasing irritation, he also became a figure of fun as his claims to know what was going on in Britain were easily discredited. He once broadcast that Eastbourne harbour had been completely destroyed – when the town has no harbour. Such nonsense was not unique on German radio – at one point it was announced that the Luftwaffe had attacked the town of Random, after a British communiqué stated that 'bombs were dropped at random.'

In September 1944 Joyce and his wife were awarded Merit medals by Hitler, but not in person: 'The Old Man was too busy,' Margaret wrote in her diary.

'...I can only say that I have day in and day out called the attention of the British people to the menace [long pause] from the east which confronted them. And if they will not hear, if they are determined NOT to hear...' [he slams the desk] '...then I can only say that the fate that overcomes them in the end will be [long pause] the fate they have merited...'

Joyce has a large scar across his right cheek that he got stewarding a political meeting in south London that turned violent. He calls it his 'Lambeth Honour'. Goebbels has insisted that Joyce keep broadcasting until the very end of the war, and so in March he had him and his wife evacuated from Berlin to Hamburg. Joyce has come increasingly to rely on alcohol, and is in pain from an ankle injury resulting from a fall into a tank trap while drunk. The night before they left Berlin Joyce wrote in his diary, 'I believe a bomb fell quite near but I was indifferent to it. Was really drunk...'

Before his final broadcast this evening, he and other members of the *Reichs-Rundfunk-Gesellschaft* had raided the cellars of the Hamburg station. His colleagues naively believe that they will be able to carry on working in broadcasting after the war. Joyce knows that's impossible, and that they will all be arrested by the Allies. 'If I cannot dodge the bill I must pay it,' he wrote in his diary four days ago.

Joyce has reached the end of his typed script: '...I say to you these last words – you may not hear again for a few months, I say – *Es lebe Deutschland*!' He drops his voice. '*Heil Hitler...* and farewell.'

> At 4am, Joyce and his wife will be driven away from Hamburg by two SS officers, with the city about to surrender to the British. Joyce has no recollection of what he's said in that last broadcast. He wrote in his diary, 'I fear I made an improper speech but what it was I don't know. I was under the influence. Was given a good bottle of wine as I left. Splendid.' The recording was never broadcast, and is found by British soldiers on 2nd May in the studios of the Hamburg Rundfunk.

At a meeting of the War Cabinet, Churchill is explaining that the war is ending with 'no friendly spirit' between the Allies, and there is a 'tendency to quarrel'.

Sir Andrew Cunningham, the First Sea Lord, agrees with the Prime Minister saying, 'Quite true – the French are very difficult and the Russians very suspicious and so difficult.'

The Chair of the British Military Chiefs of Staff, Field Marshal Sir Alan Brooke, listens with frustration. Brooke has just had a week's fishing in Inverness and feels 'a great disinclination to start work again'. He returned yesterday to such a backlog of mail that it took two dispatch riders to transport the sacks from his office to his home. This afternoon he's chaired a long meeting of the chiefs of staff and now finds Churchill 'in a bad mood', making the Cabinet meeting unpleasant. Brooke is fed up with Churchill's misunderstanding of events, refusal to listen and tendency to drink until he's 'tight'. Now he's exasperated by Churchill abusing Field Marshal Alexander. Only a day after Alexander has received the German surrender in Italy, Churchill is complaining that he hasn't yet taken Trieste and made a greater advance towards Vienna.

The Reichstag is full to the rafters with blind-drunk Russians. Where ten have been shot, twenty new ones arrive! It's terrible. Hand grenades and pistol shots rain down from above, the underground passageways and vaults echo with anti-tank grenades and rifle fire.

First Lieutenant Fritz Radloff

6.00pm

In Berlin the Russian soldiers of the 150th Rifle Division are charging the front of the Reichstag. They have finally been able to cross Königsplatz under the cover of the dark fug of smoke and with tank support close behind them. They rush at the building expecting to burst through doors and windows, but the German defence force has managed to brick up and block the entrances. The Russians have to blast their way in.

A few hundred yards away SS officer Ewald Lindloff climbs the steps from the Führerbunker to the Reich Chancellery garden, armed with a spade. He has been ordered by Otto Günsche to bury the bodies of Adolf and Eva Hitler. Shells have hit the garden in the last few hours and Lindloff finds the bodies are not only burned, but have been 'torn open' by shelling. He buries the remains in a fresh shell crater.

Admiral Dönitz arrives back at Plön Castle, following his meeting with Himmler in Lübeck police station. He is astonished to be greeted with a telegram from Martin Bormann informing him that he has been appointed as Hitler's successor.

In Mauthausen concentration camp, prisoner Henry Wermuth is getting ready for what he called later 'the performance of my life'. Three days ago the 22-year-old arrived at the camp – his eighth – and has decided that if he is to survive he must steal some extra food. The rumble of guns in the distance gives him hope that the Allies are not far away – if he can only survive until they get here.

For the first time Wermuth is alone; his father died on the way to Mauthausen. Together they had survived Auschwitz, where, convinced that they were destined for the gas chambers, his father had said calmly, 'Should we be gassed, breathe deeply, my son, breathe deeply, to get it over with quickly.' They were never sent to the gas chambers, but their forearms were tattooed. Wermuth is B3407, his father B3406.

Wermuth's barracks at Mauthausen contain two rows of three-tier bunk beds for about 6,000 prisoners. Last Friday night, his first night, he was allocated a middle bunk made for one person to sleep in. He had to share it with four others, one of whom is suffering from diarrhoea. It was so unbearable that Wermuth got out and slept under a blanket on a nearby table. He often dreams he has a machine gun and is shooting crowds of Germans. He only stops when he sees a small child in his gunsight.

In Auschwitz a small loaf of bread was shared between four

people; here it is one loaf between eight. Wermuth can feel his strength diminishing. But he has a plan.

At six o'clock as usual, the sealed metal container carrying watery soup arrives in the hut, and is placed on the floor just a few feet from Wermuth. He knows that it will be five minutes before it'll be dished out by a *kapo* (a prisoner given authority over the inmates) so he hasn't long.

Wearing his blanket like a robe over his right shoulder, Wermuth walks up and down, brushing over the soup container with his blanket as he does so. On the fourth pass he quickly bends down and opens the clasp that keeps the lid shut. Again he starts walking back and forth, then suddenly crouches, lifts up the lid, pulls out a bowl and dips it deep into the soup.

Then Wermuth walks slowly back to his bunk with the bowl and pulls out a spoon hidden under his thin mattress. He knows that he can't drink the soup openly, so crawls under the bed, taking care not to spill any.

Suddenly the bed is surrounded by angry inmates, and he only has time for a couple of spoonfuls before the rest is stolen from him. They leave him alone to lick the bowl. Wermuth reckons that if stealing the soup doesn't prolong his life by much, the thrill of carrying it out has revived his fighting spirit.

Mauthausen will be liberated by the Americans five days later. An inmate spots something unusual, and climbs onto the table that had been Wermuth's bed on his first night for a better look.

'Ein amerikanische Soldat!' he shouts.

Wermuth, lying in his bunk, too weak to move, pulls the blanket over his head and weeps for the loss of his family. He turns to share the moment of liberation with his last surviving bunkmate, but he has already died.

About 6.30pm

The Commandant of Berlin, General Weidling, arrives in the bunker and is met by Goebbels, Bormann and the generals, who show him Hitler's study where the double suicide took place. He is sworn to secrecy. He immediately summons Colonel von Dufving, his Chief of Staff, and a number of other staff members, to join him in the bunker, without giving a reason.

The stone columns of the great entrance hall of the Reichstag are covered in blood. The first Russian soldiers to force their way in are met with a storm of grenades and Panzerfaust fire from the balconies around the central staircase. As reinforcements flow into the building, climbing over the dead and injured, the Russians gradually make their way up the stairs, firing from sub-machine guns, lobbing grenades. Many of the German defenders – the Hitler Youth, the sailors, the SS – race down back staircases to hide in the cellars. Others are forced further and further upwards as the building catches fire.

'They rape our daughters, they rape our wives,' the men lament. There is no other talk in the city. No other thought either. Suicide is in the air.

Ruth Andreas-Friedrich, diary entry, April 1945

Plonzstrasse Cemetery, Berlin Records, 30th April 1945:

Gerhard N., b.1914
Rüdigerstrasse
Suicide by shooting

Ilse N., b.1914
Rüdigerstrasse
Suicide by shooting

Irma N., b.1944
Rüdigerstrasse
Suicide by shooting

It was not only Russians who were guilty of rape as they advanced through Germany. Saul K. Padover, an American officer, wrote in 1946, 'The behaviour of some troops was nothing to brag about, particularly after they came across cases of cognac and barrels of wine. I am mentioning it only because there is a tendency among the naive or malicious to think that only Russians loot and rape.' Many Allied soldiers discovered that sex was readily available to them. Major Bill Deedes of the 12th King's Royal Rifle Corps, and future journalist, wrote later, 'The Germans were very hungry. The girls would get at my riflemen for a tin of sardines.'

In the town of Berchtesgaden, near Hitler's mountain home, Albine Paul gave her 11-year-old daughter, Irmgard, a small envelope containing a teaspoon of pepper. Pepper was very hard to obtain during the war and Albine had to overcome her reluctance to use the black market in order to get hold of some. She was terrified about the expected arrival of the Russians. The town had taken many refugees from the east who had brought hideous stories of the Soviet army raping and murdering women of all ages. Albine told Irmgard that if an enemy soldier threatened to harm her, she was to throw the pepper in his eyes. In the end, however, it was not the Russians but American, French and Moroccan troops that liberated Berchtesgaden. The local women feared the French and the Moroccan soldiers the most, but Irmgard was horrified to overhear a local official telling the story of a group of American soldiers gang-raping a 16-year-old girl in the former Nazi headquarters in

269

Stangass, Berchtesgaden. Although she understood that this was terrible it would be several years before Irmgard would understand what the word rape, Vergewaltigung, meant. She had not yet learned the facts of life. Nor did she fully understand the conversations between her mother and her aunt about the many abortions carried out in Berchtesgaden during the American occupation.

Corporal Bert Ruffle is hiding in a latrine in Stalag IV-C, a POW camp in the Sudetenland. He fled before the guards came to his hut to get the night shift out for construction work at the oil refinery. Keeping true to his vow that he would never do hard labour again, Ruffle slipped out and headed to the latrine.

It's been a day of rumours in the camp: that the Russians are near Berlin, that Montgomery has crossed the Rhine, and that Hitler has finally gone mad.

7.00pm

Geoffrey Cox is staring at the diners in the restaurant of the Royal Danieli Hotel in Venice. Men in linen suits are eating with well-dressed women wearing expensive jewellery. The last of the day's sun bounces off the water of the lagoon into the room. To Cox it is an unpleasantly decadent scene – he can only think about the ambulances carrying wounded New Zealanders, and the Germans he saw lying dead in a ditch the day before. He hurries away.

Geoffrey Cox and the Eighth Army will reach Trieste on 2nd May, shortly after Marshal Tito's Yugoslav Fourth Army. A stand-off ensues, which some see as the first confrontation of the Cold War. Churchill is keen to keep the Stalin-backed Yugoslavs out of the city, but needs President Truman's backing. On 12th May he sends a letter to Truman stating, 'An iron curtain is drawn down on their [Russian] front. We do not know what is going on behind. There seems little doubt that the whole of the regions east of the line Lübeck-Trieste-Corfu will soon be in their hands.' Truman has already made up his mind to resist further Soviet expansion and demands that Tito withdraw. Stalin fails to back the Yugoslavs over Trieste, and so they reluctantly pull out of the city. But not empty-handed. Before the Allied Military Government moves in, Tito's forces strip factories, hotels and homes of their contents.

In the early dusk of the smoke filled skies, the three officers who have escaped the bunker, von Loringhoven, Boldt and Weiss, are setting off in a rowing boat they have found in a sailing club on the Pichelsdorf peninsula. Like the three men carrying Hitler's testaments, they are also heading for the Wannsee bridgehead. It is another dark and moonless night. The three men hold their oars and let the boat glide silently downstream. They can hear the conversations of the Russian soldiers occupying the villas along the river banks. These are the very same houses that have, until only recently, been used as weekend getaways by the top Nazis, and before that belonged to Jewish families who were brutally forced out.

As the bunker telephones are no longer working, a technician called Hermann Gretz brings a drum of cable to Misch's switchboard. He heads out, taking the other end to the Russian command in nearby Zimmerstrasse. Now the Führer is dead, those remaining in the bunker want to establish contact with the enemy forces.

In Plön Castle Admiral Dönitz is on the telephone to Heinrich Himmler. After hearing of his appointment as Hitler's successor, one of Dönitz's first actions was to ask his adjutant to call Himmler. He feels it is very important that he gets his support. At their meeting that afternoon, Himmler had given him the impression that he saw himself as a natural successor to the Führer. The SS chief initially refused to come to Plön, but now reluctantly agrees when Dönitz calls him back and speaks to him in person.

'Moment, moment...'

7.30pm

Gretz returns from the Russian command and plugs in the cable. Misch tests it, but says the line is dead. Gretz double-checks. It is dead. He goes back to the Russians in Zimmerstrasse.

In the upper bunker Magda Goebbels is putting her children to bed. The littlest, Heide, has a sore throat. Her mother finds her a red scarf.

This is their last night's sleep. This time tomorrow they will each be given an injection of morphine. Their mother will tell them that this is a vaccination that all the soldiers are getting to protect them against disease.

Once they are dozing, Ludwig Stumpfegger, one of the Reich Chancellery doctors, the only one whom Magda has been able to persuade to carry out this task, will crush a cyanide capsule between each child's teeth.

The three testament couriers are reunited at the Wannsee bridgehead. While waiting for his colleagues, Johanmeier has found a small German army unit and used their radio to make contact with Admiral Dönitz. Dönitz has instructed them to go to Pfaueninsel, a small wooded island further south along the River Havel, and wait for a seaplane which he is sending to rescue them.

8.00pm

Gretz the technician reappears in the Führerbunker switch-board office. 'The cable wasn't earthed. Try it again.' Misch plugs it in and hears a Russian voice. '*Moment, moment,*' he says and passes the connection to General Krebs, who has been secretly brushing up the Russian he learned when he was the military attaché in Moscow before the war. Krebs arranges to meet the Russian General Zhukov later that evening.

Constanze Manziarly is mashing potato and frying eggs, creating a dinner that she knows the Führer won't eat. Those in Hitler's immediate circle are keeping his death secret from the staff in the Reich Chancellery, and the kitchen orderlies who assist her have no idea that this meal is a charade.

8.15pm

Back in the map room, Goebbels and Bormann are drafting a letter for Krebs to take to General Zhukov. Goebbels is adamant that they will not offer an unconditional surrender.

In the Reichstag fierce fighting continues. Two Russian soldiers, bearing a red flag and heading for the roof, are mown down as they reach the second floor.

About 8.30pm

The three officers who are supposed to be delivering Hitler's testaments have reached Pfaueninsel in the middle of the River

Havel. The island's white castle looms through the darkness. This will be the landmark to guide the seaplane which Admiral Dönitz is sending. The men clamber ashore. They manage to find some civilian clothes in the castle and they dispose of their army uniforms. They begin the long wait for the seaplane to arrive. At dawn they will be joined by the three officers who have broken out of the bunker – von Loringhoven, Boldt and Weiss.

About 8.30pm/9.30pm UK time

General Eisenhower's staff are sending a telegram to the Russian General Antonov, requesting that he advance no further into Austria than 'the general area of the Linz' and the River Enns.

A guard at Stalag IV-C has found Corporal Bert Ruffle hiding in the latrine and he's marching him to the Commandant's office.

Noël Coward is in a suite at the Savoy Hotel in London (his London home having been bombed in 1941). Pencil in hand, he is updating a diary which also doubles up as his appointments book. He has an impressive set of friends – lunch dates with Fred Astaire, Laurence Olivier or Greta Garbo are not uncommon. But today has been a quiet Monday, the papers full of speculation about the war.

He's writing, 'These supremely melodramatic days are somehow anticlimactic and confusing. The *Sunday Express* announced Germany's unconditional surrender to all three Allies. This headline is mischievous and misleading as it is not true, although it probably will be in the next day or two. Rumours of the death of Hitler and Goering. Mussolini shot yesterday and hung upside down and spat at. The Italians are a loveable race.'

Coward has written two of the most successful songs of the war – 'London Pride' and 'Don't Let's Be Beastly to the Germans' (a favourite of Churchill's after Coward played it for him at Chequers), and is the screenwriter of the most popular wartime film, the navy drama In Which We Serve. *Today filming resumed on Coward's latest screenplay after the weekend break. It's called* Brief Encounter *and is being made at Denham Studios, with Celia Johnson and newcomer Trevor Howard.*

'When, oh when, is this bleeding bloody sodding WAR going to finish??'

8.45pm

Bert Ruffle is saluting the Commandant of Stalag IV-C, who then stands and returns the salute. The Commandant asks him why he was evading work.

'Sir, I was ready for work when, a quarter of an hour before I was to go on parade, my stomach was filled with pain. I was very sick and I felt as though the world had come to an end. It took me all my time to come to this office, as you can see, sir.' Ruffle holds out his grubby hands.

'I am shaking like a leaf in the wind. I shall be OK for work tomorrow, Sir.'

The Commandant tells him that he should have reported sick earlier, and lets Ruffle go without punishment. Ruffle walks back to his hut feeling extremely lucky, given that his old friend 'Lofty' Whitney is serving seven days in the jail for leaving Stalag IV-C without permission.

> ***They give us rooms and huge beds... and we sleep in the same house with them, never thinking of knives in the dark. These people want us to like them.***
>
> **Matthew Halton, Canadian Broadcasting Company**

In Braunau-am-Inn, where Hitler was born 56 years ago, BBC correspondent Robert Reid is spending the night with an Austrian farmer and his wife. When the correspondents are far from an army base, they often knock on the door of a German house asking for a bed for the night. Almost without fail they are invited in, and almost without fail, as they enjoy German hospitality, they will notice the space on the wall where a picture of Hitler once hung.

Reid is enjoying a large candlelit meal and plenty of beer. The farmer and his wife have brought out photographs of their relatives living in Seattle and Chicago and they are telling him about how they hated Hitler and the Nazis. But Reid is unconvinced by their claim – too many of the civilians he's met in Germany have said the same. Two weeks ago he was reporting from Buchenwald concentration camp, an experience he will never forget. There, Reid interviewed a British officer named Captain C.A.G. Burney who'd been in the camp for 15 months.

Reid: How would you like to sum up your whole experience here?

Burney: Well, I couldn't politely say it over the microphone.

Reid: But has it been shocking?

Burney: It's been shocking, but on the other hand it's so stunning it's almost unreal, and I think probably when one has been back among civilised people for a while one just forgets it.

Reid: You really feel like you've been out of civilisation, do you?

Burney: Oh yes, absolutely out of the world.

About 9.30pm

Back in his hut in Stalag IV-C, Bert Ruffle is updating his diary. He has been a prisoner since he was captured at Dunkirk on 26th May 1940. He's tired and he's hungry.

'Why?? Why?? am I writing this diary? Will anyone read it? What I have written is the true account of what I and my comrades have suffered in the past few months. When, oh when, is this bleeding bloody sodding WAR going to finish??'

Bert's war will end on 8th May as Britain celebrates VE Day. He and about 100 other men are in the prison camp's theatre that evening watching a concert, when a POW runs on the stage interrupting the squaddie singer, shouting, 'It's over, lads. The war is finished! We are free!'

Either side of the stage is a picture of Hitler and Göring. They are instantly torn down and someone produces pictures of King George VI and Churchill. Then two POWs unfurl a Union Flag on stage.

Ruffle wrote in his diary that night, 'Suddenly, and without a word of command, we all stood to attention, stiff as ramrods. Never, in all my life have I heard the national anthem sung as we sang it then. It was sung from the heart, with tears running down our faces. We sung that anthem – proud, unbeaten, unashamed. Life, freedom, hope and home lay before us. Then we sang "Rule Britannia" and boy, did we let it go! It was a great and wonderful feeling. We were rejuvenated, reborn.' When he left the theatre, Ruffle saw that all the guards had fled.

The next morning, he left the camp with his friends, Frank, Lofty, Harry and Bunny, to try and find the advancing Americans. Later that day, Ruffle stared at the first GI they saw.

'I was fascinated by the huge roll of fat that was hanging from the

back of his neck and over his collar. Talk about being well fed! He must have had a good lifestyle.'

Ruffle arrived home on 15th May 1945. He'd been a POW for four years and 51 weeks. Years later he wrote about his return to his wife Edna at their home at Weoley Castle in the suburbs of Birmingham, 'I stood on the corner of Ludstone Road and looked at number 5. It was so silent and peaceful. I crossed the road, sat on the fence and lit a fag. I just sat there thinking "I am here!" I just couldn't take it in. I left my kitbag by the front door and was about to kick it down to let them know I was here. I decided to climb over the back wall but, in the process, I knocked the dustbin flying. I threw some bits of grit up at Edna's window. Then a voice I had not heard in five years came from the other bedroom "I'm coming." I heard a shout "He's here!"

'I was home... at last!

'I thank God for a wonderful home-coming.'

Not all returns were as joyous and as straightforward as Bert Ruffle's. The Daily Express journalist Alan Moorehead met two British POWs who had recently been liberated from a camp outside Hanover. Moorehead's car had broken down and as they helped fix it, he chatted to them.

'You'll be home soon. Are you married?' he asked.

'Yes,' they both said, but hesitantly.

One added, 'My wife got killed in an air raid and his' (he pointed to his friend) 'has gone off with an American. She wrote to him about it.'

'I'm sorry about that,' Moorehead said.

'Well, we've thought about it and we're not sorry. How could we have gone back again after five years? It wouldn't work. No. It's better the way it is.'

10.00pm

General Krebs sets off from the Führerbunker for the Russian command post. He is accompanied by two officers and is bearing a letter from Goebbels and Bormann, which announces the death of the Führer and requests a ceasefire in order that peace negotiations may commence. They ask for safe passage for everyone in the Reich Chancellery complex.

Traudl Junge is sitting with her fellow secretary Gerda Christian in the Führerbunker corridor with the other bunker staff, drinking coffee and schnapps and making 'pointless conversation'. Constanze Manziarly is sitting in a corner. Her eyes are red from weeping. Günsche and Mohnke are talking about leading a group of fighting men to break out of the bunker. Junge's ears prick up and in one voice she and Gerda Christian say, 'Take us too!' The two men nod. Junge doesn't think it likely that any of them could survive a breakout, but it seems better to do something active rather than 'wait for the Russians to come and find my corpse in the mousetrap'.

About 10.45pm

Dr Hans Graf von Lehndorff is in the attic of the Königsberg camp hospital. It's cold and drafty, and looking up he can see holes in the roof where rain is coming in. Yet this is where, over the course of the day, over 100 sick men have been placed. Von Lehndorff has come to see how they are. The men were laid side by side on the floor, but some are now lying on top of each other. He can see a few are already dead and so he takes their coats and jackets and covers the living.

For days now von Lehndorff has been trying not to think too much about the hopeless situation he's found himself in, hoping that he doesn't have to treat someone he knows, as he may break down when he sees them.

Without thinking, von Lehndorff makes the sign of the cross as he leaves the attic, blessing those who will die before morning.

10.50pm

Russian reports will claim that this is the moment the red flag was hoisted above the Reichstag. Stalin will get his victory in time for May Day. On 2nd May Russian photographers will take the famous photograph that demonstrates their control of the building and the capital. For now the bitter fighting continues. The Battle of Berlin has cost Russia hundreds of thousands of lives. Ivan Kovchenko, a Russian soldier, summed up their experience: 'The battles for Berlin were characterised by particular toughness and resistance on the part of the Germans. Everything was on fire. We spared nothing, including ammunition, just to advance another few metres. It was even worse than Stalingrad.'

> *I increased speed from five to sixteen knots... and in a little while we had shaken off our pursuers. We heard them searching for us for quite a while after; the reason we had escaped them must have been beyond them.*
>
> **Captain Adelbert Schnee**

About 11.00pm

A revolutionary new submarine is leaving Bergen in Norway and heading out to sea. She is *U-2511*, a Type XXI U-boat under the command of 31-year-old Captain Adelbert Schnee. (The same type that British naval intelligence officer Patrick

Dalzel-Job discovered in the Bremen shipyards earlier in the week.) Schnee knows these waters well, having taken part in the invasion of Norway in 1940. For over six months Schnee has been waiting for his U-boat to be ready, and now he is excited to try out her new technology, as are his crew of 56 submariners.

In 1942, following the loss of scores of U-boats, Admiral Dönitz had ordered German naval architects to come up with a radical new design of submarine. U-2511 has powerful batteries that give her a very long range and a submerged speed of 18 knots. The fact that she is an Elektroboote *– an electric boat – means that she can run silent at slow speeds and is therefore hard to detect; she can also crash-dive very fast. U-2511 even has a freezer to store food.*

Schnee had sailed 12 combat patrols when he was brought onto Admiral Dönitz's staff to help oversee the project. It has been a frustrating two years – 118 of the new class of U-boat have been made, but only two are ready for active service because they have been plagued by technical problems (mostly because the eight pre-fabricated sections of the submarine were made by companies with little experience of shipbuilding).

U-2511 is passing the small island of Store Marstein, with its bomb-damaged lighthouse. Schnee gives the order to dive.

U-2511 will soon prove herself. The next day she manages to evade a flotilla of Allied warships, and on 4th May gets within 600 metres of the cruiser HMS Norfolk *without being detected. Schnee invites his engineering officer and the officer of the watch to look through the periscope at the remarkable sight. But Schnee can't take advantage of his spectacular position; a few hours earlier he had received a radio message (while submerged – another innovation) telling him to return to base and to surrender to the Allies. Schnee had sunk 21 merchant vessels in his career, so to let a prize like the Norfolk go was hard indeed.*

On 5th May Captain Schnee will be interrogated by a Royal Navy admiral who doesn't believe his story about the Norfolk – no submarine could get so close to one of his vessels without being detected. But once the Allies examine the captured Type XXI U-boats, they quickly appreciate its revolutionary technology.

The Soviets will get four Type XXI class U-boats, the US two, the British and the French one each. The French U-boat will remain in commission until 1967.

Adelbert Schnee's U-2511 will leave Bergen for the final time on 14th June towed by a Royal Navy vessel. She is scuttled off the coast of Northern Ireland in January 1946 and still lies there in 226 feet of water.

11.30pm/3.30pm PWT

At the UN Conference in San Francisco, Soviet Foreign Minister Molotov is giving the delegates a barnstorming performance at the podium. Without notes, he is taking apart the Argentine regime of General Edelmiro Farrell and his deputy Colonel Juan Perón, concentrating on their many years of support for the Nazis (countries could attend the conference if they'd declared war on at least one of the Axis powers by 1st March. Argentina had declared war on Germany on 27th March once German defeat looked inevitable). Molotov is insisting that if Poland, a country that fought the Nazis, is excluded, then so should Argentina be, having helped them. James Reston of the *New York Times* wrote afterwards, 'there was considerable admiration for the skill and persistence with which Molotov put his case'. Molotov impresses the US press, but not the delegates. He loses the vote and Argentina is allowed to join the United Nations.

Molotov has a secret. During his time in the United States he has constantly been asked by the press and his allies about 16 Polish underground activists who had gone missing in March on their way to Warsaw for a meeting with Red Army generals about the future of their country. Molotov denied any knowledge of their whereabouts. Then on 4th May, at a reception at the Soviet consulate in San Francisco, as Molotov is shaking hands with the US Secretary of State, he will say casually, 'By the way, Mr Stettinius, about those 16 Poles, they have all been arrested by the Red Army.' Edward Stettinius is left standing with a fixed smile on his face. UN talks about Poland are called off.

About Midnight/5.30am Burmese time

On the roof of Rangoon jail in Burma, Allied POWs are painting 'JAPS GONE' in large white letters. The Union Flag, used for three years for burials of POWs, is now flying above their heads. On Sunday night, Wing Commander Bill Hudson, who is the leader of the Allied POWs, discovered that their Japanese captors had fled, leaving two farewell notes on the gate. For the past 24 hours the men have been eating well, now that they have access to the guards' stores and livestock. They have been eating pancakes, chutney and plenty of pork. But the men still face dangers – from the Burmese population outside the gates, many of whom have supported the Japanese, and from their own bomber crews, who might attack Rangoon not realising there are prisoners in the city. Hudson yesterday ordered all Burmese and Indian collaborators within the jail to be disarmed, and he had the gates shut and fortified.

Someone has had the idea that the best way to stop the Allies bombing the jail is to paint messages on the roofs, hence the words 'JAPS GONE'. After a Mosquito bombs the jail later in the day, a pilot will suggest a more urgent message, the RAF slang 'EXTRACT DIGIT', meaning 'get your finger out now'.

To ensure the POWs safety, Bill Hudson has started negotiations in a nearby house with two organisations that in March had swapped sides and joined the Allied cause – the Indian National Army, and the Burma Defence Army led by 30-year-old General Aung San. Aung San had been such a strong supporter of the Japanese (in the hope that they would grant Burma independence) that Emperor Hirohito had awarded him the Order of the Rising Sun. Aung San soon realised that, in the words of a British general, 'he had exchanged an old master for an infinitely more tyrannical new one'. Hudson fears that if the Japanese are forced to retreat they may return to Rangoon – he wants to be ready to repel them if they do so, and he needs Aung San's support and weapons.

Hudson was escorted out of the jail by RAF Warrant Officer Donald Lomas, who carried an old rifle that hadn't been fired for years. Lomas wrote in his diary that the meetings were 'very interesting' but that he was 'rather shaky' (he had been ill for a number of weeks). Hudson had had his first full-length wash with soap for five months, but he still looked scruffy in his tatty uniform, so someone lent him an RAF cap. Somehow he managed to convince Aung San and the INA leader that he was the Allied Supreme Commander Louis Mountbatten's official representative. Within an hour they provided the POWs with 17 rifles, ammunition and 12 hand grenades. 'We were no longer toothless,' Hudson wrote in his diary.

The POWs will have no need of the weapons. They will be liberated on 3rd May. Many of them are suffering from tropical diseases and malnutrition, and the side effects of eating rich food in the last few days of their captivity, which their stomachs could not cope with. In July 1947, shortly after signing an agreement with the British guaranteeing Burmese independence, General Aung San is assassinated in Rangoon. His daughter, the future Burmese political leader Aung San Suu Kyi, is two when her father dies.

Heinrich Himmler arrives at Plön Castle in a convoy of Volkswagens and armoured personnel carriers. He has surrounded himself with a big team of bodyguards for fear that Admiral Dönitz is planning to arrest him for negotiating with the Allies.

Dönitz is equally wary of Himmler. He arranges to greet him in his office. He has placed a pistol on his desk, hidden beneath a pile of papers with the safety catch off. As he later wrote in his memoirs, 'I had never done anything like this in my life before, but I did not know what the outcome of this meeting might be.' In addition to the guards of Plön Castle, the Admiral has a detachment of U-boat sailors at the ready should Himmler's SS guard attack.

Himmler sits down opposite him and Dönitz passes him the telegram from Bormann. Himmler's face goes white. Then he stands up and says, 'Allow me to become the second man in your government.' Dönitz tells him that that won't be possible. Himmler, shocked by the news but relieved that he has not been arrested, takes his leave.

The new Chancellor of Germany gets down to work. Given the impossibility of holding back the Russians, he decides his top priority: how to get as many Germans as possible into the British and American zones.

By the light of several candles, on the second floor of the makeshift camp hospital in Königsberg, Dr Hans Graf von Lehndorff and his young assistant Erika Frölich are helping a woman deliver twins. After the horrors of the Russian invasion, and the desperate plight of the other patients around him, this scene offers some comfort.

'Life goes on,' von Lehndorff thinks.

Prime Minister Winston Churchill visiting Hitler's bunker on 16th July 1945
The petrol cans used to burn the bodies are in the foreground

After April 1945...

'So - that's the end of the bastard.'

At 11pm on 8th May, Hitler's body made an appearance in Wakefield, Yorkshire. A hearse containing his coffin was pulled through the town by 50 British servicemen and women, towards a park where a bonfire was waiting. A marching band played a funeral dirge. Walking alongside the hearse were the mayor, Winston Churchill, President Truman, General de Gaulle and Joseph Stalin (who, the local paper noted, was particularly popular with the local ladies). When the cortege reached the park, Hitler's body was unceremoniously bundled out of the hearse and into the flames. This spectacular event, staged by the members of the Wakefield Operatic and Dramatic Society, was just one of the many responses around the world to the news of the death of Adolf Hitler.

The Führer's death was announced from the Hamburg radio studios of the *Reichs-Rundfunk-Gesellschaft* at 10.30pm on 1st May. Listeners were told by an 18-year-old announcer that the Führer had 'fallen at his command post in the Reich Chancellery fighting to the last breath against Bolshevism and for Germany.' When Churchill was told the news moments later – in the middle of a meeting about the forthcoming general election – he said, 'Well, I must say I think he was perfectly right to die like that.' Lord Beaverbrook pointed out that he obviously did not.

In Moscow, Stalin's response was blunter, 'So – that's the end of the bastard.'

Although Hitler was dead there was still no ceasefire. Some German units made up their own minds about whether to fight on in light of the news. Eighteen-year-old Herbert Mittelstädt was part of an anti-aircraft unit in the Austrian province of Vorarlberg. On 1st May his commanding officer declared, 'I no longer believe that there is any way possible for us to win this war. I am going to discharge you, and whoever wants to, can continue fighting with me as a Werewolf (lone fighter).' Only one man put his hand up. Dispirited, the officer concluded, 'The whole thing isn't worth it. I'm going to discharge myself as well!'

In the Sudetenland, Michael Etkind was part of a group of Jews being forced by the SS to march away from a labour camp and the advancing Russians. Resting in a barn for the night, they heard their guards saying, 'Hitler is dead.' The news spread quickly around the exhausted prisoners. One man, who Etkind had nicknamed 'the Joker' because he kept them all going with his sense of humour, leapt up and started to sing a spontaneous song:

'I have outlived the fiend
My life-long wish fulfilled...'

The others watched in horror as he sang and danced his way to the open barn door. One of the guards took aim. Etkind recalled, 'We saw the "Joker" lift his arms again... turn around surprised (didn't they understand, hadn't they heard that the Monster was dead?) and like a puppet when its strings are cut, collapse into a heap.'

The killing only stopped in Europe, when on 7th May,

General Alfred Jodl, who had been Hitler's senior military advisor, signed a simultaneous and unconditional surrender on all fronts.

John Amery

John Amery was tried for high treason at the Old Bailey in November 1945. His family tried to prove that, during his pre-war European travels, he'd become a Spanish citizen, and therefore treason against the British Crown was impossible. But when in the dock on 28th November, Amery was asked whether he would plead guilty or not guilty, he shocked the court by replying, 'I plead guilty on all counts.' On 18th December 1945 John Amery was hanged at Wandsworth Prison.

Nicolaus von Below

Hitler's Luftwaffe adjutant was given some civilian clothes by a farmer who lived on the edge of the River Havel. He registered as a civilian under a false name on 4th May and was given an identity pass and a ration book. He then worked his way, doing odd jobs, towards his in-laws' home near Magdeburg, 100 miles south-east of Berlin, where he arrived on 20th June. He remained there with his pregnant wife and their three children, but he was recognised in the clinic where his wife gave birth to their fourth child, and was forced to flee. He hid with friends in Bonn until 7th January 1946, when he was denounced to the British. He was imprisoned and used as a 'material witness' at the Nuremburg trials. He was finally discharged on 14th May 1948. He spent the rest of his working life as a pilot for Lufthansa. He died in 1983.

Gerhard Boldt, Bernd Freytag von Loringhoven and Rudolf Weiss

The three adjutants who escaped from the bunker joined a small German army unit which had become trapped between the Great and Little lakes of Wannsee, just south of Berlin. On the night of 1st May they attempted a breakout with the aim of reaching Wenck's 12th Army. Most of the men who took part in the breakout were gunned down by Russians. Weiss was captured. Boldt and von Loringhoven managed to hide in a pine thicket.

On 3rd May Boldt and von Loringhoven succeeded in obtaining civilian clothes. They learned of Hitler's death the same day. Disguised as civilians, they made their way to American-controlled territory, which they finally reached on 11th May. They then separated.

Boldt headed to Lübeck to join his wife and child. He reached them at the end of May. He was arrested by the Allies in the spring of 1946, and wrote his memoir, *Hitler's Last Days, An Eye-witness Account*, while in an internment camp. He died in 1981.

Von Loringhoven headed for Leipzig but he was arrested by the Americans before he could reach his wife and son. He was taken to a British interrogation camp near Hannover. There he was interrogated by a man calling himself Major Oughton, who was, in fact, the British spy and historian Hugh Trevor-Roper. Von Loringhoven was very unhappy with his treatment. He had no news of his family, was often hungry and treated aggressively by guards. There was one occasion when he appealed to 'Major Oughton' for help after three days of being sprayed with water and kicked, kept cold and naked and forced to sleep on a wet floor. After he spoke to Oughton, his treatment improved. Von Loringhoven was finally freed in January 1948 and reunited with his family. In the following years he was involved in the recreation of the German army, and represented Germany at the NATO Standing Group in Washington. He died in 2007.

Weiss spent five years in a prisoner-of-war camp in Poland. He died in 1958.

Martin Bormann

Bormann had worked for Hitler for ten years before entering the Führerbunker with him in January 1945. He had originally been appointed to oversee building renovations of Hitler's property in Obersalzberg. Whenever Hitler was at his mountain retreat, Bormann would be in attendance. He began dealing with all Hitler's correspondence in Obersalzberg, and gradually took control of his personal finances. After the flight of Rudolf Hess in 1941, Bormann became head of the Nazi Party Chancellery, which gave him power over legislation and civil service salaries and appointments. He became inseparable from Hitler and he earned the nickname 'Brown Eminence' long before he was given the official title of Personal Secretary to the Führer in 1943. All communication with Hitler went through him. Throughout his career he was virtually unknown by the German public and became famous only after his death.

On the night of 1st May 1945, Bormann was in the third group to leave the bunker. The group of 15 men included a pilot, a surgeon and a small troop of soldiers. They gathered in the Reich Chancellery cellar at 11pm and watched the first two groups leave – in small subgroups of five or six, through a shell-hole. When the third group's turn came at 11.40pm they decided to run for it together through the main Chancellery doorway. They raced to the nearest underground station where they found it was pitch dark. They had to feel their way along the tracks as very few in the group had brought torches. It was a bad mistake. The group missed a crucial turning and became separated. Bormann was at a particular disadvantage as he had very little knowledge of Berlin.

At about 3.30am on 2nd May Artur Axmann, the head of the Hitler Youth who had also been in the third group, came upon the bodies of Ludwig Stumpfegger and Martin Bormann, lying side by side, close to a bridge over a railway line. He noted that they were both uninjured and assumed that they had taken cyanide. In 1973 the bodies were found and in 1998 DNA tests proved that they were the bodies of Stumpfegger and Bormann, quashing decades of rumours that the Brown Eminence had escaped to South America.

Martin Bormann and his wife Gerda had ten children. Bormann also had a series of mistresses. Gerda died of cancer in April 1946 and the children were dispersed to foster homes. Bormann's oldest son, Martin Bormann junior, became a Catholic priest before leaving the church to marry. He spent the second half of his life working as a theologian and peace campaigner.

General Wilhelm Burgdorf

Burgdorf, the man who killed Rommel, committed suicide by shooting himself in the head on 2nd May 1945.

Gerda Christian

Dara, as she was known – a shortening of her maiden name, Daranowski – escaped from the bunker, together with Hitler's other secretary Traudl Junge, in the breakout on 1st May 1945.

She succeeded in making her way to American-held territory. She died in 1997.

Winston Churchill

In the general election of July 1945, a war-weary Britain voted for Clement Attlee's Labour Party rather than Churchill's caretaker Conservative government. On the afternoon of the result, Churchill's doctor, Lord Moran, told him he thought the British people were ungrateful. 'Oh no, I wouldn't call it that,' Churchill replied. 'They have had a very hard time.' In 1951, Churchill bounced back, winning office once more. He served as an MP until 1964, dying, aged 90, a year later.

Geoffrey Cox

After the war Geoffrey Cox returned to journalism and joined the *News Chronicle* as a political correspondent, and by the mid-1950s was deputy editor. Keen to work in television, he joined ITN and was its editor-in-chief from 1956 to 1968. In 1967 he started *News at Ten*, ITN's flagship half-hour evening news bulletin. Sir Robin Day described Cox as 'the best television journalist we have ever known in Britain'. Geoffrey Cox was knighted in 1966, and died in 1993, aged 97.

Patrick Dalzel-Job

On 3rd May 1945, Patrick Dalzel-Job wrote in his diary after a skirmish with German troops, 'I realised with some feeling of regret that this was likely to be one of the last times we should face enemy fire; the German resistance was everywhere collapsing.' He had lost not a single man in his 30 Assault Unit and had enjoyed the thrill of his wartime experience.

Immediately after the war, Dalzel-Job travelled to Norway to find a girl called Bjørg Bangsund, who he had sailed with in the summer of 1939. Three weeks after he tracked her down, they married in Oslo. Their son Iain has a senior officer's report on his father that says he is 'an unusual officer who possesses no fear of danger'.

Dalzel-Job agreed he may have inspired Ian Fleming's famous spy but said, 'I have never read a Bond book or seen a Bond movie. They are not my style. And I only ever loved one woman, and I'm not a drinking man.' Patrick Dalzel-Job died in 2003, aged 90.

Admiral Karl Dönitz

Having been named as Hitler's successor, Karl Dönitz was head of the German government until it was dissolved by the Allies on 23rd May. He was tried at Nuremberg and found guilty of planning, initiating and waging wars of aggression and of crimes against the laws of war. He was imprisoned in Spandau Prison for ten years and released in October 1956. He later wrote his memoirs. He died in 1980.

Gretl Fegelein

Eva Braun's sister gave birth to a daughter, Eva, on 5th May in Obersalzberg, where she, her mother and her other sister were staying.

They had been expecting Hermann Fegelein, Hitler and Braun to join them, but that hope ended when Hitler's aide, Julius Schaub, arrived on 25th April bringing documents from the bunker, which Hitler wanted preserved. He also brought Eva Braun's last letter to her sister, which she had written on 23rd April, setting out her wishes for her jewellery in the case of her death. 'The Führer himself has lost all faith in a successful outcome. All of us here, including myself, will carry on hoping as long as we live. Hold your heads up high and do not despair! There is still hope. But it goes without saying that we will not allow ourselves to be captured alive.'

Gretl Fegelein later remarried. She died in 1987. Her daughter Eva committed suicide in 1971 at the age of 27 following the death of her boyfriend in a car crash.

Sister Erna Flegel

Flegel, who had become hysterical when saying goodbye to Hitler, remained with the patients in the emergency hospital in the Reich Chancellery cellars until the Russians arrived on 2nd May 1945. She was handed over to the Americans and briefly interrogated. She died in 2006.

Joseph, Magda, Helga, Hilde, Helmut, Holde, Hedda and Heide Goebbels

On the night of 1st May, after Dr Stumpfegger had administered cyanide to the six children, Joseph and Magda Goebbels went up to the Reich Chancellery garden and committed suicide. They probably took cyanide. They may also have shot themselves. Goebbels had given instructions for his adjutant Günther Schwägermann to burn their bodies, but Schwägermann wasn't able to source much petrol, so when the Russians arrived the following day they were easily able to identify the bodies.

Hermann Göring

The former head of the German Luftwaffe ended the war in

his Bavarian castle. On 5th May he set off to the American zone in order to avoid capture by the Russians. He was taken into custody on 6th May. In the months before the Nuremberg Trials he came off morphine and lost a lot of weight. He was found guilty on four counts: conspiracy; waging a war of aggression; war crimes, including the theft of works of art; crimes against humanity, including the disappearance of opponents, and the murder and enslavement of civilians, including 5,700,000 Jews. He was sentenced to death by hanging but committed suicide on 15th October 1946 by taking cyanide the night before he was due to be executed. It has never been finally established how he obtained the cyanide but two American soldiers claimed to have played a part.

Robert Ritter von Greim

The newly appointed head of the Luftwaffe, von Greim was captured by the Americans with Hanna Reitsch on 9th May 1945. He was by now quite seriously ill from his infected leg wound. He was interrogated by the Americans and committed suicide by taking cyanide on 24th May, having learned that he was to be handed over to the Russians as part of a prisoner exchange programme.

Otto Günsche

Hitler's personal adjutant was one of the people who broke out of the bunker on 1st May 1945. He was in the first party to leave, led by General Mohnke, and he was with Mohnke when he surrendered to a Russian army unit in a Berlin brewery cellar. He was imprisoned in Moscow and later in East Germany until May 1956.

Like others who had been in the Führerbunker at the end,

Günsche was repeatedly tortured by the Russians, who were trying to establish a detailed picture of Hitler's life and death. He returned to live in a small town near Cologne. He died in 2003.

Dr Werner Haase

After instructing Hitler on how to use the cyanide phial, Werner Haase was one of the small group who remained in the bunker until the Russians came on 2nd May 1945. He was sent to Moscow's Butyrka prison. He was probably tortured, like the others from the bunker who were imprisoned by the Russians, in order to extract information about Hitler's death. He died of the tuberculosis in 1950.

Fey von Hassell

Fey was reunited with her husband Detalmo in May 1945. Together they searched for their missing sons but it was Fey's mother who, in August 1945, tracked them down to a former Nazi children's home in Innsbruck, where they had been given new names and identities. She was just in time, as all the homes were due to be closed down in a few days and all children given up for adoption to local peasants. Fey and her husband were reunited with their sons at the end of October 1945, a year after they had been taken from them. They returned to Italy, and had a daughter in 1948.

In 1975 Detalmo and Fey returned to the Lago di Braies Hotel, but as it was filled with tourists, and surrounded by cars, it had none of the atmosphere of the days before her liberation.

Heinrich Himmler

As the war ended, the former head of the SS was at a loss. He played no part in the surrender and was isolated from his fellow Nazis. For several days he did nothing, then on 11th May 1945 he decided to flee from Lübeck with a small number of SS guards, but without planning where they would go. He was captured at a Russian checkpoint on 22nd May and handed over to the British. He was undergoing a medical examination the following day when he slipped a cyanide phial into his mouth and, to the surprise of the doctor examining him, suddenly dropped dead.

Lionel 'Bill' Hudson

For months after his release from Rangoon jail, whenever Bill Hudson heard a noise in the night, he would leap out of bed and stand to attention, expecting a Japanese guard to appear. He dedicated his memoirs to his wife Audrey, who helped him get over the trauma. Exactly 40 years on, Bill Hudson flew to Tokyo to meet Haruo Ito, the commander of Rangoon jail, who had written the letters left on the jail's main gate. In the foyer of the New Otani Hotel they shook hands and Ito gave Hudson his card – he now worked for a successful Japanese food company. They talked about the night of 29th April 1945. Ito explained that he left the camp with 60 of his men, but only 17 survived the journey through the jungle. Hudson then took Ito to meet his wife, and in his hotel room the former POW and his jailer had a beer.

General Alfred Jodl

On 7th May 1945 Alfred Jodl signed the Act of Military Surrender to the Allies on behalf of Admiral Dönitz at the supreme headquarters of the Allied Expeditionary Force, in Rheims. He was then arrested and tried at Nuremberg. He was found guilty of conspiracy to commit crimes against peace; waging a war of aggression; war crimes; and crimes against humanity. He was hanged on 16th October 1946. A German court later overturned the guilty verdict on the grounds that it had not been unanimous. His property was restored to his widow. This reprieve was later overturned by a Bavarian court, but his widow was allowed to retain the property.

Willi Johannmeier, Heinz Lorenz and Wilhelm Zander

The three couriers who had left the bunker on 29th April 1945 with Hitler's testaments spent the night of 30th April on Pfaueninsel, the island on the River Havel where Dönitz had promised to send a seaplane to rescue them.

On the night of 1st May the island was bombarded by Russian fire and they seized a canoe and paddled out to a yacht at anchor in the Havel. They hid in the stationary yacht; a munitions ship was ablaze close by and the river was brightly lit by its flames, so the men knew that any move would be easily spotted by the Russians. Unfortunately for them, it was at this moment that the seaplane arrived. The three couriers attempted to row towards it but the plane came under direct fire and the pilot flew off without them. For the next two days the men remained in hiding, moving between the island and the yacht. On 3rd May, wearing civilian clothes which they had found on the island, they set off on their journeys home, abandoning the attempt to take the documents to their destinations.

Johannmeier returned to his family home in Westphalia and

buried the documents in the back garden, inside a bottle. He was quickly found by Allied investigators, living under his own name. He refused to admit to his American interrogators that he had any papers until after his two companions had both been forced to give their copies up.

Zander succeeded in reaching Bavaria. He hid the documents in a trunk in the house of a woman he knew in the village of Tegernsee. He adopted a new identity, taking the name Friedrich Wilhelm Paustin, and created a new life working in Tegernsee as a gardener. The documents were found on Boxing Day 1945, following detective work by Hugh Trevor-Roper and American counter-intelligence agents. Zander himself was tracked down and arrested, after a short gun battle, near the Czech border early in 1946. The documents were shipped to Washington. Zander died in Munich in 1974.

Lorenz, Hitler's press secretary, was captured by the Americans in June 1945. Information he gave under interrogation led to the arrests of his fellow couriers. He was released in 1947 and returned to work as a journalist, which had been his profession before the war. He died in 1985.

William Joyce

Having fled Hamburg at the end of April 1945, by mid-May the Joyces were lodging in a house in a small Danish hamlet called Kupfermühle under the name of Hansen. On 28th May two British soldiers who were part of T-Force, Lieutenant Geoffrey Perry and Captain Adrian Lickorish, were walking in the woods nearby collecting firewood, when they met a man with a limp called 'Herr Hansen'. They started talking, and Hansen gave them a lecture on the difference between coniferous and deciduous forests. After a while, Perry said, 'You wouldn't by any chance be William Joyce, would you?' Joyce reached into his trouser pocket for his false 'Hansen' papers, but Perry thought he was reaching for a gun and shot him though the hip, knocking him to the ground. As he was driven off in the jeep, Perry recalled that Joyce 'couldn't stop talking'.

In an appropriate twist of fate, Geoffrey Perry was a German-born Jew named Horst Pinschewer, whose family had fled Nazi persecution in 1936.

Joyce was hanged at dawn at Wandsworth Prison on 3rd January 1946, having been found guilty of giving 'aid and comfort to the King's enemies'. The jury took 19 minutes to reach their verdict. One eyewitness in the courtroom said they looked as if they'd been out for a cup of tea.

The rules for those who were hanged were followed to the letter; Joyce was buried at night, within the prison precincts with no mourners present, and his grave was unmarked. At the time of the execution, three men hiding in the prison nursery garden wearing sports jackets and flannels gave a quick Nazi salute.

Margaret Joyce was never tried. She died in London in 1972.

Traudl Junge

Hitler's secretary was in the first group to break out of the bunker on the night of 1st May 1945. She was dressed as a male soldier and carrying a pistol. The sight of Berlin shocked her. In the moonlight she saw a dead horse on the pavement, its body hacked for meat. Her group stopped for some rest in a beer cellar. It soon became apparent that the beer cellar was surrounded by Russians and that their only option was surrender.

The leader of the group, General Mohnke, suddenly had an idea. He ordered Junge and Gerda Christian to take off their helmets and army jackets and even leave their pistols, and attempt to get through the Russian line under the guise of ordinary civilian women. He wrote a brief report, which he wanted them to take to Admiral Dönitz.

Junge later recalled that, to their amazement, they passed through the line of Russians 'as if we were invisible'. However, Junge was later captured by the Russians. She caught diphtheria in custody and was handed over to the British. She was released in 1946.

In later life she remarried – her first husband had died during the war – and she worked on a magazine called *Quick*. After many years of silence she wrote her memoirs in late life: 'my attempt to be reconciled... to myself'. She died in Munich in 2002 at the age of 81.

Field Marshal General Wilhelm Keitel

Wilhelm Keitel was arrested by the Americans in early May 1945. He was tried at Nuremberg and found guilty of conspiracy to commit crimes against peace, waging a war of aggression, war crimes and crimes against humanity. He was sentenced to death and was hanged on 16th October 1946.

General Hans Krebs

Krebs was ushered into the headquarters of the Russian General Chuikov at 4am on 1st May. According to Russian records, he began, in Russian, by informing Chuikov of Hitler's death, adding, 'You are the first foreigner to know.' Chuikov bluffed and pretended that he already knew. Krebs then read Hitler's political testament and a request from Goebbels for 'a satisfactory way out for the nations who have suffered most in the war'.

Chuikov telephoned Marshal Zhukov, who immediately sent his deputy to the headquarters. Zhukov then telephoned Stalin, who was asleep in his Dacha outside Moscow. Zhukov insisted he was woken.

Stalin was disappointed to learn that Hitler had not been captured alive. He ordered that Chuikov should agree to nothing less than unconditional surrender. Presented with the demand for unconditional surrender, Krebs insisted that he didn't have the authority to offer it. Goebbels and Bormann had given him strict instructions not to surrender. He argued that the Russians needed to recognise a new German government with Admiral Dönitz as leader, then Dönitz would be able to surrender.

Chuikov consulted Zhukov on the phone again. Zhukov was clear: Krebs had to get Goebbels and Bormann to agree to an unconditional surrender by 10.15 that morning or the Russians would 'blast Berlin into ruins'.

Krebs returned to the bunker. Goebbels, in particular, was implacable. The Russians waited until 10.40am and then they turned their big guns on what was left of the city centre.

Krebs committed suicide alongside General Burgdorf by shooting himself in the head on 2nd May 1945, leaving General Weidling to take on the negotiations with the Russians.

Erich Kempka

Hitler's chauffeur escaped from the bunker on 1st May 1945 and managed to make his way to Berchtesgaden. He was arrested by American troops in June and held until 1947. He died in 1975. He gave many interviews and produced memoirs, becoming well known both for the inconsistencies in his accounts and the colour of his language. For example he said of Eva Braun's brother-in-law, Hermann Fegelein, 'he had his brains in his scrotum.'

Dr Hans Graf von Lehndorff

Dr Hans Graf von Lehndorff stayed in Königsberg until October 1945, when he fled to West Prussia on the run from the Russians, often giving medical aid in return for food and a bed for the night. In May 1947 he made his way to West Germany, where he worked for the rest of his life as a surgeon. In 1967 von Lehndorff published his harrowing diaries covering the years 1945–47. He died in 1987. In Bonn there is now a street named after him.

Ewald Lindloff

The SS officer who buried Adolf Hitler and Eva Braun broke out of the bunker on 1st May 1945 and was killed by Russian tank fire as he attempted to cross Weidendammer Bridge on 2nd May.

Heinz Linge

Hitler's valet was one of the last to leave the bunker on 1st May 1945. He was captured by the Russians the next day and held in Moscow's Lubjanka prison where he was frequently tortured. He was released in 1955. He travelled to London shortly afterwards and gave an interview to the BBC's *In Town Tonight* programme. He settled in West Germany, wrote his memoirs and died in 1980.

Heinz Lorenz
See Johannmeier above.

Bernd von Loringhoven
See Boldt above.

Constanze Manziarly
Hitler's cook was in the group lead by General Mohnke which broke out of the bunker on 1st May 1945, but she became separated from the others and was presumed dead. Her body has never been found.

Nina Markovna
Within days of the end of the war, the Americans left Triptis and the Russians moved in; the town was now part of their zone of occupation as agreed at Yalta. All Russians were forced to return to the Soviet Union, but Nina and her family managed to escape to the French zone, and for a while Nina found work dancing with a ballet troupe. In 1947, while working in a Red Cross club, she met a young GI, and they married. They crossed the Atlantic as soon as they could, as Nina wanted the child to be born in America.

Emil Maurice
Maurice served in the Luftwaffe for much of the war. He was captured by the Russians in 1948 and served four years in a labour camp. He died in 1972.

Rochus Misch

Misch was one of the last people to leave the bunker, making his escape early on 2nd May. He was soon captured by the Russians and held in labour camps until 1953. Like others who had been in the bunker, he was frequently tortured for information about Hitler. On release he returned to his wife in Berlin and became a painter and decorator. He died in 2013 at the age of 96. He insisted for the rest of his life, 'He was a wonderful boss.'

General Wilhelm Mohnke

Mohnke led the first party to break out of the bunker on 1st May, and surrendered to the Russians the following day. He was held by the Russians until 1955, spending the first six years of his incarceration in solitary confinement. On his release he returned to live in West Germany and became a dealer in trucks and trailers. He died at the age of 90 in 2001.

General Bernard Montgomery

In the 1946 New Year's Honours list, Montgomery was named a viscount. His staff already knew, as he'd been practising his signature for weeks. Montgomery remained hugely popular with the British public and retired from the army in 1958. He died on 24th March 1976.

Heinrich Müller

Müller was last seen in the bunker on 1st May 1945. There were many rumours that he went to work for the Russians or the CIA, but both the Soviet and US secret services have now released archives which show that they were never in contact with him. In 1967 West Germany sought the extradition from Panama of a man called Francis Willard Keith, whose physical appearance was so close to Müller's that his wife, Sophie Müller, was convinced it was him. Fingerprints proved otherwise. It is now presumed that he died in Berlin in early May 1945.

Liesl Ostertag

In the last surviving letter from Eva Braun to her sister Gretl she wrote, 'The faithful Liesl refuses to abandon me. I've proposed several times that she should leave. I should like to give her my gold watch.' Anneliese Ostertag escaped the bunker and survived. She was interviewed by Nerin E. Gun for his 1968 biography of Eva Braun.

Captain Sigismund Payne-Best

After a short stay in an Italian hospital, Payne-Best flew home to England on 22nd May to be reunited with his wife, whom he had not seen since 9th November 1939. In 1950, with the permission of MI6, he published a memoir of the war, which became a bestseller. Sigismund Payne-Best died in 1978, aged 93.

Harald Quandt

Magda Goebbels' oldest son was released from a British prisoner-of-war camp in 1947. With his half-brother he inherited his father's industrial empire in 1954. This made him one of the richest men in Germany. He married and had five daughters. He died in a plane crash in Italy in 1967.

Hanna Reitsch

After a couple of days at Plön Castle, Hanna Reitsch and Robert Ritter von Greim set off together on a flying tour of army outposts. Their aim was to encourage troops to keep on fighting and ignore calls to surrender.

However von Greim's injury became so painful that they had to stop, and she spent several days nursing him. They were captured by the Americans on 9th May 1945. Reitsch told her interrogators that von Greim would never have allowed himself to capitulate if he had not been so ill from his infected wound.

When she was arrested Reitsch was carrying the letters from Joseph and Magda Goebbels to her son Harald. She had, however, destroyed Eva Braun's last letter to her sister Gretl. She was not a fan of Eva Braun. She told her American interrogator that Braun occupied most of her time with 'fingernail polishing, changing of clothes for each hour of the day, and all the other little feminine tasks of grooming, combing and polishing'. Reitsch claimed she destroyed Eva Braun's letter on the grounds that it was 'so vulgar, so theatrical, and in such poor, adolescent taste' that its survival would damage the reputation of the Third Reich. For her own safety, in case she was captured, Reitsch had also destroyed the official letters that she had been given by Bormann.

Reitsch was held by the Americans for 18 months. She learned that on 3rd May her sister had killed her three children and herself, alongside both Reitsch's parents, fearing that they were about to be handed over to the Russians. She also learned of von Greim's suicide.

After her release, Reitsch returned to gliding. The Allies had introduced rules banning Germans from flying powered planes. She became German gliding champion in 1955 and set many endurance, distance and altitude records. In recognition of her competitive flying, John F. Kennedy invited her to the White House in 1961.

She set up gliding schools in India and Africa and spent much of the rest of her life in Ghana. She died in 1979 at the age of 67.

Lieutenant Wolfgang F. Robinow

For the young German-born GI, the rest of 1945 consisted of interrogating prisoners and arresting Nazis – the most famous of whom was the film maker Leni Riefenstahl 'because the commanding officer wanted her autograph'. He once asked a Gestapo officer how many people he had killed. He replied, 'Are you in the habit of counting the number of slices of bread you have for breakfast in a year?'

Robinow stayed in Germany and lived in Munich until 2003, when he moved to Frankfurt to be closer to his children and grandchildren.

Bert Ruffle

After the war, Ruffle found it hard to settle down to regular work, but in the end became a qualified coppersmith. He often told his three sons the story of his 1945 six-week winter march; the boys made the snow deeper each time he recounted it (it got up to 45 feet). Bert retired in 1975 and died on 9th November 1995 aged 85.

Yelena Rzhevskaya

Together with her colleagues in the SMERSH intelligence detachment that found Hitler's bunker, Rzhevskaya was forbidden to talk about what they discovered there, and in particular about finding Hitler's body. After the war she returned to live in Moscow to work as a writer and won prizes for her fiction and journalism. Eventually, in the late 1960s, she was allowed to publish a memoir and at last help, in her own words, 'prevent Stalin's dark and murky ambition from taking root – his desire to hide from the world that we had found Hitler's corpse'.

Dr Ernst Schenk

Schenck took part in the breakout from the bunker on 1st May 1945. He was quickly captured by the Russians and held until 1953. He returned to live in West Germany and tried to track down surviving patients from the emergency hospital in the Chancellery cellar. He was unable to find any. He died aged 94 in 1998.

Claus Sellier

In May 1945 Sellier started work in Munich as a cook at the Hotel Excelsior. Young German men were so scarce that the fact Claus could peel potatoes was qualification enough. He soon lost contact with his friend Fritz. Claus took English classes and in 1953 got a job as a trainee chef in New York. Claus became a US citizen and ran a number of restaurants and clubs across the country. He now lives in California.

Joseph Stalin

The people of the Soviet Union celebrated the end of the European war on 9th May 1945, but they had not won any greater freedom. If anything, Stalin's grip grew tighter over the next few years. He showed no mercy for those Red Army soldiers who had been captured by the Germans – they were considered traitors, and over a million were imprisoned in Soviet gulags. There was a bloody purge of Russia's successful wartime generals, of party members, intellectuals and Jews. The scientists in the Soviet nuclear weapon project were tolerated. 'Leave them in peace. We can always shoot them later,' Stalin said.

Relations with his former Allies deteriorated further. In June 1948, furious at the Americans and British for introducing the Deutschmark as the official currency in their occupied zones in Berlin (he preferred the weaker Reichsmark), Stalin ordered a blockade of the city. To Stalin's surprise, America and her allies responded with an airlift that successfully supplied food and fuel to their occupied zones. The blockade ended in May 1949.

Always obsessed with his place in history, Stalin oversaw a film called *The Fall of Berlin*, made by the state-controlled Mosfilm studio as a 70th birthday present for the dictator. In the film, it is Stalin alone who directs the battle and who later is surrounded by a grateful crowd made up of many nationalities chanting, 'Thank you, Stalin!'

Stalin collapsed on 5th March 1953 after suffering a massive cerebral haemorrhage. His daughter Svetlana said that in his final moments his eyes were 'full of the fear of death'.

Fritz Tornow

Hitler's dog handler remained in the bunker and surrendered to the Russians when they arrived on 2nd May 1945. He was showing signs of post-traumatic stress. Four other people remained in the bunker including the nurse, Erna Flegel, and the doctor, Werner Haase.

President Harry Truman

The UN Charter was finally agreed and signed in San Francisco, and on 28th June was put in a safe which was put onto a plane bound for Washington. In case of an air crash, on the safe was written: 'Finder! Do Not Open. Send to the Department of State, Washington.' The safe was also wrapped in a parachute.

On 16th July 1945 President Truman was in Berlin for a conference with Stalin and Churchill. Truman was driven to the Reichstag, which by now had graffiti scratched on its stones by Russian soldiers ('Ivanov, all the way from Stalingrad'; 'Sidorov from Tambov'), and then on to the Brandenburg Gate. They passed a park bench that still had a sign saying 'NICHT FÜR JÜDEN' – 'Not for Jews', before heading into what was now the Russian sector. Truman was shown the Reich Chancellery and he stared at the stone balcony where Hitler had addressed the crowds so many times. Reporters clustered around the car. 'They brought it upon themselves. It just demonstrates what man can do when he overreaches himself,' the President told them.

Truman was President until 1953, when he was succeeded by his former Supreme Commander, Dwight D. Eisenhower.

General Helmuth Weidling

Following the suicide of General Krebs, Helmuth Weidling, commander of Berlin, took over the negotiations with the Russian General Chuikov. He signed an unconditional surrender in the early hours of 2nd May. He was then arrested by the Russians and died in KGB custody in 1955.

Rudolf Weiss

See Boldt above.

General Walther Wenck

Wenck's forces spent 1st and 2nd May moving General Busse's depleted 9th Army from the forests south of Berlin to the River Elbe with the aim of enabling as many German soldiers as possible to cross over to the American zone. Hearing of Hitler's death on 3rd May, Wenck sent negotiators to the Americans and immediately gave orders that the Nazi salute be replaced by the traditional German army version. He withdrew fighting troops from the Elbe.

The Americans agreed to receive the injured, unarmed soldiers but not to rebuild bridges across the Elbe to facilitate the speedy evacuation of all soldiers. US General William Stimpson felt he was under an obligation to their Russian allies not to rescue soldiers or civilians from the Soviet zone. He did not, moreover, have the resources to feed and house such a mass surrender. Wenck's 12th Army was still under attack from the Russians advancing westward, and the force of that attack was such that, on 6th May, the Americans withdrew from the Elbe to protect their troops from fire. At this point the Germans surged across the river on rafts cobbled together from fuel cans and planks of wood. Some strong swimmers swam across with signal cable in their teeth, which they fastened to trees on the west bank. Women and children, and those who couldn't swim, then tried to haul themselves along these lines. Many who couldn't cross committed suicide. On 7th May the remnants of the 12th Army blew up their guns. That afternoon Wenck was in one of the last boats to cross the Elbe. He surrendered to the Americans and was held as a prisoner of war until 1947. He died in a car crash in 1982.

Alan Whicker

After the war, Whicker worked for the Exchange Telegraph

news agency covering events all over the world, including the Korean War. In 1957 he joined the BBC and his best-known series *Whicker's World* started soon after, running until 1988. Alan Whicker was given a CBE for services to broadcasting in 2005, and died in 2013.

Wilhelm Zander

See Johannmeier above.

The first Russian soldiers to enter the Reich Chancellery on 2nd May quickly established that the place was not wired to explode. They discovered the charred remains of Joseph and Magda Goebbels in the Reich Chancellery garden, and the bodies of their six children on the bunk beds in their room in the upper bunker. The intelligence officer, Yelena Rzhevskaya, found ten fat notebooks containing Joseph Goebbels' diaries, and came across one of her female colleagues trying on Eva Hitler's dresses. The Russians also found the remains of Eva and Adolf Hitler and, on 9th May, Rzhevskaya was in the team that managed to track down an assistant of Hitler's dentist who was able to provide the dental records. The corpse believed to be Hitler's had a well-preserved jawbone. Rzhevskaya expected that the whole world would be told within days that they had found Hitler's body.

However, by now Stalin refused to recognise any evidence that Hitler was dead, almost as if he was clinging onto his long-held dream of a show trial. The Soviet press published numerous articles speculating about whether Hitler had fled to the American zone in Bavaria or to Franco's Spain or Argentina. A hunt was launched. On 26th May, Stalin told Truman's representative in the Kremlin that 'Bormann, Goebbels, Hitler and probably Krebs had escaped and were in hiding'. He repeated the assertion when he arrived at the Potsdam Conference on 16th July 1945 to meet Churchill and Truman.

That day – ten days before he lost the British general election – Winston Churchill had visited the Reich Chancellery just ten minutes after President Truman left. Russian soldiers showed him the wreckage of Hitler's study and handed out souvenirs of bits of the Führer's smashed marble desk. Sir Alexander Cadogan, one of Churchill's party, used his as a paperweight.

Churchill was then taken down into the bunker, where by torchlight, he wandered through the corridors that were littered with broken glass, upturned furniture, strewn books and papers. The debris was six feet high in places and there was a smell of death.

When Churchill emerged into the sunshine, mopping the sweat off his forehead, he stared at the spot where Hitler's body was burned, then gave a swift V sign. Before he walked away he said, 'This is what would have happened to us if *they* had won the war. We would have been in the bunker.'

Acknowledgements

I would like to thank John Schwartz, Dietlinde Nawrath and Annette Yoosefinejad for talking about their memories and family stories; Patrick Mueller and Myfanwy Craigie for help with translation; the late Elizabeth Bruegger for the information about Harald Quandt in Latimer House; Joanna Hylton, Richard Oldfield, Gillian Rees-Mogg and Charlotte Rees-Mogg for showing, lending and giving me books and Kate O'Brien for recommending sources. I'd also like to thank my family for allowing me to shirk domestic duties in the run-up to Christmas and Jonathan for being a great collaborator – in the best sense.
  EC

Many thanks to Sibylle Harrison for her invaluable German translations; the Ruffle family, and in particular Alan Ruffle, for permission to reprint Bert Ruffle's 1945 diary; Robin Mortimer for the book loans; Phil Critchlow for his on-going minute by minute support. Particular thanks to my family who have put up with a husband and father whose head has too often been in April 1945 rather than the present day. I couldn't have asked for a better writing partner in Emma – whose idea this book was.
  JM

Thanks to Aurea Carpenter and Rebecca Nicolson for their support and enthusiasm, and to Paul Bougourd for his wise and focused editing.

Bibliography

Alanbrooke, Field Marshal Lord, War Diaries 1939-45, ed. Danchev, Alex, and Todman, Daniel (Weidenfeld and Nicolson, 2001)

Aldrich, Richard J., The Faraway War (Doubleday, 2005)

Anonymous, A Woman in Berlin (Picador, 2000)

Arthur, Max, Forgotten Voices of the Second World War (Ebury Press, 2004)

Atkinson, Rick, The Guns at Last Light (Henry Holt, 2013)

Bagdonas, Raymond, The Devil's General (Casemate, 2014)

Beevor, Antony, Berlin, The Downfall, 1945 (Viking, 2002)

Beevor, Antony, The Second World War (Weidenfeld and Nicolson, 2012)

von Below, Nicolaus, At Hitler's Side (Greenhill, 2010)

Benn, Tony, Years of Hope (Arrow, 1995)

Best, Nicholas, Five Days that Shocked the World (Osprey, 2012)

Boldt, Gerhard, Hitler's Last Days (Sphere, 1973)

Bullock, Alan, Hitler, A Study in Tyranny (Penguin, 1990)

Bullock, Alan, Hitler and Stalin: Parallel Lives (BCA, 1991)

Bunting, Madeline, The Model Occupation (HarperCollins, 1995)

Buruna, Ian, 1945 Year Zero (Atlantic Books, 2013)

Calder, Angus, The People's War (Pimlico, 2008)

Campbell, Christy, Target London (Abacus, 2012)

Capa, Robert, Slightly Out of Focus (The Modern Library, 2001)

Churchill, Winston, and Truman, Harry S., Defending the West: The Truman-Churchill Correspondence, 1945–1960 (Praeger, 2004)

Clarke, Nick, Alistair Cooke (Orion, 1999)

Coward, Noël, The Noël Coward Diaries, ed. Payn, Graham, and Morley, Sheridan (Little, Brown, 1982)

Cox, Geoffrey, The Race for Trieste (William Kimber, 1977)

Crick, Bernard, George Orwell: A Life (Penguin, 1992)

Crosby, Harry H., A Wing and a Prayer (Harper Collins, 1993)

Dallek, Robert, John F. Kennedy: An Unfinished Life (Penguin, 2003)

Dalzel-Job, Patrick, From Arctic Snow to Dust of Normandy (Leo Cooper, 2005)

Davenport-Hines, Richard, Auden (Minerva, 1995)

Davidson, Martin, The Perfect Nazi (Viking, 2010)

Delaforce, Patrick, Marching to the Sound of Gunfire (Wrens Park, 1999)

Delaforce, Patrick, The Hitler File (Michael O'Mara, 2007)

Dimbleby, Richard, Broadcaster (BBC, 1966)

Dobbs, Michael, Six Months in 1945 (Hutchinson, 2012)

Eisenhower, David, Eisenhower at War 1943–1945 (Collins, 1986)

Farndale, Nigel, Haw Haw: The Tragedy of William and Margaret Joyce (Macmillan, 2005)

Fest, Joachim, Hitler (Harcourt Brace, 1973)

Fest, Joachim, Portraits of the Nazi Leadership (de Capo, 1999)

Fest, Joachim, *Inside Hitler's Bunker* (Macmillan, 2004)

Field, Roger, *Rogue Male* (Coronet, 2011)

Gardiner, Juliet, *Wartime Britain 1939–1945* (Headline, 2004)

Gilbert, Martin, *The Holocaust* (William Collins, 1986)

Gilbert, Martin, *The Road to Victory: Winston Churchill 1941-1945* (Heinemann, 1986)

Gilbert, Martin, *Second World War* (Fontana, 1989)

Gilbert, Martin, *The Day the War Ended* (HarperCollins, 1995)

Görtemaker, Heike B., *Eva Braun, Life with Hitler* (Allen Lane, 2010)

de Guingand, Sir Francis, *Operation Victory* (Hodder and Stoughton, 1947)

Gun, Nerin E., *Eva Braun, Hitler's Mistress* (Coronet Books, 1969)

Hamilton, Nigel, *JFK: Volume One* (BCA, 1993)

Hargrave, Michael John, *Bergen-Belsen: A Medical Student's Journal* (Imperial College Press, 2014)

Haslam, Jonathan, *Russia's Cold War* (Yale University Press, 2011)

Hastings, Max, *Armageddon* (Macmillan, 2004)

Hastings, Max, *All Hell Let Loose* (Harper Press, 2012)

Hawkins, Desmond ed., *War Report: From D-Day to VE Day* (BBC Books, 1994)

von Hessell, Fey, *A Mother's War* (John Murray, 1990)

Hibberd, Stuart, *This – Is London* (MacDonald and Evans, 1950)

Hitchcock, William I., *Liberation: The Bitter Road to Freedom* (Faber and Faber, 2008)

Holmes, Richard, *The World at War* (Ebury, 2011)

Hood, Jean, *Submarine* (Conway, 2007)

Horne, Alistair, with Montgomery, David, *Monty 1944–1945* (Pan, 1995)

Hudson, Lionel, *The Rats of Rangoon* (Arrow, 1987)

Hunt, Irmgard, *On Hitler's Mountain* (Atlantic, 2006)

Jenkins, Roy, *Churchill* (Macmillan, 2001)

Jones, Nigel, *The Venlo Incident* (Frontline, 2009)

Junge, Traudl, with Müller, Melissa, *Until the Final Hour*, translated by Anthea Bell (Phoenix, 2005)

Karpov, Vladimir, *Russia at War 1941–45* (Guild Publishing, 1987)

Kempowski, Walter, *Swansong 1945* (Granta, 2004)

Kenny, Mary, *Germany Calling* (New Island, 2003)

Kershaw, Alex, *The Liberator* (Arrow, 2013)

Kershaw, Ian, *Hitler 1889–1936 Hubris* (Penguin, 1998)

Kershaw, Ian, *Hitler 1936–1945 Nemesis* (Penguin, 2000)

King, Greg, *The Duchess of Windsor* (Aurum Press, 1999)

Klabunde, Anja, *Magda Goebbels* (Little, Brown, 2001)

Lambert, Angela, *The Lost Life of Eva Braun* (Century, 2006)

Lehmann, Armin D., with Carroll, Tim, *In Hitler's Bunker* (Mainstream, 2004)

von Lehndorff, Hans Graf, *Ostpressisches Tagebuch* (DTV, 2005)

Lewis, Jon E., *World War II: The Autobiography* (Robinson, 2009)

Linge, Heinz, *With Hitler to the End* (Frontline Books, 2013)

Longden, Sean, *T Force* (Constable, 2010)

Longmate, Norman, *How We Lived Then* (Pimlico, 2002)

von Loringhoven, Bernd Freytag, *In the Bunker with Hitler* (Weidenfeld and Nicolson, 2006)

van Maarsen, Jacqueline, *My Name is Anne, She Said, Anne Frank* (Arcadia, 2003)

Markovna, Nina, *Nina's Journey* (Regnery Gateway, 1989)

McKinstry, Leo, *Lancaster* (John Murray, 2009)

Meissner, Hans-Otto, *Magda Goebbels* (Sidgwick & Jackson, 1980)

Michel, Ernst, *Promises to Keep* (Barricade Books, 1993)

Milburn, Clara Emily, *Mrs Milburn's Diaries* (Fontana, 1979)

Millgate, Helen D. ed., *Mr Brown's War: A Diary of the Home Front* (The History Press, 1998)

Moorehead, Alan, *Eclipse* (Hamish Hamilton, 1946)

Nicolson, Harold, *Diaries and Letters 1939–45* (Collins, 1967)

Niven, David, *The Moon's a Balloon* (Penguin, 1971)

O'Donnell, James P., *The Bunker* (Da Capo Press, 2001)

Overy, Richard, *Russia's War* (Penguin, 1997)

Palmer, Svetlana, and Wallis, Sarah, *We Were Young and at War* (Collins, 2009)

Reuth, Ralph Georg, *Goebbels* (Constable, 1993)

Roberts, Geoffrey, *Stalin's General* (Icon, 2012)

Royle, Trevor, *Patton* (Weidenfeld and Nicolson, 2005)

Sarantakes, Nicholas Evan, *Seven Stars* (Texas A&M University Press, 2004)

Schellenberg, Walter, *Hitler's Secret Service* (Harper, 1956)

Schlesinger, Stephen C., *Act of Creation: The Founding of the United Nations* (Westview Press, 2003)

Sellier, Claus, *Walking Away from the Third Reich* (Hellgate Press, 1999)

Sereny, Gitta, *Albert Speer, His Battle with Truth* (Macmillan, 1995)

Sereny, Gitta, *The German Trauma* (Penguin, 2000)

Service, Robert, *Russia* (Penguin, 1997)

Service, Robert, *Stalin* (Pan, 2004)

Shelden, Michael, *Orwell* (Heinemann, 1991)

Shepherd, Ben, *After Daybreak: The Liberation of Belsen* (Jonathan Cape, 2005)

Smith, Marcus J., *Dachau: The Harrowing of Hell* (State University of New York Press, 1995)

Stafford, David, *Endgame 1945* (Little, Brown, 2007)

Stargardt, Nicholas, *Witnesses of War* (Pimlico, 2006)

Swaab, Jack, *Field of Fire: Diary of a Gunnery Officer* (Sutton, 2005)

Taylor, Frederick, *Dresden* (Bloomsbury, 2004)

Trevor-Roper, Hugh, *The Last Days of Hitler* (Pan, 2002)

Truman, Harry S., *1945: Year of Decision* (New World City, 2014)

Tyas, Stephen, and Witte, Peter, *Himmler's Diary 1945: A Calendar of Events Leading to Suicide* (Fonthill, 2014)

Vassiltchikov, Marie 'Missie', *The Berlin Diaries 1940–1945* (Pimlico, 1999)

Weale, Adrian, *Patriot Traitors* (Viking, 2001)
Wermuth, Henry, *Breath Deeply My Son* (Vallentine Mitchell, 1993)
Whicker, Alan, *Within Whicker's World* (Elm Tree Books, 1982)

Other Sources

The Observer, 29th April 1945
The Times, 30th April 1945
The Daily Telegraph, 30th April 1945
New York Times, 30th April 1945
Der Spiegel
The Atlantic Times Archive, http://www.the-atlantic-times.com/archive
BBC, WW2 People's War, http://www.bbc.co.uk/history/ww2peopleswar/
History, 'Ten Days to Victory', http://www.history.co.uk/shows/ten-days-to-victory/videos/ten-days-to-vicyory-gerda-petersohn
YouTube, 'Ten Days to Victory', https://www.youtube.com/watch?v=LejBUZ41b9o Ten Days to Victory
Bomber Command Museum of Canada, http://www.bombercommandmuseum.ca/
Audrey Hepburn Timeline 1929-1949, http://www.audrey1.org/biography/16/audrey-hepburn-timeline-1929-1949
Seigel, Jessica, 'Audrey Hepburn on a Role', Audrey Hepburn: A tribute to her humanitarian work, http://www.ahepburn.com/article8.html
BACM Research, 'Adolf Hitler, "The Last Days in Hitler's Air Raid Shelter": Hanna Reitsch Interogation', http://ia801400.us.archive.org/19/items/HitlerLastDaysHannaReitschInterrogation/Hitler%20LastDays%20HannaReitsch%20Interrogation.pdf
YouTube, 'Traudl Junge Interview', https://www.youtube.com/watch?v=h3I0pm14cRU
Uboat.net, http://uboat.net
BBC, '29/10/1955', *In Town Tonight*, http://www.bbc.co.uk/programmes/p00nw1kn
BBC, '1st May', *On this Day*, http://news.bbc.co.uk/onthisday/hi/dates/stories/may/1/newsid_3571000/3571497.stm
http://www.scrapbookpages.com/DachauScrapbook/DachauLiberation/Allach.html
http://individual.utoronto.ca/jarekg/Ravensbruck/LastDays.html
Yale Law School, Lillian Goldman Law Library, The Avalon Project

Index

Also Available in the Minute by Minute Series